The Complete Idiot's Reference Card

W9-AYA-849

Top Ten List for Investing for Your Future

1. **Start small, do it often.** You don't need a gazillion dollars to begin your investing program. Even $100 a month is a great way to start creating your wealth. In fact, if you are 25 years old and invested only $100 a month *every month* that earned 12% a year until you retired, you would have close to a million bucks. You don't need a lot of money to get started—just discipline.

2. **Think long term no matter what.** Investment success isn't rewarded overnight. Unless you were fortunate to have Uncle Louie leave you a fortune in his will, you're going to have to work at creating your wealth over the long term.

3. **Understand that investing and saving are not the same thing.** Investing your money allows you to make your money work for you as hard as you do for it. Saving your money—either in a low interest-bearing savings account or under your mattress—only guarantees you two things. Low interest and dust bunnies.

4. **Shop around for a financial adviser and compare services.** Don't just rely on cousin Mort, family broker extraordinare. You'll pay a high price for investment advice even if it's a family member. Learn how to do your own investment research and create your own investment plan. Ultimately, you can save thousands of dollars in commissions and fees.

5. **Treat yourself like a bill, and pay yourself first.** Even before you pay the cable man, the electric bill, and your daughter's Girl Scout dues, pay yourself. Write yourself out a check and put it away. (You'll learn where in this book.) This habit guarantees that you're putting you and your family ahead of all other obligations. It's a great way to build your wealth.

6. **Don't just buy—diversify!** This rule follows the old adage "Don't put all of your eggs into one basket." By allocating your money into several different investments, you reduce your risk. If you put all of your eggs in one basket and drop the basket, they all break—egg yolk everywhere. Put your eggs in different baskets and drop one basket, voilà! Only one cracked shell… and the others are still intact.

7. **Don't follow John Q. Public.** One of the riskiest investment decisions to make is based on what other people are saying or doing. You can listen to your friend's stock tips or watch market gurus on financial TV programs, but don't blindly invest in the product without doing your research.

8. **Do your homework.** It is amazing how many people spend so much time investigating what house to buy or where to go on vacation but give such little time to researching their investments. Learn as much as you can about the investment, such as its performance history and how risky it is.

9. **Know that if it sounds too good to be true, it probably is.** Be wary of the investment pro who tells you about a "sure thing" in which you should invest all your money. First, it doesn't practice the art of diversification. Second, the investment pro is probably an investment clod.

10. **Don't let your investments keep you up at night. If you can't sleep, sell!** If there is an investment that is making you nervous and you can't catch those Zs, sell it. There is no investment worth losing sleep over—except our children, of course.

alpha books

The Complete Idiot's Guide to Making Money on Wall Street Teaches You How to Make Money

1. **Get M-O-T-I-V-A-T-E-D.** You work hard for your money, now let's do something about it! Forget the self-help tapes and the financial guru seminars. The key to successful investing is self-motivation and education. Motivation is the beginning to all of life's achievements. You have to want to learn first.

   What do you usually do to get yourself motivated about something? Suggestion: Use creative visualization. Actually picture yourself with your bills paid and your investment goals reached.

   _____

2. **Kick the two bad financial habits—fear and greed.** It isn't uncommon to be afraid of losing money. Personally, I hate to lose money, but that fear shouldn't stop you from investing because you have such an enormous potential to create a wealthy investment portfolio. Keep in mind not to get greedy, either, because your investments will control you instead of you controlling them.

3. **Figure out what goals you are working toward.** What do you want? Before you can even learn what different types of investment products are right for you, you need to determine what you're working toward. You can't invest your hard-earned cash just for the sake of watching your money grow.

   Are you investing for a house? A child's education? Retirement?

   _____

4. **Determine how much money it's going to take to reach these goals.** Buying a house, paying for a child's college education and retiring comfortably all require a substantial wad of dough—so do any other financial goals you're trying to reach. Now that you know what you want, you need to figure out how much it's going to cost.

   ➤ How much money are you going to need in the future?

   $1,000 __ $5,000 __ $10,000 __ $25,000 __ $50,000 __ $100,000+ __

   ➤ When do you need this money?

   a. Three years from now

   b. Five years from now

   c. Ten years from now

5. **Eliminate your debt *first*.** Compare what you own to what you owe. What does the result look like? You can't put a bandaid over your financial picture by only meeting monthly minimum payments. Make the commitment to get rid of the debt.

What I Own	*What I Owe*
_____	_____
_____	_____
_____	_____
_____	_____

6. **Ask yourself how much you can afford to lose, not how much you can afford to invest.** You need to figure out how much risk you can bear from an investment. By doing this, you'll be able to pinpoint which investments are best for you.

7. **Investment success isn't rewarded overnight.** You should know that when you're working on your financial plan, creating your financial goals, and determining your risk tolerance, you're planning for a long-term time horizon. It's best to work at creating your wealth for the future—not just for tomorrow.

8. **Understand that you have to do your homework.** You're on the right track, folks. You're motivated, you're eliminating bad debt, and you've assessed your risk-comfort level. Now what? Homework time! Learn as much as you can about the products you are investing in. Why? Well, have you ever bought something through the mail without seeing it, only to receive it and find out it's the wrong size, color, or style?

9. **You don't need a million to make a million.** Really! It only takes a little bit. You'll find out in this book that you can start with as little as TEN DOLLARS for an initial investment. And the earlier you begin, the better—you'll have more time on your side. How much money do you spend on frivolous things per week? $10? $25? $50? What if you took that money and invested it over a long-term time horizon?

10. **Always watch to see how your investments are performing.** Simply sending off a check to a mutual fund company or blindly investing in stocks is wrong. You have to set aside time to monitor your investments consistently. In this book, you'll learn where to find the information you need to monitor your investment portfolio.

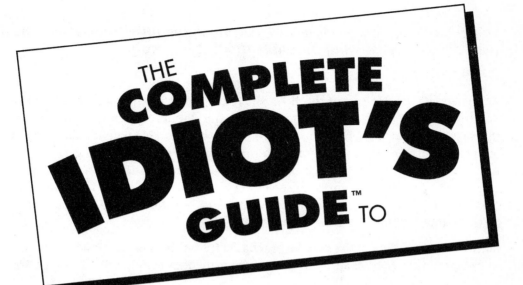

THE **COMPLETE IDIOT'S GUIDE** TO

Making Money on Wall Street

Second Edition

by Christy Heady

alpha books

A Division of Macmillan General Reference
A Simon and Schuster Macmillan Company
1633 Broadway, New York, NY 10019-6785

To my husband, John, whose love, devotion, and unselfishness encourage me every day to surpass what I initially thought impossible.

©1998 Alpha Books

All rights reserved. No part of this book shall be reproduced, stored in a retrieval system, or transmitted by any means, electronic, mechanical, photocopying, recording, or otherwise, without written permission from the publisher. No patent liability is assumed with respect to the use of the information contained herein. Although every precaution has been taken in the preparation of this book, the publisher and author assume no responsibility for errors or omissions. Neither is any liability assumed for damages resulting from the use of information contained herein. For information, address Alpha Books, 1633 Broadway, 7th Floor, New York, NY 10019-6785.

Macmillan Publishing books may be purchased for business or sales promotional use. For information please write: Special Markets Department, Macmillan Publishing USA, 1633 Broadway, New York, NY 10019.

THE COMPLETE IDIOT'S GUIDE name and design are trademarks of Macmillan, Inc.

International Standard Book Number: 0-02-861958-7
Library of Congress Catalog Card Number: 97-073185

00 99 98   4 3 2 1

Interpretation of the printing code: the rightmost number of the first series of numbers is the year of the book's printing; the rightmost number of the second series of numbers is the number of the book's printing. For example, a printing code of 98-1 shows that the first printing occurred in 1998.

Printed in the United States of America

This publication contains the opinions and ideas of its author. It is intended to provide helpful and informative material on the subject matter covered. It is sold with the understanding that the author and publisher are not engaged in rendering professional services in the book. If the reader requires personal assistance or advice, a competent professional should be consulted.

The author and publisher specifically disclaim any responsibility for any liability, loss or risk, personal or otherwise, which is incurred as a consequence, directly or indirectly, of the use and application of any of the contents of this book.

Alpha Development Team

Brand Manager
Kathy Nebenhaus

Director of Editorial Services
Brian Phair

Executive Editor
Gary M. Krebs

Managing Editor
Bob Shuman

Senior Editor
Nancy Mikhail

Development Editor
Jennifer Perillo

Editorial Assistant
Maureen Horn

Production Team

Development Editor
Nancy Warner

Production Editor
Mark Enochs

Cartoonist
Judd Winick

Cover Designer
Michael Freeland

Designer
Glenn Larsen

Indexer
Chris Barrick

Layout/Proofreading
Tricia Flodder, Angela Perry

Contents at a Glance

Contents

Foreword

In the 1970s, when I was a newspaper financial edition and syndicated columnist, I would occasionally speak at meetings of newspaper publishers and editors. Even then, they were bemoaning the fact that most Americans were getting most of their news from television. But there was one area of news, I asserted, where newspapers were way ahead. That was in the coverage of business news, which was the great wasteland of TV news coverage. And that was a serious problem. Because most Americans were getting most of their news from television, and because the tube was ignoring business and financial news, we were in danger of creating a nation of economic illiterates.

Well, I don't make those kinds of speeches anymore. Not only because I'm in television myself these days, but because the situation no longer exists. With the advent of Cable News Network, CNBC, and additional programming on public television, there's now a solid amount of TV coverage of business, financial, and economic news. The broadcast networks are still a wasteland, but there's enough else out there to enable anyone interested in the subject to be well-informed.

Unfortunately, though, too many people remain ill-informed about such elementary matters as taking control of their own personal finances. The financial media sometimes contributes to that situation by cloaking our reporting in jargon and by failing to show how seemingly complicated financial and economic developments can affect the daily lives and fortunes of ordinary Americans.

How refreshing it is to find a clear mind and a fresh voice to put these things in perspective and bring them to everyone's level of interest and comprehension. Christy Heady has done this for the small investor, in *The Complete Idiot's Guide to Making Money on Wall Street*, with a user-friendly guide to success in the investment world. Her advice is simple, yet so intelligent that some of the so-called Wall Street pros could benefit from it as well. For beginners, it's must reading.

Myron Kandel
Financial Editor

"Moneyline...with Lou Dobbs"
CNN (Cable News Network)

Introduction

I once knew a gentleman who wanted to invest a little money he had. He wasn't wealthy by any means, but he wasn't stupid either. He knew that his little bit of money, wisely invested, could be working a lot harder for him than it was parked in his savings account. He also knew that he needed to learn about investing if he was to do it wisely. So he bought books—he had more books on investing than anyone I knew—and as far as I know, his money is still parked in the bank. Why?

He never got past Chapter 3 in any of the books he bought. They were dry; they were tedious; they made history books on 17th-century France look fascinating by comparison. And they made this gentleman, who wasn't stupid, feel like an idiot. I wrote this book for him and for the thousands of others like him...like you...who know their money could be making more money, but don't know where to begin.

I know you're not an idiot (after all, you bought this book). That's the first assumption I've made about you, and I'm presumptious enough to make a few other assumptions, too. For example:

➤ You're not an economist and you're probably not a stock broker or even a certified public accountant.

➤ You work hard for your money and you can't afford to lose much of it.

➤ You are smart enough to realize that unless you provide for the future, the future may be very bleak indeed.

➤ The very thought of buying stocks—let alone futures or options—sends a prickle of fear down your spine.

Although Wall Street looks like a shark tank and you feel like bait, you CAN make it work for you, and that's what this book is all about. It contains the fundamental information you need to make sensible decisions about your money. It offers tips—not hot tips on a real deal ("trust me"), but tried-and-true tips on investing from pros who've been there. It gives you useful worksheets and formulas that help you plot your course through some-times choppy waters. And it isn't boring. Yes, you can get past Chapter 3 without falling asleep. Here's how it works.

Part 1, Show Me the Road to Wall Street, grounds you in some basics. It helps you establish your financial goals, determine an acceptable level of risk, learn how to research different investment opportunities, and get disciplined about spending and saving (so you have money to invest).

Part 2, Megabanks: One-Stop Shopping, helps you get the most out of your bank accounts (checking and savings), and understand how both fit into an overall investment plan. And, a quick update on how Cyberspace fits into your banking behavior is included.

Part 3, Mutual Fund Mania, shows you how to make even small amounts of money grow through managed portfolios, how to pick reputable mutual funds, and how to select the best time for mutual fund investing.

Part 4, Stock Market 101, introduces you to your first really scary (and potentially really profitable) investment product. This section helps you understand what stocks are and how their performance can build or evaporate profits from your investment dollars.

Part 5, Looking for Income? Consider Bond Investing, walks you through another popular investment tool—government and corporate bonds—complete with tax considerations.

Part 6, Taking the Plunge with the Commodities Market, explains the risks and opportunities in this volatile area of investing and helps new investors understand the culture of this particular Wall Street avenue.

Part 7, Make That Money Grow, provides specific strategies for investing dollar amounts from $100 to $10,000, plus tax tips for handling profits from your investments.

Plus, you get four appendixes listing "freebies" that may be available to you just for becoming a corporate shareholder, several no-load mutual fund companies, Federal Reserve Banks and their U.S. branches, and the major U.S. financial exchanges. There is also a glossary of investment terms that will help you understand how "money talks."

While you may not need to read this book cover to cover, I strongly recommend that you read Part 1 before you dive into a specific investment area that interests you. From there you can pick and choose, based on your goals and how much risk you can handle without losing sleep.

Extras

In addition to clear and interesting explanations and advice, this book offers other types of information that point you in the right direction, help you avoid dangerous and costly traps, define confusing jargon, or provide sidenotes that may simply be of interest. Look for these easy-to-recognize signposts in boxes:

Bet You Didn't Know

These little boxes contain interesting or useful background information about investment opportunities or the fascinating world of Wall Street. It's information you can ignore...but you probably won't want to.

What?

Yes, it's true. Wall Street is full of mysterious and unnecesary jargon, but you should get familiar with some of it. These boxes will put you in the know, so you can talk to your broker without embarrassment, and impress your friends at cocktail parties.

Secret

Tips show better ways to get things done—ways to save money or time. Think of them as a friendly word whispered in your ear.

Careful

Cautions help you avoid costly mistakes so you don't end up like this pitiful character.

Acknowledgments

I could not have created this book without the help of many people. These people were kind enough to provide me with timely, accurate information—usually at the drop of a hat so I could meet my deadlines (once again!).

Many thanks to Dr. Warren Heller of Veribanc, Don Phillips of Morningstar, Richard Lehmann of the Bond Investors Association, Jay Sherman of the *Mortgage-Backed Securities Letter*, Fritz Elmendorf at the Consumer Bankers Association, Nancy Judy, American Bankers Association, and John Hall, Investment Company Institute.

I would also like to thank those people who have encouraged me to believe in helping others through my work: Tom Siedell and Dennis Fertig of *Your Money Magazine*, for no matter how many stories I now write, I cannot thank you enough for my first chance when I started out on my own; John Wasik of *Consumers Digest*, your confidence and encouragement in my journalistic ability has allowed me to reach new heights in my career; Myron Kandel, CNN, thank you for your belief in me educating the public with my first book; and to the folks at America Online's Personal Finance Department whose introduction to the financial end of cyberspace created a new and exciting outlet for my work.

And for those family and friends who know me better than I know myself, thank you for your encouragement: in particular, my mother, Diane, who is one of my closest friends, thank you for sharing your spirit with me and keeping me motivated to meet life's challenges; my father, Robert, thank you for instilling in me how important independence and integrity are in this business, a lesson I will *never* forget. And to my husband, John, thank you for showing me that whatever I set my mind to, I can do. Your love and faith has shown me that together our universe is possible.

Part 1
Show Me the Road to Wall Street

Twenty years ago, not many consumers would talk about Wall Street, let alone spell it. Today, however, Wall Street is the subject of many conversations. It's not uncommon to hear the phrase "So what did the market do today?" while you're waiting at the train station or standing in line at the grocery store. Headlines that scream "The Dow Jones Industrials Soar to New High" are common these days. But what does this all mean? Simply put, O-P-P-O-R-T-U-N-I-T-Y. Case in point: If you invested $10,000 in the S&P 500, a weighted index comprised of a basket of 500 stocks, at the end of 1986, your initial investment would be worth $49,766.61 today, counting reinvested dividends. That's an increase of almost 400% on your money! There are no secret formulas or magic potions to maximize your investments to meet your financial goals. You can do this if you learn how to invest wisely. This part of the book will explain that it doesn't take a lot of money to begin—just a little know-how and commitment.

Before you begin, you need to know yourself very well. What are your financial goals? How much risk can you handle? What bad spending habits do you have to break before you can invest a dime? What you do today will affect you for the rest of your life. Making mistakes will cost you, especially on Wall Street. But doing nothing is the biggest mistake of all. So, are you ready? Let's see how today's markets will set the tone for your financial future…and let's find out more about you.

Chapter 1

You Can Get There from Here

In This Chapter

➤ Motivating yourself to wealth—even on a limited budget

➤ Learning how the future of finance will affect you and your wallet

➤ Knowing the Top Ten Tips for Successful Investing

Lucille Ball, the redheaded comedic American icon, once said, "I don't know anything about luck. I've never banked on it, and I'm afraid of people who do. Luck to me is something else: hard work—and realizing what is opportunity and what isn't."

Lucy was right. You can't bank on your lucky stars to help create your fortune. The best way to predict your financial future is to create it. Today.

Wall Street is nothing more than opportunity, and there's no better time than the present to begin thinking about the opportunities that will make your money work as hard for you as you do for it.

Sit down right now and take a few minutes to make a list of the desires you have for the next ten years. It's okay to reach for the sky. Go on a shopping spree at your favorite mall. Buy your dream house—two-car garage included. Or send your kids to college with their tuition paid in full! Now pick out two goals for this year. Make a list of reasons why you want to reach these goals. With enough reason—and Wall Street opportunities—you can accomplish anything.

Focus on Your Investments—Not the Lottery

Winning the lottery may be the quickest path to wealth, but *playing* it is not. You have a 1 in 7,397,685 chance (or something like that) of winning a zillion dollar lottery. Sure you can dream, but if you want to make your dreams a reality, you're going to have to do more than fill in the little boxes on a lottery ticket. Let's say you spend $5 a week on lottery tickets and never win, you are throwing away $20 a month. That's $240 a year, which can be a week's worth of pay for many Americans. That's like working a week for free—you might as well just set your paycheck on fire and watch it burn.

What?
A *mutual fund* represents a pool of different stocks and bonds.

What if you take that same twenty bucks and invest it? You're probably thinking: "Twenty bucks? I need more money to start investing." No, you don't. You can invest as little as $20 a month in a stock or mutual fund and watch it grow into hundreds and possibly thousands of dollars.

Let's take a $100 bill and see what it can do. Suppose that on the 15th of each month you invest $100 into a mutual fund of your choice—no matter what the change in price of the mutual fund.

One hundred dollars a month invested over a twelve-month period is $1,200. Easy enough. Of course, we don't live in a perfect world, so there are times when the price, (also known as Net Asset Value or N.A.V.) of your mutual fund rises and falls. However, the long-term benefit of dollar cost averaging is that it gives you the opportunity to invest a small amount of your savings to build long-term wealth.

Now check out Table 1.1.

Table 1.1 Watching Your $100 Grow

When Do I Invest?	How Much Do I Invest?	What's the Price?	How Many Shares Do I Own?
January 15	$100.00	$15.00	6.67
February 15	$100.00	$16.00	6.25
March 15	$100.00	$14.00	7.14
April 15	$100.00	$12.00	8.33
May 15	$100.00	$14.00	7.14
June 15	$100.00	$15.00	6.67
July 15	$100.00	$16.00	6.25
August 15	$100.00	$15.00	6.67
September 15	$100.00	$17.00	5.88
October 15	$100.00	$18.00	5.56
November 15	$100.00	$20.00	5.00
December 15	$100.00	$22.00	4.55

When Do I Invest?	How Much Do I Invest?	What's the Price?	How Many Shares Do I Own?
Totals:	$1,200.00	$16.17 average price/share	76.11
Total amount I invested:	$1,200.00		
Value of my portfolio now:	$1,674.42		
Net profit:	$474.42 (does not include dividends being reinvested)		

From Table 1.1, you can conclude that if you were to invest $100 a month into a mutual fund whose share price fluctuated, at the end of a year you would have a profit (in this example). Keep in mind that prices of mutual funds can rise and fall. This method of investing is known as dollar cost averaging. Its true definition is that it's the method of making a regular investment in a mutual fund (or stock) of a fixed amount of money at a predetermined time.

Careful

Dollar cost averaging does *not* guarantee against loss. If the overall trend of the market is down, then you will wind up with a loss for that period of time. That's why you should plan a dollar cost averaging program to last at least several years.

And, another word of caution, for those investors who believe the market trend is on the upswing for a long period of time, and who can afford more than the $100 a month (for example, they have a $10,000 or even $50,000 lump sum to invest): You would be better off to invest that lump sum in the market at once rather than always paying a higher price on a monthly basis in a rising market.

Dollar cost averaging is a great "blind formula" for those of us who, for example, can only afford that fixed monthly amount versus the others who can make the decisions to implement other strategies because he or she has a lump sum to invest today.

Mutual funds aren't the only investments to consider. There are stocks, bonds, futures, and options. Each of these specific investments may work for you, based on your financial goals, your initial investment, your risk-comfort level, and your age. In this book, you'll get the best answers to your financial questions and learn which investment products are most ideal for you. You'll also discover that there are ways to maximize your investments using your own knowledge without having to rely 100% on financial experts who promise you oodles of money and astronomical returns. However, there are situations where you may need a financial adviser, as discussed in Chapter 5, when you're doing the legwork.

It may look like Greek to you now, but the language of investments is easy. You can learn to make money on Wall Street *and* understand and practice this new language. It's the same as learning how to play the tuba, taking up underwater basket weaving, or making a cheese soufflé in ten minutes or less; the jargon of investing is easy once you know how to do it. The knowledge you are about to gain is powerful, if and *only if* you use it. And remember: The oldest rule on Wall Street is that it fools the greatest number of people. Don't let it fool you.

Save or Invest?

If a 25-year-old were to invest a little over $100 a month until age 65, and his investment earned 12% annually, he would have a million bucks by the time he retired. Even if you are in your 40s, $600 a month for the next 25 years would get you a million bucks, too.

Can you save your money over the same time frame and have a million bucks? Good question.

You can always save money. Whatever is left over after you've paid all your expenses can be savings. That's good—most people try to have money left over. But if it's tucked away in a *non*interest-bearing checking account, what good is it? It's just sitting there...well, earning no interest. Savers that earn less than 3% do little more than make banks wealthy by paying outrageous banking fees.

Investing the money is a different story. As an investor, you do your homework to see what investments pertain to your style, your level of risk, and your financial goals. You can earn more if you invest it. You can even double and triple your money. But you can also lose it all. You'll learn that there is more risk to investing than just losing money later on in Chapter 4.

What?
Dividends are simply a distribution of earnings to shareholders. *Capital gains* simply means that it's the difference between an asset's purchase price and selling price, where the end result is positive.

Typically when you think of saving money, you think of a savings account. Deposit your money and earn around 3%–4% interest. You can sleep at night knowing all of your cash is there. Some of you might even stash your cash in an old shoe box or a special hiding place under your mattress—no interest earned there, though!

If you were to invest your money, where would you put it? Many people choose stocks, bonds, and mutual funds when they invest their money.

To compare the differences between saving and investing, take a look at Table 1.2. This shows what would happen if you allocated $100 a month to a *savings account* or an *investment* over certain periods of time, assuming the following:

➤ Money under your mattress earns no interest (0%).

➤ Savings accounts earn less than 5% interest.

➤ All dividends and capital gains from an investment are reinvested.

Table 1.2 Save or Invest?

Return (%)	5 years	10 years	15 years	20 years	30 years
0%	$6,000	$12,000	$18,000	$24,000	$36,000
5%	$6,829	$15,592	$26,840	$41,275	$83,573
8%	$7,397	$18,418	$34,835	$59,294	$150,030
10%	$7,808	$20,655	$41,799	$76,570	$227,936
12%	$8,247	$23,334	$50,457	$99,915	$352,992

Table 1.2 charts the results of saving your money in the following three ways:

➤ **Under your mattress (0%).** You would have $36,000 at the end of 30 years. $36,000 is a lot of money, until you compare it with…

➤ **A savings account.** Earning less than 5% on a savings account in the 1990s really equates to an average 2%–3% annual yield. You can turn $100 a month for the next 20 years saved in a savings account into *almost* $40,000. But there's a better avenue to turn down…

➤ **Stocks, bonds, or mutual funds.** Any of these investments can boast higher returns than if you were to save your money in a savings account. Just look at the table. If you *invested* your $100 a month *every* month—even at a 10% annual return—after 15 years you'd more than double the amount earned by leaving it under your mattress. After 30 years of investing, you'd have six times the amount sewn up in your bed for the same period of time. Of course, investing your money in stocks, bonds or mutual funds does not guarantee stellar performance or profits.

What?

In general, a *yield* refers to a return on an investor's capital investment. It has different meanings, depending on the investment. For example, in real estate, a piece of property may "yield" a certain return. When you borrow money, it is the total money earned on a loan; that is, the annual percentage rate of interest multiplied by the term of the loan.

But what about in the markets? With bonds, for example, it is the coupon rate of interest divided by the purchase price. And for stocks, it is simply the percentage rate of return paid on a common stock in dividends.

History, Technology, and Your Future

In order to create your future, you must learn from the past. For example, the Great Depression affected thousands of today's seniors, leaving them searching for ultra-conservative investments. Baby boomers, on the other hand, experienced the "Greed is Good" money style. The result? Inflationary times during the '80s with sky-high interest rates. And today's young-30-somethings, along with their Gen-X counterparts? They get to experience the effects technology has on their investments today, which will ultimately drive them into the future.

No matter which part of history you've experienced, you can leverage today's technology to help you on your path to future wealth. Online banking and online trading technology provide convenience. They allow you to access your bank account or brokerage account at any time of day, rectify statements and execute transactions—all from the ease of your armchair.

By utilizing this new technology, you can stay on top of Wall Street, too. America Online, the world's fastest-growing online service, allows you to maintain several investment portfolios, monitor the financial markets at your convenience, and execute trades, and search for Wall Street performance information.

Microsoft Investor, available through the Microsoft Network (**http://www.msn.com**), provides Internet users a "community" aspect to online investing complete with news stories, columns, quote service(s), and electronic trading transaction capability. The caveat? You must pay to subscribe to this service—$9.95 per month.

Also available to you "'Netizens" (those of us whose lives involve a computer and a modem hookup) are several large online brokerages—complete with electronic trading capabilities. They include Charles Schwab (**http://www.schwab.com**), PCFN (**http://www.pcfn.com**, which stands for Personal Computing Financial Network), and E*Trade (**http://www.etrade.com**).

You can trade right online—buy and sell shares, move money between accounts—all for a fee, of course. Often the costs involved with online trading are posted right on the home page, along with basic information about the company, its products (similar to an online marketing brochure), quote service(s), and security transaction information. Check with each firm to see if they offer discounts on trades for completing electronic transactions.

The bottom line? It's going to pay off to stay connected.

The Process for Successful Investing

So you want to be investment-savvy? Many people want to be a smart investor, and everybody wants to be a rich investor. Why not? As a smart investor, you control your investments and don't let fear or greed get the best of you. You work too hard for your money to throw it away. If you're a rich investor, then it shows that your smarts have paid off.

But you can't be a rich investor without first being a smart one. Smart investors know that knowledge is power. They're not looking for an immediate payoff but have a stick-to-it attitude that guarantees wealth and success. The two most important words in managing your money and creating your wealth are *getting control*. The more you learn about what some of the investment products are and how they work in different economic and financial climates, the more control you'll have creating your own wealth.

This isn't a cakewalk, though. You have to commit to the following steps first:

1. **You have to want to learn.** Motivation is the starting point of all achievement. You have this book, that's motivation right there. Believe you can do it, because you can. Actually close your eyes and imagine your financial dreams come true.

2. **Get rid of the negative emotions—fear and greed.** Many people are afraid of investing, usually because of a lack of knowledge or confidence. Others are greedy, only caring about improving the bottom line. These same people let their investments control them rather than the opposite. Kick these emotions, and you can control your financial destiny.

3. **Set some goals.** This is probably the most important step. What do you want? Where do you want your money to take you? Setting specific financial goals—such as paying for your children's college tuition, retiring at an early age and living comfortably, or buying your dream home—needs to be done before you know what a stock or bond even is. You cannot invest just for the sake of watching your money grow. You'll see how to set a goal and how to reach it in Chapter 3.

4. **How much money is it going to take for these goals?** How much will your new home cost? Do you have any money for your child's college education? Take your goals from the previous step and figure out how much money each will require.

5. **Figure out where you are financially.** Are you deeply in debt? Can you barely make ends meet? Are you scared of really knowing what your financial situation is like? It's not uncommon—believe me! By using the recommendations in Chapter 3, you will be able to find out where you are financially and how much you can afford to invest.

6. **Determine how much you can afford to lose.** This step in the process of successful investing concerns risk. By establishing your tolerance of how much risk you can take, you will be able to pinpoint which investments you should be in.

7. **Plan for the long-term.** Investment success isn't rewarded overnight. You are going to have to work at creating your wealth.

8. **Do your homework.** You've got the motivation, you know where you are financially, and you know how much risk you can take. Now what? Time to do your homework. You need to learn as much as you can about as many different types of investment products that are out there. This may entail:

    ➤ Definitely buying this book.

    ➤ Subscribing to a few investment newsletters on the investments of your choice.

    ➤ Taking a course or two in basic investing.

    ➤ Watching television programs that talk about investing.

    ➤ Buy computer software programs specifically for budgeting and investing.

    ➤ Subscribing to an online service and researching investment information online.

Secret
The best way to start learning about the financial markets is to get some free sample copies of financial newsletters. It's cost-effective (because they're free) and they give you a quick introduction into the world of investing.

9. **Start small and start early.** You don't need a million to make a million. It only takes a little bit. Recall what as little as $100 a month can do. Even if you only have $50 or even $25 a month, you can still continue the process of successful investing. The earlier you start, the better. Why? You have more time on your side to make your money grow—and take more opportunities of potential rising financial markets. Don't think it's too late—better late than never.

10. **Constantly monitor your investments.** You can't just sink a week's pay into stocks or bonds and ignore it. You have to set aside time to monitor your investments and keep up with the latest financial information. Once you learn where to find your stock symbol or bond quote in the newspaper, you'll be hooked.

Your Financial Toolbox

Think of what a toolbox looks like. Not very big, but it can hold a lot. Now, open the lid, and inside there's a top shelf. You can store a few things in there: pencils, fishing line, bolts, and a few lugnuts or whatever. Pull up the lid and underneath you find several shelves that open like an accordion. These shelves are at different levels. Many times a handyman puts the heaviest items on the bottom, such as a hammer or phillips-head screwdriver. The lighter items are left on top.

The concept of investing works in the same manner. Each investment product sits on a different shelf in a financial toolbox. What goes into each shelf depends on how risky it is, how much of it you own, and how long you own it.

Within this toolbox are the investment products. You may have heard how you can make money investing in these products: buy low and sell high! It's an old trick, but one that works. But what are you buying and selling? You are trading investment products, such as certificates of deposit, stocks, bonds, mutual funds, futures, and options. For a great discussion on how these products (and a few others) work, check out Chapter 2.

The Big Payoff: The Magic of Compounding

Let me ask you a question. If I could give you a million dollars today—right now—or a penny that you could double in value today, tomorrow, and every day thereafter for the next thirty days, which would you pick? Most folks want the up-front cash. The smart ones, however, would take the penny. Why?

Because if you took the penny today and doubled its value each day thereafter for the next 30 days you will have almost $5.4 million dollars. Really. It's easy to figure out. On a piece of paper, write down the next 30 days, starting with Day One and ending with Day Thirty. At the beginning of Day One put down .01, for one penny. Day Two should have .02 next to it because doubling one penny gives you two pennies. How much does two pennies give you? Four. Put that down for Day Three. Complete your worksheet, making sure you double each day's amount.

> **What?**
> *Compounding* is the money you earn on the interest you earned in the previous period. To maximize the benefits of compounding, let an investment compound over a longer time period. The more time you give it to work, the better.

Why does this work? Because of the magic of compounding. It is one of the most powerful ways to double, triple, and even quadruple your wealth.

Compounding works if you understand its theory. Here's an example: There's a tale of a young boy who used to buy used Matchbox cars for $1.00 at garage sales. He would clean them up and make them look brand new. Then the boy would turn around and sell each of them for $2.00 apiece to the next child that came to his house. That kid made 100% profit on his initial investment. What a grand idea. (Eventually his mother found out what he was doing and was miffed, but boy, was his stockbroker father proud.)

The kid doubled his money because he knew the basic essence of compounding without even picking up an investment book. Not everyone can do that, especially when you're trying to make money on Wall Street. Oh, sure you can make 200% profit on some of Wall Street's riskiest investments, but you could also lose all of your money—and more!

Ultimately, the more you invest, the more compounding goes to work for you. Now, to practice its theory, you must:

➤ Have already established the time horizon for your financial goals.

➤ Practice the self-discipline—like $100 a month, *every month*, for example.

➤ Learn the Rule of 72.

One of the biggest secrets to learning how the method of compounding works is understanding the Rule of 72. You don't need to break out the calculators or even sign up for a statistics course to see how this works.

The Rule of 72 tells you how long it will take you to double your money. Many financial advisers have used this rule. The formula is pretty easy. Take any fixed annual rate of return and divide that number *into* 72. The end result should be the number of years it will take to double your money. Keep in mind the rule is based on a *fixed* annual rate of return.

Use some math. A $1,000 investment with a 10% annual rate of return would take 7.2 years to double and grow to $2,000. Figure it out. 10.0 divided into 72 = 7.2.

Buying and Selling Your Way to Success

It's funny, but many investors don't follow the process for successful investing. Instead, they look for a "get-rich-quick" investment, but that investment usually tends to leave them without a big payoff—and empty pockets.

The big payoff in investing comes from an old trick—one that's easy to grasp:

Buy Low and Sell High!

Generations of experts have calculated financial formulas and tested hypothetical theories, but no one has designed one specific set of rules except for this one!

Unfortunately, statistics indicate that 70 percent of all investors lose money in the stock market. Many investors lose money in the other financial markets as well, especially if they don't do their homework and follow up on their investments. Why do so many people lose money? For example, in the case of investing in stocks, they buy stocks at too high a price and let greed overcome their sense of reality. Or maybe they get really greedy and want more profit. So they don't sell the investment and the price of it drops. Then the investor has a loss.

When you buy low and sell high, the big payoff is a profit. This is also known as a capital gain.

The Slow and Steady Method

Secret
Dividends that you receive are taxed on federal and state levels. Make sure you record all of your dividend payments so that you are organized during tax preparation.

Where else is there a payoff? In dividends, for one. Typically these are quarterly payments sent to stockholders that represent a company's profit. For example, when you buy stock, you become part owner in the company, and your proportion of ownership depends on how many shares you buy.

As a part owner, you may share in the company profits when the company sends you a dividend check. Technically, it is the proportion of net earnings (kind of like a profit) from a company paid to you. So, as a stockholder, not only do you benefit from the price of a stock rising (the buy low and sell high concept), you also get a perk—a dividend.

It's in Your Best Interest

You can also make money from *interest* payments you receive from some investments. Typically, these interest payments come from fixed-income investments, which include all types of bonds.

Interest payments are paid to you every six months. The amount of interest you receive depends upon the interest rate that is given on the bond. Many investors choose fixed-income securities as a way to earn steady income.

Investing for Tomorrow

Those people who are saving for a rainy day will find themselves all wet. Today, the focus is on investing for retirement.

Why should you place so much emphasis on retirement, especially if it's 10, 20, 30, or even 40 years away?

Because it will be here sooner than you know it. Many folks can attest that retirement comes too quickly. Today's senior citizens who live on a fixed-income are faced with very, very limited budgets. Their incomes have fallen so dramatically because they either didn't plan for retirement properly, saved their money instead of invested it, or counted on Social Security to be their cure-all.

The average household income for a senior citizen is just over $22,000 a year, according to the U.S. Census Bureau. Can you live on that?

If you are getting ready to retire or are already retired, it's not too late. In fact, it's *never* too late! Start working your plan as if it were day one. Check out the top ten steps to the process of successful investing and plan accordingly.

If you're a baby boomer, you're in your peak earning years and you know that retirement is just around the corner; however, you have a shorter amount of time to invest for retirement than you had ten years ago. You can still reach your million by retirement; it's just going to take a few more dollars for you to invest per month to get there.

The group who has the longest time—and therefore the power—to plan for retirement are you 20- and 30-year-olds. Remember, only $100 a month invested every month over the next 40 years can practically get you a million bucks. (Of course, there's no guarantee.)

Don't believe that Social Security will take care of *all* of your financial necessities when you retire. Receiving Social Security benefits should be looked upon as a "bonus" during your retirement years—not the panacea. If you work your investment plan to its fullest potential, you won't have to count on Social Security. (You should still apply for benefits, though, when the time comes.)

Secret
Because the life expectancy of people is increasing, it isn't necessary to be ultra-conservative with your retirement investment objectives. Retirees tend to live 20 years within retirement and still need capital appreciation on their investments.

The Least You Need to Know

➤ You can motivate yourself to wealth by planning your work and working your plan. Sit down right now and think about what you would like to accomplish over the next 5, 10, and 20 years.

➤ Start small, and start early. Realize that you don't need a lot of money to participate in the opportunities on Wall Street. Even $50 or $100 a month will do it. As you keep reading this book, you'll find out you can work with even less!

➤ Let history be your guide to your financial future and don't be afraid of the changing technologies. Online banking and trading, as well as online services, will enable you to stay on top of Wall Street more than ever before.

➤ The top ten steps to the process of successful investing include (among others): motivation, setting some financial goals, determining how much money you're going to need for these goals, learning *how* to do your homework, and then doing it!

➤ Keep in mind that the oldest rule on Wall Street is that it fools the greatest number of people. Don't let it fool you. Do your homework.

Chapter 2

Everyday Economics

In This Chapter

➤ Discovering how economics affects everything you do—especially investing

➤ Learning the economic buzzwords

➤ Understanding the language of money

Are you a Fed watcher? If you want to make money on Wall Street, you should monitor the actions of the nation's central bank: The Federal Reserve.

Some of you may query, "Why do I have to worry about the direction of interest rates? My investment portfolio is allocated among stocks and mutual funds."

While you may not have to follow every single economic report generated by economic gadflies, it is imperative to know how economics affects your ability to invest your money—and its potential future growth.

The Big 3: Economics, You, and Your Wallet

Here's a classic example that shows how economics affects your wallet. I had a grandfather, George, who when I was a little girl, happily reminded me how expensive money was. "Money, Grandpa? How can *money* be expensive?"

He shared examples with me, such as how gasoline only cost a nickel a gallon when he was a little boy, a loaf of bread was a quarter, and that the deficit of the U.S. Government didn't have as many zeros behind it as it does today.

My grandfather also spoke of how bad things were, and, for a reason: he lived through one of the most depressing financial times of the century—the stock market crash and the Great Depression. Terrible unemployment. War rationing. He can attest to poverty and explain how the basic essentials of life that used to cost a few pennies now cost a bundle. His generation can also discuss how our economy has changed over the years and how it has affected the financial markets. I'm sure his generation probably can even tell stories of a few financial windfalls that they've enjoyed. Listen to them!

The point is that things—such as gasoline, a loaf of bread, clothing, and so on, known as *consumer goods*—do cost more today than yesteryear. Why? The law of supply and demand. And that, my friend, is economics.

But what does all this mean? How do economics affect you and your investment decisions? Plenty.

Bet You Didn't Know

The most outstanding economics book, *The Wealth of Nations* by Adam Smith, was written the same year Paul Revere took his ride and declared "The Red Coats Are Coming! The Red Coats Are Coming!" What year was that? 1776.

You should care about economics. Why? If you understand...

➤ Where you are in the business cycle

➤ The general direction of interest rates

➤ The economic indicators

...then you will be able to make better decisions for your investments. Many investments are affected by these three factors.

First, if you know where you are in the business cycle, you will have a better understanding of how well or how poorly companies are doing. This may help you choose stocks, corporate bonds, and mutual funds to invest in, since stocks and corporate bonds are issued by companies and mutual funds invest in both stocks and bonds.

Second, if you follow the general direction of interest rates, you will be able to determine at what point in time you should be investing in bonds. For example, if interest rates are really low, would you want to invest in an investment product that doesn't pay a high rate of interest—such as a bond—for a really long time? Probably not. But on the other hand, if interest rates are high, you may choose to invest in a bond so you can get higher interest payments that are paid to you on a semi-annual basis.

Secret
The cardinal rule of economics? Learning that there is no such thing as a free lunch! There is always a cost involved. Know this and you understand the first lesson in economics.

Third, knowing the major economic indicators will help you because of how these economic reports affect the financial markets. Many times if the news is good, the financial markets react favorably; on the other hand, if the economic news is really bad, the financial markets don't do very well at all. Following these indicators can help guide your investment decisions. Plus, these indicators let you know where you are in the business cycle...and the process just starts all over again.

What Do Inflation and Recession Have to Do with Me?

Prosperity is when the prices of the things that you sell are rising; inflation is when the prices of things that you buy are rising. Recession is when other people are unemployed; depression is when you are unemployed.

Anonymous, taken from *Economics: Private and Public Choice* by James D. Gwartney and Richard L. Stroup.

A perfect economic world would be a pretty stable environment: steadily increasing business production, full employment (when the rate of unemployment is normal—not because everybody is working), and keeping the prices of products on an even keel. But you don't live in a perfect world—you live in a *business cycle*.

What?
Normal employment is when 94 percent of the entire labor force is working.

WHAT?

You can make better investment decisions by finding out where the economy is in the business cycle. In the following figure, the business cycle looks like nothing more than a squiggly line drawn by your two-year old on your dining room wall. This line reveals a lot, however.

Riding the roller-coaster of the business cycle.

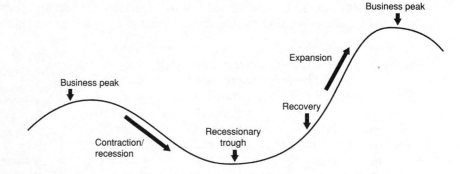

What?

The *business cycle* reflects changes in the general levels of economic activity as measured by certain economic indicators, such as the unemployment rate and changes in the gross domestic product (GDP), the final measure of goods and services produced within a year.

When you hear reports that the economy grew at a rate of 3% for the first quarter of this year, what does that mean? When unemployment is at its highest level in six years, what does that indicate? The answers are in the business cycle.

A business cycle is a roller-coaster motion that shows whether the economy is moving up or down. This changing motion has to be measured by economic indicators that not only tell you whether the economy is moving up or down but also give more detailed information on how the economy is doing.

When businesses are operating at a good capacity level—meaning their production of goods and services is up, running, and steadily humming along—a business peak or economic boom may be occurring. On the other hand, if business starts to slow down a bit and sales of goods and services drop, the market may be entering the contraction part of the business cycle and possibly headed for a recessionary phase.

Economics + You = Understanding Wall Street

By understanding basic economic buzzwords, you'll have the ability to make better-educated investment decisions.

First, when you invest in a stock, a bond, a stock or bond mutual fund, or even futures and options, what are you investing in? Businesses. Determining the position of the business cycle helps you determine how these businesses are doing.

Here's an example. Let's assume the nation's general business production is on the upswing. Sales are rising everywhere in every industry. Now let's assume I own a publicly traded company that makes sleepwear for children. My company's business production has been steadily increasing as parents buy their children the sleepwear that my company produces.

As a result of the parental demand for my company's sleepwear, my profits in my company are rising, too, assuming I've kept my company expenses at a fixed level. Ultimately, this is good news for my company stock, and let's say the stock price rises also. However, not only are you "consuming these goods," you also are a shareholder in my company stock, since it's a publicly-traded company. As my company's profits increase, resulting in a positive bottom line (meaning, I'm taking in more money than I'm spending), the demand not only for the sleepwear increases, investors take notice at the improved finances (healthy bottom line), and the result? Investors demand to invest in the company (in the form of stock), which pushes the stock price higher. As a shareholder and a parent, you're a happy camper.

What?
A period of rising prices is *inflation,* meaning it costs you more to purchase a typical bundle of goods. You'll see in Chapter 4 how inflation affects your buying and investment decisions.

But a new twist occurs within this hypothetical example. The manufacturers who I buy my material from to make the sleepwear have had to raise their prices by five percent. Why? It costs them more to buy cotton from their supplier to make the material that they sell to me. Of course, I still need this material because I need to continue my business. If it's costing me five percent more to produce the same number of pajamas, I have less money in profits. This hurts my bottom line, and possibly my company's stock price, which means the price of the shares of stock that you own in my company drops. I probably have to raise my prices on the sleepwear to increase profits, (or try to reduce company expenses) but that can dampen consumer demand because parents may not want to buy their children expensive pajamas.

This is a pretty cut and dry example of how the economy's position in the business cycle—the expansionary phase, because sales are rising and production is increasing—affects the financial markets.

Let's take this example one step further. Suppose I raise my prices on the sleepwear that I distribute to stores and consumer demand does drop a little—not a lot, but enough to make a small dent in my production. As prices on my products and possibly other company products rise simultaneously, talk of inflation starts nationwide. Because of the higher prices on these products (think consumer goods), everyone's dollars purchase less than they did. Inflation is a decline in your purchasing power.

What happens if sales fall for most companies and they're not getting as much money coming in? The production of goods and services decreases. If my company has a reduction in the number of pajamas manufactured, I might not need as many workers, for example. I might have to lay some of them off. Those workers are then unemployed, which affects the unemployment rate.

What?
Technically, the *unemployment rate* is the percent of persons in the labor force who are not working, but are either actively seeking a job or waiting to begin or return to a job.

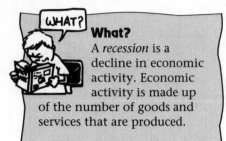

What?
A *recession* is a decline in economic activity. Economic activity is made up of the number of goods and services that are produced.

At this point, the economy approaches the recession part of the business cycle. Economists usually say it takes about two successive quarters (six months) of declining performance or no growth to result in a downturn in economic activity. Remember how this downturn in economic activity was defined? It's a decline in goods and services produced—which is gross domestic product—and a rise in unemployment. As an investor, you probably don't want to invest in a company that is experiencing a decline in production.

Second, think of the biggest component of economics—interest rates. If you follow the general direction of interest rates, whether they are rising or falling, you can determine what types of investments you should look for.

For example, there are investments that are interest-rate sensitive, meaning for every blip up or down an interest rate takes, the value of those investments will move accordingly. An example? Bonds. Bonds are IOUs. You know when you have an IOU to pay, you have to pay the amount you borrowed plus interest. The interest rate on these bonds fluctuates (rises and falls).

Here's the point. If the general direction of interest rates in the economy is rising or falling, it will affect investments that carry an interest rate, such as bonds, and the rates on the bonds will shift accordingly.

The Power Players

Businesses play a big part in the economy. But so do others. The power players are the ones who affect your investment decisions, whether you're trying to earn a gazillion percent on your bond investments or figuring out when is the best time to invest.

Who are these players? The federal government, for one. The legislators and the President of the United States. The Federal Reserve, for another, composed of the chairman and twelve Federal Reserve Board governors who monitor and control our nation's banking system—specifically, interest rates. Our foreign friends who lend the United States money have an impact, too. Finally, there's another player—you. See why in a minute.

Big Brother

The government controls our economy in several ways. First, it receives its money, or revenues, by taxing you. Then it takes this money and spends it on a number of things: bridges, defense, transportation, education, and so on.

The government keeps a budget similar to a family one. You work at a job and get a paycheck. That's your income. The government relies on revenues from the taxes that they collect from you. That's its income. If it doesn't collect enough money from taxes, it can borrow it from you by selling you U.S. Treasury securities (more on this in Part 5).

You have expenses—food, clothing, rent or a mortgage, credit card bills—and plan to meet these expenses and, of course, have a little left over. That's balancing your budget. The government does the same thing—well, sort of. It tries to balance the books every year, but the feds haven't been able to balance the budget for a quarter of a century. They have been running a budget deficit.

What?
Gross revenues are money received before expenses and taxes are taken out.

Every year the deficit keeps growing. In fact, in 1983, it got as high as $200 billion. In 1990, the budget deficit was $220.4 billion, $100 billion more than forecasted. In 1996, the budget deficit soared to $107 billion.

Let's take the next step. If you add up all the budget deficits, you come up with the national debt. So, when you hear someone say, "The national debt is running at $3 trillion" (or whatever the figure), the federal budget deficit is where that figure comes from. Unfortunately, many people also say, "Oh, don't worry about this. Our children and grandchildren will pay for it." Guess what, folks, you have to pay for it. How? Tax increases, for one.

Every time the government has to borrow money, they sell Treasury securities to people. Bingo! Here's where investing and the financial markets enter the picture.

What?
When the government spends more than it takes in (the normal state of affairs these days), it's operating with a *budget deficit*. This is spending more than is brought in, so there's not enough money left over to keep up with expenses.

When the government sells these securities, you give them money, and they pay you interest on these same securities. That's why Treasury securities are also known as IOUs. These interest payments are what you and all other investors in Treasury securities receive if you invest in Treasuries.

So what does this have to do with making money on Wall Street? Plenty. You've invested with the government. That's the investing part. Because this money is out of your pocket, you're not spending it on groceries, or homes, or anything. It isn't circulating out there in America. That's the economics part. (Hang in there. This makes sense in a minute.) Because there's a reduced amount of money floating around in the system, the supply of money shrinks. And guess what happens when something that you need shrinks? It becomes more scarce.

What?
The total amount of debt the country is in is our *national debt* (the total of our annual budget deficits over time).

If the money supply shrinks, interest rates go up. Couple that with the government borrowing more money—well, that just pushes interest rates higher. Nine times out of ten, a change in interest rates has a major impact on the financial markets and ultimately, your investment decisions.

The Fed

Speaking of interest rates, let's check out what the Federal Reserve (also known as the Fed) does. As our country's central bank, it watches the activities of all banks nationwide.

What?
Economists call the total stock of money that is circulating in the economy the *money supply*. Your personal money supply is the dollar bills in your pockets…plus what you have in your piggy bank, and so on.

However, its biggest influence is on the direction of interest rates. How does it do this? The Federal Reserve chairman raises or lowers the rate at which smaller banks borrow from the Fed. This is known as the discount rate. Think of it this way. Imagine a teller window (which technically is the discount window) that smaller banks use to borrow from the Fed. When one takes out a loan from this window, there's interest to pay. The interest rate in this case is the discount rate.

When the Fed changes the discount rate, other rates usually follow. Here is a list of interest rates that shape our economy.

Federal Funds Rate. When your bank needs to have at least 20 percent of its customers' deposits in the vault overnight but falls short of that, it borrows money from my bank. But this borrowed money isn't free. My bank charges your bank an interest rate (the federal funds rate) to borrow the money. The Fed doesn't necessarily "set" this rate but rather affects it by adding or draining the reserves to and from the banking system. If they add more money, it costs less to borrow, and the federal funds rate declines. If they take money out of the system, it costs more to borrow money, and the federal funds rate increases.

Prime Rate. This is the interest rate that banks charge to their largest customers—big customers, such as huge corporations—when these customers want to borrow

Secret
Individuals never get a loan at the prime rate, but other loan rates are based on the prime rate. That's what it means when a loan is "tied to the prime."

money. If an individual wants to borrow money, either for a house, a car, or a personal loan, that loan rate is based on the prime rate, with a few extra percentage points added in. If the prime rate was 7.50%, big customers would borrow money at this rate. If you wanted to buy a house, your rate would be the prime rate plus an additional rate (the percentage points) that the lender would charge you.

Discount Rate. The Fed has to make money, too, and it does so by assessing an interest rate (discount rate) on the money banks borrow from the Federal Reserve.

Discount Window. Almost like a private bank teller window, this is the place where banks go to borrow money at the discount rate.

The Federal Reserve is the entity that controls the supply of money. When the Fed decides there is too much money in the system, it dilutes the supply by selling the government bonds that it owns. But the Fed has to be cautious because when there's not enough money in the system, a recession can result. Recall 1991, when the U.S. was in a full-blown recession. Businesses struggled as they tried to borrow money that was in short supply. As it did then, the Fed can pump more money back into the system by printing more money and circulating it throughout the economy. However, sometimes when there's too much money in the economy, it can lead to inflation because it tends to raise prices of goods and services that are produced.

The bottom line is that the Fed's job is to put enough money into our economy to keep it running smoothly—without having interest rates skyrocket or drop too quickly.

Foreign Countries

The United States depends on foreign countries, such as Germany, China, and England, to buy the products that it makes—those are exports. Americans, in turn, buy products from other countries—called imports. Unfortunately, the United States spends more on imports than it collects from exports.

Foreign countries also invest in the U.S. by purchasing Treasury securities—basically the government's debts and IOUs. The amount of Treasury securities foreign countries purchase makes up about 22 percent of the total amount of Treasuries that exist. The interest rates offered on these securities have to be attractive enough to entice foreign buyers. If they aren't and foreigners don't buy them, the rates have to rise in order to attract other buyers.

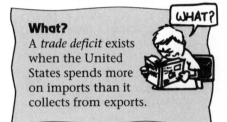

What?
A *trade deficit* exists when the United States spends more on imports than it collects from exports.

You

Now for that last factor that controls the economy. You stare at it in the bathroom mirror every day. It's you—the American consumer. The decisions you make on a day-to-day basis influence the economy. For example, if Americans decide to purchase Japanese cars rather than American cars, money is being spent on cars that are imported. If enough American products aren't sold overseas, the trade deficit increases.

Perhaps consumers are not spending a lot of their disposable income on any extra goods besides necessities. Consumer spending is down and not a lot of money is exchanging hands in our economic system. What happens then? Ultimately, interest rates are affected because the Fed has to pump more money into the economy to give it a kick. Businesses begin to increase production, and that helps their profits. If

What?
Look at your paycheck stub. See that little box labeled Gross Pay? That's your gross income. Now check out all the little boxes where taxes are taken out, and social security, medicare (you name it). Guess what you're left with? *Disposable income.*

you've invested money in stock in that company, the price should rise, and you'll either realize a profit or buy more shares.

Check In with Dr. Econ

Because our economy affects the financial markets (although some theorists say it's the other way around), there are critical reports that need to be monitored the same way a doctor monitors your vital signs. Each can send the price of an investment really high or reduce it to a fraction of its original value. Here's a thumbnail sketch of a few economic buzzwords and phrases that you should know.

Secret

If you really want to follow the direction of the economy and determine where we are in a business cycle, follow all of the economic indicators listed here. Then watch the financial markets to see how they react. It's a great way to familiarize yourself with the relationship between economics and Wall Street.

The *consumer price index (CPI)* tracks the changes in prices of food, housing, clothing, transportation, and electricity. You might also know it as the cost-of-living index. Economists and market watchers use this figure as an indicator of inflation. If the price of cereal increases, it's reflected in the CPI.

The *index of leading economic indicators* usually forecasts the future of the economy and is the most widely watched figure. In this index are 11 different reports, including the number of unemployment claims made, weekly average hours of work completed by factory workers, and stock prices. This indicator is highly regarded because its analysis can predict when there will be an economic slowdown (recession and higher unemployment) or even an upturn in business productivity (possible inflation).

The *gross domestic product* is a total measurement of the goods and services produced in the U.S. by American companies. Along with the index of leading economic indicators, the gross domestic product is the standard by which the health and growth of our economy is measured.

The *durable goods report* is an economic indicator that discloses information about those big-ticket items (refrigerators, televisions, washers and dryers, and automobiles—only the basic necessities in life!). If they're not bought, they stay on the shelf. When companies can't get rid of them, their business slows down…and so does the economy.

The *unemployment report* measures the unemployment rate. Many people watch for this report because the stock market reacts to this figure immediately.

Set 'Em Up, Knock 'Em Down

Economics is about people and the choices they make. Think of the economy and the financial markets as dominoes: when the first one gets hit, all the others are affected.

Remember the sleepwear company I owned? The first domino that was struck was my material supplier. As he increased his prices, I had to make changes to compensate for the price increase. That was the next domino. As more changes were made, more dominoes were affected.

Understanding where the country is in the business cycle affects your investment decisions. Once you understand economics and how these important economic reports affect your investments, you'll make better-educated decisions as an investor.

Learn How Money Talks

Money talks. So what's it sayin'? It's talking about terms you should know. You were introduced to a few in the first chapter, such as an *investment product*. Many times in the investment world, investment product will be used interchangeably with *investment security*, *financial security*, *financial product*, *investments*, and *financial instrument*.

You also learned in the last chapter one of the trade secrets to making money on Wall Street: Buy low and sell high. But let's take the next step. What are you buying and selling? Some potential investment products are the following:

Bank products. "Why bank products?" you query. The banking industry is changing. Banks are catching up to their Wall Street competitors by offering comparable investment products. The mainstay of their business has traditionally been savings accounts, checking accounts, certificates of deposit, and money market deposit accounts. Today, it's not uncommon to see your bank offer mutual funds and insurance products.

Stocks. When you hear of the word "investing," most people think about stocks. Buying low and selling high is a strategy that works best here. A share of stock represents a piece of ownership you have in a company. If my sleepwear company has a total of 100,000 shares of stock and you own 100 of those shares, you own one 1/100 of my company. I can change the number of shares that exist by either selling more shares to you, your family and friends, and the general public or by buying these shares back. Then your proportion of ownership changes, too.

> **What?**
> When you buy one hundred shares of stock, that is known as a *round lot*. Anything less than 100 shares of stock is known as an *odd lot*.

Bonds. Think of a bond as an IOU. A bond is a certificate that stands for a loan *from* the investors buying the bonds to the company that issued them. Here's an example. Let's say you own a company that makes the little plastic rings on the outside of shoelaces. Your product is selling like hot cakes, and you need to increase production to make more little plastic rings. But you have no more money left. To raise more money (also known as capital) you "take out a loan" by issuing a bond certificate to me. In return for loaning you my money for a specific period of time, you promise to pay me a fixed amount of interest every six months. At the end of the specified time period, I receive the amount I loaned to you.

Mutual Funds. A mutual fund is an organization whose only business is investing your money. They don't make widgets or gizmos. They invest everyone's money by "pooling" it together to buy or sell stocks, bonds, or a combination of the two. You can choose from different types of mutual funds based upon your investment objective. Do you want your money to grow or would you rather have income from it? Mutual funds either carry a load (a sales charge) or they are no-load (no sales charges at all).

Options. When you invest in options, you have the right but not the obligation to either *buy* or sell the underlying security (typically stock). Options that give you the right to buy the underlying security are known as *calls*. Options that give you the right to *sell* the underlying security are known as *puts*. These rights allow you to buy or sell the investment for a certain price at a later date.

Bulls, Bears, and Such

Those are just the basics about a few investment products. Now here's a few more words to get you going.

You hear about these bulls and bears all over Wall Street. What are they?

1. Animals from the city zoo.
2. Investors dressed up in costumes running up and down the streets of New York.
3. Animal crackers from a cookie box.
4. Names for market watchers.

I sure hope you picked number 4. There are two animals on Wall Street—two four-legged ones, that is. The bulls and the bears. When industry experts claim "Oh yes! We're heading toward a bull market!" do you know what that means?

A bull is a pretty ferocious animal that stomps its hoof on the ground several times when it's ready to CHARGE. A bull in the financial markets means the same thing—full steam ahead. If prices on many investment securities are rising and the general consensus is that they're going to continue upward, it is a long-term *bull market*. A bull market pushes its way up and takes prices with it.

If you think prices on different investment products are going up and you are optimistic about the general direction of the financial markets, you are said to be *bullish*.

On the flip side are the bears. Bears meander through the wilderness and fish for salmon in cold streams. They are huge and sometimes awkwardly clumsy (no offense to the Chicago Bears, please). They don't charge forward and at times catch people by surprise. But once they get moving—boy, can they hustle.

In financial terms, bear markets react the same way. A *bear market* brings prices down. Party poopers and prophets of doom rejoice. These market watchers tend to be big-time pessimists. If you think prices on different investment products are going down and you are pessimistic about the direction of the financial markets, you are said to be *bearish*.

Keep in mind that whether it's a bull market or a bear market, you can make a profit. You'll learn how later on.

Technical Versus Fundamental Differences

You know what the products are. Good. You learned that buying low and selling high is a good financial strategy. Great! But what's low and what's high? Obviously, that depends on price. Many times, when the price is right, you can make a bundle. Here's a few more terms that will help *you* learn what's low and what's high.

Many times, prices of an investment rise and fall, and rise and fall, eventually creating a pattern. Investors who base their buying and selling decisions on these patterns—known as price patterns—are referred to as *technicians*. These are the market wizards with dozens of colored pencils and reams of graph paper. They don't care if a company makes widgets, gadgets, or gizmos. They just look at the charts they've created and determine the target price at which to either buy or sell an investment. They often look at past price history (past performance) to aid in their decision. This function is known as *technical analysis*.

What about those financial geniuses who place more emphasis on the value of an investment rather than its price? These intellectuals analyze the financial conditions of companies and markets and buy when the price of the investment has not realized its real value and sell when it is considered to be overvalued. These value-oriented investors are known as *fundamentalists* and the function they perform is *fundamental analysis*. They crunch numbers from a company's annual report and try to make sense out of them. They also investigate why a particular security is out-of-favor among market watchers. Or they may study why a security is so hot that everyone seems to be lapping it up.

These are just the basic terms in the world of investing. In each chapter you will find a definition box that explains some not-so-common terms. You can also check the Glossary in the back of this book. Good luck!

The Least You Need to Know

➤ Economics isn't boring. In fact, if you know how our economy operates, you can make educated investment decisions.

➤ The economic reports that the government releases give a good indication about the strength and weakness of our economy.

➤ The biggest players in our economy are the federal government, the Federal Reserve, foreign countries, and you, the consumer.

➤ In the world of investing, there are many different investment products, which are also known as securities or instruments. You'll learn more in this book about bank products, stocks, bonds, mutual funds, and options.

Chapter 3

Your Personal Financial Battle Plan

In This Chapter

➤ Determining your financial goals and planning to reach them

➤ Knowing a financial rule you can't afford to live without

➤ Discovering where to find money to invest

The single most important financial goal is that you want your money to work as hard for you as you do for it. Making an investment plan is half the battle. Not only does it tell you where you stand financially right now, it will help determine where you want to be in the future. This chapter helps you put together your personal financial battle plan.

Setting a Goal—And Figuring Out How to Reach It

So where do you want to go? What do you want? It's time to set some goals.

Setting goals isn't difficult. Think back to grade school when you were the top contender in the 6th grade spelling bee. You had a goal of getting through the word "zoophagous" (look it up!) and winning the championship. Or in high school when you were on the football team, you set a goal to score the most touchdowns in a single quarter. All you are doing now is applying the same discipline to your investment plan.

Secret
Don't put off making a financial plan until tomorrow. Tomorrow always comes, you know.

Take out a piece of paper. Divide up the time frames and what your goals are into four categories: Five years, Ten years, Twenty years, and Thirty years. Write these down. It may look something like this:

➤ Five years—Pay off school loans, credit card bills, auto loans, any other "bad" debt.

➤ Ten years—Buy a new home.

➤ Twenty years—Pay for children's college education.

➤ Thirty years—Invest for retirement—and enjoy it!

Now, next to these goals write down how much money each goal is going to require. Don't be surprised at your results. Unless you already have the money socked away somewhere, most people will have to put up additional funds to reach these goals. The amount of the additional funds will determine what types of investment products you will buy and sell.

To continue with the example, it may look like this:

Secret
Want to calculate your savings needs for retirement goals using the Web? Then log on folks...SmartCalc (in partnerships with many websites and online services) provides more than 100 borrowing, investment, or financial planning calculators, including a retirement calculator. You can specifically, for example, see if you're saving enough for retirement, calculate your *future* living expenses, and what effect inflation may have on your retirement savings. Check it out at **http://www.smartcalc.com** in their "Calculator" page.

➤ Five years—Pay off school loans, auto loans, credit card bills, or any other bad debt: $10,000.

➤ Ten years—Buy a new home (twenty percent down payment, $200,000 home): $40,000.

➤ Twenty years—Pay for one child's college education: $100,000.

➤ Thirty years—Invest for retirement: $1,000,000.

When you add up the total of what you'll need monetarily to meet all your financial goals, you'll realize that the bottom-line number is more than $1,000,000. If you're like most hard-working people living paycheck to paycheck, or paying off high-rate credit card debt, reaching these goals may seem impossible. But they don't have to be.

You can meet those financial goals as long as you make the commitment. You've got the first part down: You are in the midst of planning your work and working your plan. Now, can you see why investing is so important? You need to use the magic of compounding and the essence of time to work for you to attain these goals.

Don't change your goals. Do not look at the bottom line and say "Oh, these numbers are too high. I'll never get there." With that attitude, you won't. But this book will help you get there. How? Discipline.

Let's put together a plan to meet your goals.

Buying a Home

Let's take the goal of buying a house. Ah, the American dream. This is the most expensive purchase you can make. But it is probably the biggest investment you can make, too. There's a lot of pride in home ownership—not to mention the tax breaks and the potential for appreciation through the years.

It will take more money to save for a house than any other major purchase. If the median price of a three-bedroom, two-bath home in your area is $180,000, you may need up to 20 percent of that for a down payment—that's $36,000. For many hard-working people, that's more than an average annual salary. If you save $200 a month over the next ten years and earn an annual rate of 6% (which is considered conservative), you'll almost make it, having saved $32,940 at the end of those ten years.

Secret
Even though you can get a mortgage with as little as 3 percent down, try to put down as much as possible. In fact, if you can meet the standard twenty percent down payment, do so. Why? This way you avoid paying private mortgage insurance (PMI), which insures the insurer for lending you the money to buy a house without a lot of money as a down payment. Keep in mind that closing costs also tack on an average $4,000, depending on which state you live in.

But what if you want the house sooner? Well, then you're going to have to allocate more than just $200 a month and/or invest in an investment product that pays a better return than 6%. You may wish to refer back to Table 1.2 in Chapter 1 as a guide or you can check out the "Investment Pyramid" in Chapter 4, which lists an investment product, its level of risk, and the type of annual return you can expect.

Education

And a college education for the kids? Sending them to the school of hard knocks seems a bit easier on the wallet. Perhaps, but if you incorporate the principle of discipline, Junior can go to the school of his choice.

True, the average cost of tuition, room, and board at a four-year public university has skyrocketed—and the increases aren't going to cease. Experts now project that a four-year education at a public university will cost more than $120,000 15 years from now. Private college for four years will set you back a quarter of a million bucks.

What?
Don't forget to look into financial aid and student loans where necessary. Call 800-4FED-AID. And tap into your computer, Internet service provider, and your modem to find the most comprehensive resource on student financial aid at **http://www.ed.gov/prog_info/ SFA/StudentGuide/**, which is published by the U.S. Department of Education.

To meet the rising costs of sending your children to school, implement a planned investing program. If you invest $50 a month for the next 20 years with an 8% annual return, you will have almost $25,000. Double the monthly investment to $100 a month and you'll get $59,294. Even $200 a month over 20 years equates to almost $93,000.

If you are investing your money for a child's education, the earlier you begin, the better. Many mutual fund companies are implementing college savings programs for parents to invest in for their children's future. For example, T. Rowe Price (800) 638-5660 is a no-load mutual fund company that will send you a college planning package for free. This package of information gives you projections for college costs in the future as well as tells you how much money you have to save per month. Or, simply log onto their website at **http://www.troweprice.com** and get discount brokerage information, mutual fund performance data, and an update on the new tax law changes.

Retirement

Planning for retirement? Just like planning for a kid's college education, the earlier you begin, the easier it will be to achieve your goal.

One of the best ways of planning to reach your goal of retirement—and defer paying taxes until then, too—is setting up an IRA, which is an individual retirement account. The IRA was designed in 1975 for people who were not covered by a company-sponsored retirement plan to help them save for retirement. You can set up this account with a brokerage firm, a discount brokerage firm, or a mutual fund company. It's not an investment, like a stock or a bond, but an account that you put your money in and buy and sell different investment securities.

Bet You Didn't Know

If you invest $2,000 a year every year for 30 years (assuming a modest 6% annual return) in an IRA instead of a taxable account, you will have accumulated almost $50,000 *more* in the IRA in the same amount of time!

Once the account is set up, you are allowed to make an annual contribution of up to a legal maximum of $2,000 or 100 percent of your earned income for that year, whichever is less.

Tax Law Changes of IRAs in '97: Now What?

With the new tax law changes in 1997, the IRA structure has been liberalized. Congress, who would've thought?

You now have more opportunities to shelter your earnings from federal taxes beginning in 1998. You can make a fully deductible IRA contribution—up to a $2,000 maximum—even if you participate in a company retirement program. One caveat: Your income level must be below $50,000 on a joint return or $30,000 on an individual one.

What can you do if your adjusted gross income is higher? Consider the Roth IRA, initially dubbed the IRA Plus. Benefit: If you don't qualify for tax-deductible contributions to traditional IRAs you have the chance to avoid (not evade) all federal tax as long as the money is used for retirement or other "qualifying" purposes. Your $2,000 contribution can be made even if you earn as much as $150,000 on a joint return and $95,000 on an individual return.

> **Secret**
> Don't wait until the last minute—such as April 14th or your 58th birthday—to make your IRA contribution. The earlier in the year you make your contribution, the longer your money will grow tax-deferred. Make your contribution as early as you can.

Uncle Sam is also providing some relief to parents trying to reduce staggering tuition costs. Parents can open an educational savings account, set up like a Child IRA, for children under age 18. Beginning in 1998, contributions of up to $500 a year can accumulate tax free on earnings, and would be tax-free when withdrawn for education prior to age 30. Just in case you were wondering, an annual contribution of $500 for 18 years—jettison taxes—is a $9,000 investment, not including any potential return you could earn, depending in your investment product choices. However, (there's always a however), the contributions are not tax deductible if your household income is more than $150,000 on a joint return and $95,000 on a single return.

No matter what, keep the following in mind:

➤ The $2,000 annual contribution must come from earned income, such as from your salary.

➤ You may begin taking distributions as early as age 59 1/2—if you withdraw the money earlier than that, you face stiff penalties according to IRS rules, although as of this writing, Congress is debating IRS withdrawal rules on education, emergency medical, and unemployment expenses. Mandatory age for distribution is 70 1/2, except with the Roth IRA.

➤ You don't have to pay taxes on the money that accumulates (even the profits you make in the IRA). That's why this is known as tax-deferred investing. (You pay taxes when you begin taking distributions.)

Here's how the new changes look:

IRA Change	Tax Deduct.	Participate in Co. Plan	Joint Return	Single Return
New twist on old IRA	Yes, $2k max	Yes	$50,000	$30,000
Roth IRA (must use for retirement)	No, $2k max	Yes	$150,000	$95,000
Child IRA (children must be under age 18)	No, $500 max	Yes	$150,000	$95,000

You have time on your side. You are figuring out your goals now years before you plan to reach them. This part of the process is letting you know the following:

➤ What your goals are.

➤ When you want them.

➤ How much they'll cost.

➤ How much you'll need to invest to get there.

A Few Tools to Help

Secret
Even if you don't get a tax deduction, you still receive the benefit of tax-deferred compounding when you invest in an IRA. This is also known as sheltering your investments from income taxes. Check it out.

Before you start digging into the desk drawers that are filled with your financial records, please be aware that there are a few tools to help you become organized—and none of them is a shovel!

The mainstay to organizing your finances in the future is computer software packages. They range from simple to downright computer-nerdy. Each computer software package is designed specifically for you with one goal in mind: To help you GET CONTROL (there's that phrase again) of your finances.

Most financial software packages enable you to:

➤ Pay your bills electronically.

➤ Create a budget and track your expenses.

➤ Create and monitor your own personal investment portfolio.

➤ Update investment security prices (via modem, typically).

➤ Figure out how much you'll need for your children's college education.

➤ Assist you in planning for retirement.

The only thing these programs can't do is make you breakfast.

You can use a financial software program to its fullest potential—projecting your budget on an annual basis and consistently managing your investment portfolio. Or you may wish just to get your financial records in order. In any event, transferring the mess from your desk to your computer will pay off!

My favorite software package for working with your budget and developing investment goals is Quicken Deluxe. This isn't a commercial, but rather, my humble opinion. Quicken Deluxe provides you with features to pay your bills electronically, track your investments daily, create financial records, such as asset and liability statements, and updates security prices for you on all your investments listed in your portfolio. The cost of the software package is around $80, but you can purchase it online at **http:// www.quicken.com**.

If you do not have access to a personal computer, you can always create your own on a notebook or purchase *The Budget Kit* (Dearborn Financial Publishing, (800) 322-8621) for $15.95, one of my favorite budgeting books. Author Judy Lawrence gives you step-by-step instructions on how to create your own budget categories, track your monthly expenses, and determine how much money you can invest. The Budget Kit is also available on CD-ROM. Check with Dearborn Financial Publishing for details on pricing.

A Look at Your Budget

Before you can improve your financial condition and start investing, you need to complete the following three steps:

1. Clean up the mess and get organized—it's not difficult, trust me.
2. Add up the pluses and minuses—good debt versus bad debt.
3. Create your own budget.

Clean Up the Mess

Getting organized is the key. At one point or another, many people have had the motivation to sort out their financial affairs. Some even go as far as making a New Year's resolution to develop a sound financial system for themselves and their families. This usually lasts about as long as a New Year's diet does, although I'm sure people stick to their diets better than they maintain their financial records.

Don't worry—this won't be nearly as painful as dieting. If you've kept pretty good records over the years, pat yourself on the back. Nearly six in ten Americans do not organize their financial records.

Careful
Having the ability to update your portfolio and trade your stocks, bonds, mutual funds, and so on at your fingertips can work against you if it leads you to place more trades than necessary. This isn't a Nintendo game. The money you are working with is for real. Carefully monitor your trading.

The numbers increase for those people who do not even balance their checkbooks. If you have set up a filing system, great! But if your underwear drawer is stuffed with unopened envelopes that hold your monthly bank statements, shame on you.

First, let's make this easy. You don't need years' and years' worth of information. Just use information and receipts from the past six months or even three months. Just get started. You'll be able to project for the remaining months of the year what you'll spend.

Some of you may want to be super-organized and get together all the information that you'd need if you were preparing your tax returns. The idea is not to be overwhelmed but just to be organized. You can't make educated investment decisions if you don't do the following:

➤ Start with organized records.

➤ Create a budget that you can work within.

➤ Learn how much money you can afford to invest.

The first step to organization is a file cabinet. A shoebox should just be meant, well, for shoes. You need a separate, organized space for your financial records. Why? Because this material needs to be kept for at least three years according to the IRS. It will help you to set this up as an annual filing system. These materials should include but are not limited to the following:

➤ Copies of your old federal and state tax returns (front *and* back!).

➤ Copies of canceled checks paid to the IRS for income tax payments.

➤ Paycheck stubs.

➤ Copies of the W-2s that you receive from your employer(s).

➤ 1099s from any independent contracting work that you have done, or from dividends and interest that you have earned.

➤ Bank statements and brokerage statements (if you have any yet).

➤ Checkbook registers (make sure you start a new one each year).

➤ Records of mortgage interest paid if you own a house.

➤ Records of medical expenses and other deductible expenses (see Chapter 32 for further explanation).

Make sure all of these records are stored safely in a file cabinet in a folder labeled "Tax Returns for 19XX." Do this from now on. Second, gather your tools. Purchase a three-ring binder, 12 sheets of paper dividers with tabs, a paper hole punch, a stapler, a box of legal-size envelopes, and a box of extra-large 8 1/2" × 11" envelopes.

Label one drawer of the filing cabinet for tax returns, the other "January to December." Put the 12 dividers with tabs in the three-ring binder. Label the tabs with the months of the year. Every time you receive a bill—telephone bill, electric bill, charge card bills—put the tear-off stub of the bill in this three-ring binder.

For example, suppose it's November 9th and you just received your telephone bill. Tear off the bill payment portion and put it with its envelope and your payment. Next, using your stapler and paper punch, staple together the parts of the bill that you save and punch three holes in it. Write your check number on it and the date you sent the payment. Finally, put it in the three-ring binder, and you're on your way to organization!

Do this with all your bills. You can even paper punch bank statements, paycheck stubs, and any loan statements and place them in the corresponding months.

Those of you who like to save all your receipts can do so with envelopes. For example, I like to save all my ATM receipts. At the end of every month, I put them in date order, cross-reference them with my check register, staple them together, and put them in an envelope marked ATM Receipts. I do the same thing with taxi receipts, gas receipts, grocery receipts, and clothing receipts.

Why? Because I'm an organizational freak? No way! Because if all of my receipts are in order, at the end of the year I can add them up and figure out how much I spend on each annually. Believe me, it really puts your financial affairs in perspective when you find out that you spent more money on shoes than you did on groceries in a single year!

> **Secret**
> Software programs, such as Quicken and Microsoft Money, can also help you organize your records. These products let you enter all of the information relevant to your personal finances and investment portfolios. Then, you can have the program analyze the information to help you budget and forecast your financial situation. While this gives you an electronic record, you should still keep copies of the "paper" records on file in a safe deposit box or a fireproof safe at home.

Adding Up the Pluses and Minuses

Now that you have this information organized, you can start determining where you are financially. That means figuring out your pluses and minuses. By doing the exercises in this chapter, you can see how your assets (the pluses) match or mismatch with your liabilities (the minuses). Here are some terms you should know before you embark on adding it all up:

Secret
The more debt you are burdened with, the longer it will take to dig yourself out of a hole. Your first priority should be to *eliminate* nonproductive debt.

WHAT?

What?
Your *investment portfolio* represents the sum of all of your stocks, bonds, mutual funds, futures, options, and so on, that you have invested in.

Assets. What you own, such as the *equity* in your house, your car (if paid for, otherwise the lender owns it), your furniture, your property, and your bank accounts.

Liabilities. What you still owe on your house, your car, credit cards, unpaid taxes, student loans, medical bills. If you owe it, it's a liability. There are good liabilities (good debt) and bad liabilities (bad debt).

Good Debt. What you still owe on your house. Why is it a good debt? Because the value of the asset (the house) can appreciate. The more you pay off on this good debt, the more equity you will have in your home.

Bad Debt. What you still owe on your car, your credit cards, student loans, and medical bills. These debt monsters don't work for you, rather they work against you. Plus, it's bad debt because you receive no tax breaks.

The name of the game is to have as few *bad* liabilities as possible and increase your assets substantially. You can do this by building wealth through your investment planning; however, that does not mean also increasing your credit card debt or buying an extra car. That only defeats your entire plan.

Let me give you an example of how bad debt works against you. Assume you made a $1,000 purchase last month on your 19.8% APR VISA, and you don't pay it off in full when the bill comes next month. You're the meet-the-minimum-payment type of consumer. At that rate, it will take you about *15 years* to pay off that 1,000 bucks. (This is how credit card companies make their money.) Plus—get this—there's an additional $4,100 in nondeductible finance charges.

Let's take it one step further. You have started building an investment portfolio of a few stocks, a couple of bonds, and a mutual fund or two. Let's assume the average annual return you make on your entire *investment portfolio* is 12%.

Here's where the bad debt attacks you, even if you are investing your money. If you're making 12% interest but are paying off a credit card balance of 19.8% on your $1,000 purchase, the money you make on your investments turns into *minus 7.8% (12% – 19.8%)!* You end up working even harder for that $1,000 purchase.

Of course you want to invest your money. However, equally as important is to get rid of the bad debt first. You can't get ahead in this investment race if you still have one foot in the ground. Once you reduce bad debt, your net worth will increase. You will also feel a sense of security with your growing net worth and will be able to change jobs and meet personal emergencies as they arise. Use the worksheets in the following figures to determine where you stand.

Financial Property	Date Purchased	How Much Did You Pay?	Today's Date	What's It Worth Today?
Bonds (type)				
Bond mutual funds (type)				
Certificate of deposit				
Checking accounts				
Coin collections				
Money market accounts				
Pensions & profit sharing plans				
Savings accounts				
Savings bonds				
Stocks				
Stock mutual funds				
Treasury securities				
Other				
Total Financial Property				

A financial property assets worksheet.

Once you figure out your financial property and your personal property, you can calculate your total assets. Then add up how much you owe on your liability worksheet. That sum is your liability statement. Now subtract your liabilities from your assets and you should have a positive number. That's your net worth. If it's negative, you're not alone. Hundreds of thousands of Americans have a negative net worth. This process is to identify more than just the mere importance of increasing your net worth through wise investing. That's just one itty-bitty part of the entire picture.

Secret
Keep in mind that not all debt is bad. Your mortgage debt isn't bad; you get tax breaks (all mortgage interest is currently 100% tax deductible) and you'll own a home that you hope will appreciate. Your payments contribute to building up your net worth through your biggest asset, your house.

A personal properties assets worksheet.

Personal Property	Date Purchased	How Much Did You Pay?	What's It Worth Today?
Appliances (washer & dryer, etc.)			
Automobiles			
Boats, campers			
Computers			
Furniture			
Fur coats			
Home			
Home furnishings			
—curtains			
—rugs			
—tableware (glasses, dishes)			
—blankets			
—lamps			
—silverware			
Jewelry			
Paintings			
Stereos			
Televisions			
Miscellaneous			
Total Personal Property			

What You Owe	To Whom	Interest Rate %	When Is It Due?	How Much Do You Owe?
Bills, bills, bills				
—electric				
—gas				
—retail stores				
—telephone				
—other				
Loans to family				
Loans to friends				
Automobile loans				
Bank loans				
Credit cards				
—credit card #1				
—credit card #2				
—credit card #3				
Furniture loans				
Student loans				
Mortgage				
Home equity loans				
Miscellaneous				
Total Liabilities				

A liabilities worksheet.

Creating Your Budget

Tracking where all your money goes is important. Figuring out your assets and liabilities to calculate your net worth assists you in determining how you spend your money. To keep these expenses in line, create a budget. Keeping a budget gives you insight into any nasty spending habits you might have. You can't afford a champagne lifestyle when you have a beer budget!

A common misconception is that following a budget means you can't start investing, which is untrue. You will learn in this book there are ways to budget your money, meet your expenses, and still have a few dollars left over that you *can* invest. Remember, it doesn't take a lot of money to begin.

After calculating your net worth and creating a healthy budget, you'll realize that in order to invest the money, it has to come from somewhere. You're either going to have to reduce some of your expenses or get another job. Unfortunately, millions of Americans already live in a two-paycheck family, and there are only so many hours in a day.

So where do you begin? You need to calculate your income on a monthly basis. Consider this Budget Number #1. Then, because you have organized all your receipts and financial papers from the past few months and have (I hope!) put them in their respective categories, it'll be easy to figure out how much the following regular expenses are:

Auto expenses—Car payment, auto insurance, maintenance, gas (save your receipts and payment stubs!).

Clothing expenses—Clothing, shoes, coats.

Dental expenses—Teeth cleaning, and so on (anything not covered by insurance if you have it).

Dining expenses—Restaurants, even if it's fast food (they add up!).

Entertainment—Movies, miniature golf, zoo.

Education—Kids' tuition, your tuition, books, and school supplies.

Gifts—Birthdays, holidays.

Groceries—Food, drugstore items (including cosmetics, contact solution, toothpaste, and so on).

Home business—Subcategories including equipment, supplies, taxes, and so on.

Household items—New things you buy for the house—furniture, plants, curtains, and so on.

Household expenses—This is different from the items above. These are things you buy for the upkeep of the house, such as paint, aluminum siding, lawn maintenance equipment and services, and so on.

Insurance—Life insurance, disability insurance, medical insurance, nursing home insurance, renter's insurance, homeowner's insurance.

Mortgage—If you own a home, fill in your mortgage payment.

Parking—If you have to pay to park (at work, when shopping, and so on).

Rent—If you are renting, fill in your monthly rent.

Taxes—Income taxes paid, real estate taxes.

Utilities—Including telephone bill, gas bill, electric bill.

Vacations—Including airplane tickets, hotel/motel accommodations, meals, sightseeing, and so on.

(These are just a few categories to get you started. Depending on your own situation, you may wish to add or delete a few.)

Calculate how much you spend on each category in a month. When you have determined each total, add them all up. That should be Budget Number #2.

Now complete this calculation to find out what you can invest each month:

Budget Number #1 – Budget Number #2 = What You Can Afford To Invest

If you break even or are "in the hole," you may have to cut some expenses. It's up to you to decide which expenses are necessities and which are just plain frivolous. If you are ahead of the game, congratulations!

An integral part to creating and working within a budget is monitoring—and possibly cutting—some spending habits.

> **Secret**
> If you want to forecast your annual budget, remember to take into account the changes in utility bills, (higher in winter, lower in summer) or non-monthly expenses, like car insurance and real estate taxes.

How Much Can You Afford to Invest?

Whatever money you have left over after subtracting your expenses from your income should work just as hard for you as you do for it. That's why you should choose to invest it, and you don't have to invest all of it if you don't want to. That decision is up to you. However, the more money you invest over a longer period of time, the more it has the potential to grow.

One rule of thumb is the 10 percent rule. Why 10 percent? Because it's easy to figure out in the math calculations. For example, if your monthly income is $2,500, 10 percent would be $250.00. Easy enough.

If you cannot afford the 10 percent rule, try and have at least $50 a month to begin your investment portfolio. If that is too much, start with $25—but no less. (You'll learn where you can invest with these amounts in Chapter 16.) Even if it means making holiday gifts instead of buying them or staying at home on vacation, the potential reward over the long-term is greater than any gift you could buy or any sightseeing tour you could take. Use the $50 or $25 as your own guideline. Once you start trimming your expenses (or perhaps receiving more income), add to the monthly amount as much as you can.

Pay Yourself First

Secret

One of the biggest expenses you can cut right now is debt. How? Getting rid of all but one credit card—just for emergencies—is a great way to begin, considering all the debt problems that many Americans face today. One way is to take that remaining credit card and put it in a container of water and freeze it. By the time it thaws out, your itch to spend may be gone.

WHAT?

What?

Your company may offer a *401(k) retirement plan*, which allows you to save for retirement with pretax dollars by sheltering your money and the profits you make from taxes until you retire. If your company has one, check into it! Usually the employee benefits department or human resources will carry information on this type of company-sponsored retirement program.

Treat yourself as if you were a monthly bill. On your budget worksheet, create another category. Call it the "Pay Yourself First" category. Remember that 10 percent rule? That's where this money goes.

This commitment requires you to further develop the habit of investing on a consistent basis. Before all of the other utility bills, before the kids' shoes, even before Monday night bowling, pay yourself first every time you receive your paycheck. Take this money and invest it. By earmarking it in your monthly budget, you are creating your fortune without even realizing it.

A number of financial strategies use this principle. In fact, you can pay yourself first by using automatic deductions that are taken directly out of your paycheck before you even see the money.

For example, if your company has a 401(k) retirement plan, you can automatically contribute a substantial percent of your *pretax* dollars. The rule of thumb is to contribute the maximum amount allowable, according to your company plan's rules. Companies sometimes match your contribution, which allows you to save even more.

The contributed moneys are invested in various types of money market, stock, or bond mutual funds, depending on what the company offers. The advantage of a 401(k) retirement plan is that you can shelter all the money that is invested in the plan from taxes until you retire as well as reduce your gross income.

The 401(k) retirement plan is definitely long-term and the crux of all retirement planning. With time on your side, you can see your investment grow substantially. Remember, doing something (something smart, that is) is better than doing nothing!

Contributing to your company's 401(k) plan is one way to pay yourself first. Another way is to have your paycheck directly deposited into your bank checking account or savings account. Why? Well, first you earn interest as soon as it hits the account (if it's an interest-bearing account) and don't have to wait in long teller lines during your lunch hour to deposit your check. Plus, you don't see it; it's automatically deposited. No temptation!

Secret
Some companies even match 401(k) contributions dollar for dollar up to a certain percentage of what you contribute. Where else can you earn 100% on your money?

Once you establish a direct deposit feature, have your bank take ten percent a week from your account and electronically transfer it into a money market account. This is a great way to get your feet wet in "dollar discipline." Plus, it eliminates the temptation to withdraw a few bucks for things that you don't really need. Plus, you'll earn better rates of interest than you do in a *noninterest*-bearing checking account. The money that accumulates in this money market account can eventually be invested in stocks, bonds, mutual funds, futures, or options as it grows.

Reducing your expenses is a smart move. So is paying yourself first!

Cash You Didn't Know You Had

You have hidden cash resources that can grow into a substantial investment nest egg.

If you were able to catch the dip in mortgage rates when they see-sawed in the first half of 1997 and refinanced, you could have saved hundreds of dollars over the life of your loan. Plus, for example, even $50 from an $875-a-month mortgage bill allows you to save and invest an extra $600 a year. If you invest $600 every year into an equity mutual fund that earns an average annual rate of 13% a year, it can grow to roughly $4,139 in five years—and that's not even counting dividends being reinvested in the fund.

You can find extra money by asking for discounts on your automobile insurance coverage. They include breaks for having air bags or antitheft equipment (such as a car alarms), for keeping annual mileage to less than 10,000, and for having no claims against your policy. Check with your insurance agent. These discounts can save you up to 20 percent of your average annual car insurance premiums. That could mean an extra $240 a year if your annual premiums are $1,200.

Another gold mine of extra money to invest is in your home-owner's insurance policies. By increasing your deductible to $500 or $1,000, you can lower your premiums and save as much as 10–20 percent a year.

Above all, ask yourself:

➤ **How much is my net worth?** If you're competing with a negative net worth and high credit card debt, you must eliminate your credit card debt. This will help increase your net worth, and you'll eventually be able to allocate more dollars to your investment plan.

➤ **What is 10 percent of my weekly take-home pay?** Calculating this figure is easy. Once you establish self-discipline and put that amount in investments, you'll see how much your money can grow.

➤ **At what rates of return over how long a period of time do I need?** This depends on what you're investing for (the house, the college education, your retirement). By determining how long you have until you reach these milestones, you'll know how conservative or aggressive you must be in your investing.

These are just a few questions you should ask yourself. As you learn more from each chapter of this book, you'll be able to judge how well your investment plan is going.

The Least You Need to Know

➤ Everyone needs a plan before he can make his dream a reality. Work your plan and plan your work!

➤ Organizing your financial records is the key to successful investing. Once you know where you stand financially, you'll be able to determine which investments are right for you.

➤ Automatically save at least 10 percent of your paycheck. This strong discipline will pay off handsomely as the money accumulates. If you can't, you should begin with $50 or $25 a month. As you trim your expenses, you will be able to add to it.

➤ Only you can determine what you are going to do with your money. Determine what you want, how much money you're going to need, and how long you're going to have to invest your money to reach those goals.

Chapter 4

How Risk Plays a Part on Wall Street

In This Chapter

➤ Knowing how much you can afford—and can't afford—to lose

➤ Discovering your investment style

➤ Learning the trade-off between risk and reward

Investing on Wall Street is nothing more than balancing the rewards of risk and return. Let's face it, there are risks involved in everything you do these days. If you decide to eat a greasy hamburger instead of a sprout-laden tofuburger, boom! Clogged arteries. How about whitewater rafting through the Grand Canyon instead of the annual family vacation to Disney World? Somehow being tossed around in a six-by-four-foot inner tube, trying to avoid submerged boulders seems quite risky.

This chapter will help you assess how much risk you can, and should, build into your investment plan.

How Much Risk Can You Take?

What?
Your investment's *liquidity* depends on how easily and quickly your investment can be converted into cash. Every investment product has a time factor determining how quickly that product can be converted into cash. For example, a savings account is very liquid; you can easily get at your cash. The harder it is to convert your money from an investment to cash, the more risks there are.

Investing in stocks, bonds, mutual funds, futures, and options all carry some type of risks and all to varying degrees as you'll see in the Investment Pyramid in this chapter. How risky your investing becomes depends on you. How quickly do you need the money? How much can you afford to lose? What do you want from the investment?

Determining how much risk you can tolerate from an investment is an element of creating (and following) your investment profile. To get a very general and basic idea of what your risk-comfort level is, ask yourself the following three basic questions:

➤ What is the amount of time between now and when you need your money?

➤ What are your investment goals?

➤ How much risk are you willing to take to achieve those investment goals?

Answers to these questions vary with each individual. Many people don't have a lot of extra money to invest. Others haven't put together a personal financial battle plan to determine how much they can afford to invest.

Take a look at the following figure. The least risky investments are at the base. As you climb the pyramid, the more risky it becomes. Like Mt. Everest, the higher you climb, the scarier it is. This pyramid gives you an idea of how the different risk levels are involved in investing, but there is a trade-off. The higher you travel on the pyramid, the greater the possibility for a higher investment return on your money. That's trading "risk" for "reward."

Now let's review the answers to the questions. Your answers should determine how comfortable you are with investing. Investing in stocks, bonds, mutual funds, and even futures and options can reap great rewards, but you can lose money, too.

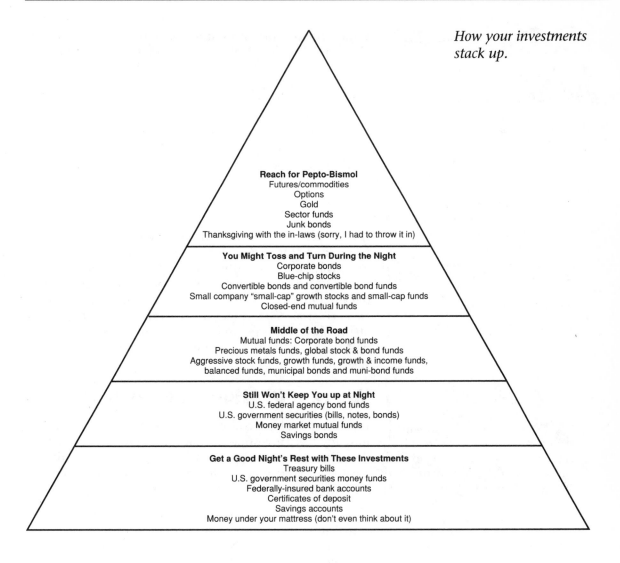

How your investments stack up.

Reach for Pepto-Bismol
Futures/commodities
Options
Gold
Sector funds
Junk bonds
Thanksgiving with the in-laws (sorry, I had to throw it in)

You Might Toss and Turn During the Night
Corporate bonds
Blue-chip stocks
Convertible bonds and convertible bond funds
Small company "small-cap" growth stocks and small-cap funds
Closed-end mutual funds

Middle of the Road
Mutual funds: Corporate bond funds
Precious metals funds, global stock & bond funds
Aggressive stock funds, growth funds, growth & income funds,
balanced funds, municipal bonds and muni-bond funds

Still Won't Keep You up at Night
U.S. federal agency bond funds
U.S. government securities (bills, notes, bonds)
Money market mutual funds
Savings bonds

Get a Good Night's Rest with These Investments
Treasury bills
U.S. government securities money funds
Federally-insured bank accounts
Certificates of deposit
Savings accounts
Money under your mattress (don't even think about it)

What is the amount of time between now and when you need your money? Many investors need the capability of getting at their cash immediately in case of emergency that cannot be covered by a sound insurance plan. Your answer will help you determine whether or not you'll choose an investment that can be volatile (ups and downs) or doesn't tie up your money for a long period of time (liquid).

Secret
All investors should have some portion of their portfolio allocated to cash. That means a money market deposit account or even just a savings account earning a comparable rate of interest. In case of an emergency, you can access that money quickly. For the highest yielding money market deposit accounts nationwide, subscribe to *100 Highest Yields* (800) 327-7717, or search Bank Rate Monitor's website at **http:// www.bankrate.com**.

Careful
Putting all of your assets into a single low-risk investment can be considered more risky than investing in many high-risk investments. If you don't diversify your portfolio, you could wind up with the rare low-risk investment that loses some or all of your money.

What are your investment goals? What are you going to do with this money? What are you saving for? It's probably not just for the sheer joy of watching your investments go up and down in price. Determining your financial goals helps set your risk-comfort level. For example, if you need the money next fall when Junior starts State U., you won't be comfortable tying up your money in a security that doesn't mature for another ten years or more, such as a thirty-year Treasury bond. You'd be better off putting your money into something that's shorter term, such as a one-year Treasury bill or one-year CD, depending on the general direction of interest rates.

How much risk are you willing to take to achieve those investment goals? Assess how much money you can afford to invest without wiping out the family fortune. You want to balance out the potential risk and reward and invest when that balance is most promising. *Don't risk your life savings with high expectations of unattainable returns.* If an investment is keeping you awake at night, it's not worth it. No investment is worth losing sleep over.

You're a Die-Hard Conservative

If you're a die-hard conservative, don't put a lot of money into any risky investments that sound promising. Stick to the lower half of the pyramid. But that doesn't mean putting all of your eggs into one super-safe investment basket...or under the mattress, either.

Every investor's portfolio should have different "baskets" of investments. If one of your assets takes a nose-dive, you'll have alternate assets to fall back on. Your risk tolerance, financial goals, and age help determine what you'll put into those baskets.

Moderately Speaking

If you don't mind risking a little safety in exchange for a better return on your money, your investment style can be a little more moderate. You can hold on with a few market bumps. The products listed in the middle of the pyramid in the figure shown earlier typically have an average return of 8%–10%.

R-I-S-K Is Your Middle Name

Finally, if you're the type of person who lives moment to moment, well, you will probably withstand a few market fallouts and still hang on for the ride just for the sake of watching your money grow. Your investment style is aggressive and sometimes speculative. The investments listed toward the top of the pyramid are the most risky. However, in exchange for this risk, the returns you may receive are quite high. Over the long-term, studies indicate that investors may be able to achieve higher returns in exchange for taking on more risk.

Keep in mind that no matter how old you are or what your risk-comfort level is, a segment of your investment pie should always be allocated to safe, liquid investment—for example, an emergency fund, where your money is available for emergencies.

One theory suggests using your age as a factor in determining how you allocate different investment products within your portfolio. For example, let's say you are 35 years old. Subtract your age from 100, giving you 65. This result, according to the theory, means you should have 65 percent of your portfolio in growth/aggressive investments (such as stocks) and 35 percent in more conservative investments (fixed-income instruments, such as bonds). That's just one theory and there are a zillion others that follow. You may refer to Chapter 31, which discusses how you can allocate your investment portfolio.

> **What?**
> By putting your money into several different investments—*diversifying* your portfolio—you reduce your risk. How? If you put all of your eggs in one basket and drop the basket, they all break. Spread your eggs among different baskets, and when one of them breaks, you only have one cracked shell—the others are still intact.

No Pain, No Gain

Unfortunately, no one eliminates risk. Remember, the greater the potential payoff, the greater the risk.

However, it's impossible to be a successful investor if you are living in fear all of the time. You don't need to jump in headfirst. Establishing what level of risk your investment portfolio can take is based on the following:

➤ **Your age.** How old are you?

➤ **Your financial goals.** What is it that you are investing for?

➤ **Your time horizon.** When are you planning on reaching these goals?

➤ **Your wad of dough.** How much money are you allocating to investing and how much are you going to need in the future?

Here's a basic guideline to further your knowledge of how much risk you can tolerate from your investments:

How old are you? Generally, the older you are, the less risk you could take in your investments. Why? Because as you get closer to retirement, your focus shifts from investing in products that can appreciate and grow (such as stocks and stock mutual funds) to income-producing investment products, such as those that pay interest (for example, bonds). The younger you are, the more aggressive you can be in your investment approach. However, because many people are living longer these days during retirement, sometimes 20 years or longer, more retirees are allocating a higher percentage of their portfolio to more aggressive positions, such as equity mutual funds.

What are you investing for? College education or a home or whatever? If you absolutely cannot withstand losing any of the money you are investing because you need to reach that goal, then the more conservative you may have to be in your approach. However, you may not be able to afford to be too conservative depending upon your time frame for reaching the goal.

When are you planning on reaching these goals? Available time is a major determinant in factoring risk in your portfolio. If you have a lot of time to reach the goal, you may be able to take on more risk. That doesn't mean sinking Junior's college fund into pork belly future contracts, but you can be a little more aggressive in your approach *as long as you follow your investments' progress on an ongoing basis.*

How much money are you allocating to investing, and how much do you need for your goals? A few investments require initial minimum amounts, and you may have to slowly work your way to meet those minimums. Figuring out how much money you're going to need for those goals will help you determine if you need an investment that appreciates greatly in value, but carries more risk.

Above all, when you buy and sell an investment product, you always have the risk of losing your money. Investing is a risk, but the degrees of risk vary with each investment product:

➤ The more risk you take, the greater your potential is for a substantial reward, but you also have a greater chance of losing money.

➤ The less risk you take, the less your potential is for a substantial reward, but you also have less chance of losing money.

Now that you've established what level of risk you can handle, let's take a look at some other risks involved with making money on Wall Street.

There's That Inflation Word Again

Think of inflation this way. You go to the grocery store and find that your favorite cereal is now $4.29 a box instead of $3.69 like it was last year. The price has increased, but not just on this manufacturer's cereal. Other cereal makers have increased their prices, too.

Or maybe you're car shopping. The last time you bought a car, the 1964 Dodge Charger was in its stellar year. Today, you'll probably have sticker shock because the average price of a new American automobile is $21,000. Ten years ago it was $10,725—a substantial increase of almost 100%.

Does this mean the country is in a financial crisis? Not necessarily. What it means is that as time passes on, most things become more expensive. How does this affect you? Your purchasing power is reduced. The same thing happens in investing. If prices are rising about 5% a year, the value of your dollar is steadily eroding over time.

Here's an example. Suppose the cost of living rises about 4% every year, and you want to invest $1,000 each year. Today's dollar can't buy the same thing five years down the road. Therefore, the loss in purchasing power of every $1,000 you invest today is cut to $822 in five years and then to $703 in ten years. That $1,000 in 1997 will be worth $822 in 2002. No fair, but it's reality.

> **What?**
> *Purchasing power* is how much bang you can get for your buck. What you buy today for a dollar will not buy you the same product ten years from now.

> **Careful**
> Don't be too conservative. Suppose you invest $1,000 every year for five years in an interest-bearing savings account that earns 3%. Think you're happy earning 3% a year on your money? Think again. If inflation is at 4% a year, you still won't come out ahead five years from now. In the long run, you're earning a –1% on your savings.

How Quickly Can I Get At My Money?

The most liquid investments are usually those with moderate-to-low risk—with the exception of options and futures. Options and futures are two liquid investments because you can get at your cash rather quickly, however they are extremely risky. Chapters 29 and 30 show just how risky these investments can be.

The investment pyramid shows a number of different investment types. Investments from the pyramid that aren't too risky and are pretty liquid follow:

➤ Savings accounts are very liquid because they're already cash.

➤ Treasury securities are safe because the full faith and credit of the U.S. Government insures them. They are liquid because it takes only two days to convert the securities into cash.

Secret

No matter how much money you have to invest, make sure you allocate a portion of it to a liquid investment. This way, in case of an emergency, you can get at your cash rather quickly.

➤ Savings bonds can be turned in for cash at the bank.

➤ Money market accounts are basically cash to begin with.

➤ Stocks, some bonds, and mutual funds are pretty liquid. They usually only take about three business days to sell them and receive your money.

What makes an illiquid investment? Well, a good example of an illiquid investment is real estate. It takes time to find a buyer for your home or property. Many times if you are forced to sell an investment because you need cash quickly, you have to accept a lower price.

And What About Those Interest Rates?

Interest rates on bonds, mortgages, savings accounts, and CDs have risen and fallen...and risen and fallen...and—okay, you get the picture. These investments are known as being interest-rate sensitive. Because these investments have an interest rate as a feature, the general direction of interest rates (which you learned about in Chapter 2) affects the interest rate that is on the investment product. In some cases, the general direction of interest rates directly influences the price at which you buy the investment.

Secret

When, because of changing market conditions, the money that you get when your investment matures or you sell it cannot be invested in another instrument that produces the same investment return, you've experienced *reinvestment risk*.

Here's an example. Bond investments have a fixed interest rate and a price at which you can buy them. These fixed interest rates and the bond prices move in the opposite direction of each other. When the interest rate goes up, the bond price goes down, and vice-versa. Therefore, if the general direction of interest rates, which influences the interest rates on bonds, goes up or down, the price at which you can buy or sell the bond goes down or up.

In the early '80s, the prime rate was as high as 21.5%. CD investors were enjoying double-digit yields of 12%–15%. Yields on bonds, mortgage rates, and other financial instruments soared. However in the early '90s, the prime rate fell to 6%, and all other interest rates followed. Yield-hungry investors who grew accustomed to double-digits were astonished when their investments started earning anemic rates. This type of rate environment affects you in two ways: reinvestment potential and lifestyle.

First, if you are earning double digits on your investments and they either mature or you have to sell, the yield on your investment declines when you have to reinvest, which is also known as reinvestment risk.

Here's an example. Back in the '80s, you could invest $5,000 in a five-year certificate of deposit that earned 12% annually. Because when you invest in a CD you lock in your money for a specified period of time, you also lock in the interest rate, regardless of the rates going up or down.

Five years later when the CD matured, the same $5,000, five-year CDs *were not* earning 12%, but instead were yielding 8%. You couldn't reinvest your money in the same CD and earn the same return, because interest rates had dropped. And by mid-summer of 1997, five-year CDs were yielding a nationwide average of 6.35%.

Second, those investors who rely on income from their investments had to make lifestyle adjustments. Why? Because in a declining rate environment, the interest payments that you receive decline also. Therefore, there's less money received…and less you can spend.

Risk Is Not a Four-Letter Word

Unfortunately, the word "risk" gets a bad rap. It shouldn't. Risk tells you a lot about yourself. If you know how much risk you can tolerate from an investment—how comfortable you are in the investment decisions you make—and if you educate yourself about other inherent risks associated with investing, you're on your way to making your money work for you.

Let's use an analogy here regarding risk and reward, according to the American Association of Individual Investors, a trade association based in Chicago, Illinois. For a moment, suppose you could choose between two investments. One offers $1 up front, and the other $1 per spot on the roll of the die. Which investment is riskier?

According to the AAII, "The roll of the die is riskier—your return could vary anywhere from $1 for one spot to $6 for six spots. But you would probably not think of it as riskier, because it has no chance of underperforming the sure thing. In other words, the worst you could possibly do with the roll of the die is to receive $1—the same return that you would receive with the sure thing—and the probability is large that you will receive more than $1."

Risk, or uncertainty, can be viewed in a variety of ways. If it is defined in absolute dollar returns, the first investment—the $1 outright—is certain, since the return will always be $1. However, if uncertainty is defined in relative terms, the roll of the die presents the certain alternative, because it is certain that the outcome will always be equal to or greater than the first investment.

The AAII queries, "is a portfolio that contains an equal amount of stocks and long-term bonds riskier than a portfolio that simply contains Treasury bills, which are commonly thought of as "riskless" investments?"

It all boils down to your investment timeframe. The answer depends upon the length of your investment horizon. The stock market is very variable, but over the long-term the returns have been positive and much higher than those of Treasury bills, for example.

Here's the twist—if your investment horizon is sufficiently long, the relative riskiness of a balanced portfolio is akin to that present in the dice example. The absolute dollar return on the balanced portfolio of stocks and debt is less certain than the absolute dollar return on the Treasury bill portfolio. But it would be difficult to call the balanced portfolio riskier, because it is almost certain over a long-term period to provide a return that is higher than the Treasury bill portfolio.

The bottom line? According to AAII, "The probability of receiving a return that is less than that of Treasury bills decreases markedly as the investment horizon increases. Thus, the relative riskiness of an investment depends on the length of the investment horizon. It is also clear from the probability figures that the portfolios traditionally viewed as more "risky" because of their volatility over short-term periods—the stock portfolios and the stock-bond-T-bill combinations—are less risky on a relative basis over long-term periods than the bond portfolios."

The AAII points out that the risk of a portfolio depends upon the length of the investor's planned investment time horizon. A portfolio may be highly risky if the investment horizon is short, but of modest risk if the investment horizon is long. There are substantial benefits to diversification across time.

The Least You Need to Know

> ➤ Figure out what your risk-comfort level is. Are you a conservative investor? Middle of the road? Aggressive? This helps you determine what types of investments make you uncomfortable.

> ➤ Determine when you want to reach your goals. Available time is a major element in factoring risk in your portfolio. If you have a lot of time to reach the goal, you may be able to take on more risk.

> ➤ Keep some of your money liquid, that is, available for withdrawal on a moment's notice. A good example of a liquid account would be money that you set aside for an emergency in a money market account. For the highest-yielding money market accounts, check out Bank Rate Monitor's website at **http://www.bankrate.com**.

> ➤ Diversify. You can lose all your money if you invest in just one type of financial security. Spread the risk around by investing in various types of products.

Chapter 5

And Now for the Legwork

In This Chapter

➤ Making money on Wall Street—do your homework *first*

➤ Knowing where to go for research information

➤ Deciding if you can—and should—do it on your own

In the first edition of the *Complete Idiot's Guide to Making Money on Wall Street*, I said that "making money is easy once you become an educated investor."

Boy was I wrong.

Making money is never really easy, it's a constant challenge. Sure, you can achieve being an educated investor, but how long do those set of rules last before new information comes out that changes the rules you learned in the first place?

These days, often.

Fortunately, there are some tried-and-true how-to's that you can use no matter how much information-overload you receive (even that hot stock tip from your Great Aunt Lorraine), how much of an education you get, or how much technology tries to make our lives—and Wall Street research—easier. You'll always be learning on Wall Street, and with the information provided in this chapter, you'll learn how to research potential investments.

Learn About the Company and Market

If you had $100,000 to invest, anywhere, and you know you want to create an investment portfolio of stocks, bonds, and a few mutual funds, which stocks would you invest in?

One of the initial steps in creating an investment portfolio is deciding *what* you should invest in. You make this decision by determining what each investment product is, how it works, and how risky it is. Once you figure that out, the next step is to decide which stocks or bonds you should consider. That decision is based upon investment research. Yup, folks, it's homework time. What if you don't know how to do any research? Well, you've come to the right place.

Anytime you are researching an investment, you are typically investigating a company. Why? Because that's who issues stocks, bonds, and so on. Before you get out the paper and pencils, know that you already have the ability of one of the greatest resources around—your eyes. Look around you and what do you see? Many times a good investment choice will come from paying attention to your surroundings. One of the easiest—and most often overlooked—elements to investment research is observation.

Bet You Didn't Know

The Beardstown Ladies are a perfect example of utilizing the best tool we have that we're even born with: our eyes. Simple observation, they say, are the windows to future investment opportunities. Several years ago, the Ladies had been discussing how they noticed how many families were eating out more often than not. It was fast-food-mania, as hectic lifestyles and dual-income parents needed to work to provide for their families. A sad situation? Well, the Ladies took this observation as an opportunity at noticing the increased customer traffic at places such as McDonald's, Taco Bell (owned by Pepsi), and Wendy's. That observation, along with their research into company annual reports and other financial details, lauded them a Golden (dare we say Arches?) opportunity. And, a 59.5% annual return on their investment club portfolio in 1991 didn't hurt the investment pie either.

So, let's say, you notice everyone is choosing Burger King for their fast-food takeout choice and not frequenting McDonald's as much as before; it might be a trend. Why is this happening?

Consider going to the library and looking up the latest news articles about Burger King and McDonald's, in particular. What changes have taken place at the company? These changes can include new services, improved equipment, or a new line of products. Here, you are performing your own *fundamental analysis*.

You can learn about a company by contacting its headquarters and finding out where they're located. If they are nearby, you may wish to see if you can tour the facilities or at least pick up some information about what type of business the company is in.

Speak with a representative in shareholder services or investor relations to see if the company is a private or a public company. Most often, whenever you have a question regarding the company's business or past history, you contact either of these departments. They are there to serve investors. Request documentation from them such as financial reports and brochures on general company information. Ask to be put in their mailing list. Find out the following:

➤ **Who is running the company?** If there has been poor management in the past, it will be indicated in the company's track record. However, if the company is managed well, chances are that good results can be repeated. If there is a change in management, you may wish to look into the background of the new managers.

➤ **How long has the company been in business?** Is it a brand-new company? If so, realize these companies are relatively risky. Companies who have a stable background and have been around for years probably won't go belly up overnight.

➤ **How profitable is it?** See if you can get at least a five-year history on its profitability. This information is found in a company's *balance sheet*. Make sure that the company isn't constantly running itself into the ground without any profits at all. The more profitable a company, the greater the possibility for increases in dividends for shareholders.

➤ **How much bad debt versus good debt does it have?** Companies are just like you! They carry both good and bad debt. The idea is to eliminate the bad debt. Companies also break out their debt into short-term debt and long-term debt. Watch and compare the numbers year-by-year.

➤ **Who is the competition?** Think of McDonald's versus Burger King or Pepsi versus Coca-Cola. How strong are the company's competitors? How much of a market share does the company have? If the company is new and entering an already saturated market, what type of competition does it face? Does its product have an edge over the others?

➤ **Are there any new products or services coming out on the market from this company?** In an already-established company, new products or services can be either good or bad. Find out if the company has ever ventured into that territory before and if it faces any stiff competition.

Once you have done all your research and have answers to your questions, check out the entire market or industry. Using the Burger King versus McDonald's example above, you would look into the fast-food or "restaurant" industry. Many brokerage firms have departments where people analyze specific industries and write reports. Business publications such as *Barron's*, for example, draw upon these analyst reports.

You should also consider the following questions when continuing your research:

➤ Is the industry a stable one or is it based on fads?

➤ How well does it perform overall in each phase of the business cycle? (Now you can see why the discussion of economics in Chapter 2 is so important to understand.)

Realize that your research will be an ongoing process. Learning about the company and the industry is just the first part. You need to consistently monitor the company after you have invested by following its performance information.

Think of the research part as a three-step process:

1. Learn about the Company
2. Learn about the Industry
3. Monitor the Company and Industry

Sources of Performance Information

One day you're standing at your mailbox and open it up to find it crammed full of envelopes. There's a few bills, some junk mail, and an envelope that looks unfamiliar.

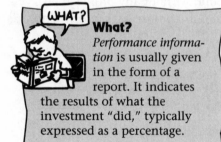

What?
Performance information is usually given in the form of a report. It indicates the results of what the investment "did," typically expressed as a percentage.

You open up the unfamiliar envelope and find what looks like a research report, but you can't make heads or tails out of it—you'd have an easier time spelling out your name in a bowl of alphabet soup. Then you remember that you had contacted the shareholder services department at a company you were researching. This slick, glossy brochure and the unintelligible research reports included with it must be the information you need to wade through.

Is this the only avenue to pursue? No. There are so many sources of *performance information* available to you that you could wallpaper your whole house with them.

Most of the resources described next track performance of individual stocks and mutual funds. Individual bonds aren't necessarily "tracked" for performance, but they are assigned special ratings based on the risks involved in each individual bond. Futures and options are both such volatile investments that most of your information will come from financial newsletters covering those markets or the day-to-day coverage found on financial television programs such as CNNfn (CNN Financial News) or CNBC, as well as on the Internet.

Some organizations were created solely to provide performance and statistical information to the public about companies and businesses. Following are descriptions of the most popular research companies that analyze stocks, bonds, mutual funds, futures, and options.

Hook, Value Line, and Sinker

Value Line Investment Survey is a definite must-read report that is provided by the research company Value Line for researching potential stock investments. This one-page report gives you the background of a company's business, current happenings in the company, information from its financial statement (such as net income and profits), and performance information, which is its stock track record. These reports are available through brokerage firms, your public library, or Value Line (800) 634-3583.

Value Line also publishes a one-page report called the *Value Line Mutual Fund Investment Survey*, which tracks the performance information of 2,000 mutual funds, including in-depth coverage of 1,500 equity and fixed-income mutual funds for subscribers. You can contact (800) 284-7607, but it's also available in your public library. You can also access their product information online at **http://www.valueline.com**, but to get performance data you must subscribe.

Oh, What a Beautiful Morning(star)!

The most popular—and most comprehensive—survey of mutual fund performance is given by *Morningstar Mutual Funds* in its full-page reports. Each page gives detailed performance information and a bit of history about each load, low-load, and no-load mutual fund. Morningstar not only tracks performance but also assigns a special star-rating system to each fund. The rating is a measure of performance based on risk and gives investors a way to narrow down the group of funds they want to look at in more depth. You can subscribe to their three-month trial subscription. It's also available at your public library.

Secret
For those of you who have America Online, simply go to keyword: **Morningstar** to access their mutual fund database or visit them on the Net at **http://www.morningstar.net**.

Wise Guy, Huh?

CDA Weisenberger is a mutual fund rating service that tracks performance on a large database of funds, and performance information is available in two of their reports, the *Mutual Fund Report* and the *Mutual Fund Update*. Both reports are available on a monthly basis either on hard copy or in several of its software packages. For information about either of the reports or software packages, call (800) 232-2285, or write to CDA Wiesenberger, 1355 Piccard Drive, Rockville, MD 20850. Or, visit their website at **http://www.cda.com** for further information.

Secret
Performance reports don't show you how well or how poorly a company has performed—they just give facts. It's up to you to decide if the track record is good or bad.

Ticker Talk

The most readily available source of performance information is in the financial section of your local newspaper where you'll find the biggest performance indicator, the closing price of an investment. Your local paper, for example, lists the closing prices for thousands of stocks, bonds, mutual funds, futures, and options that traded the previous trading day. These investments are listed either by their *ticker symbol* or an abbreviation. (Or if there's room, it's completely spelled out.)

> **What?**
> You use a *ticker symbol* (an abbreviation of the investment name) to get current quotes (prices) from a broker. For example, American Airlines' ticker symbol is "AA." McDonalds' is "MCD."

These closing prices represent the last price at which the investment security listed was either bought or sold. That price is usually what people look for—and you will, too, once you begin investing. It is one way to monitor your investments.

In addition to the closing prices, other performance information is given. These include but are not limited to the following:

➤ **High and Low.** Typically the numbers in these columns represent the highest and lowest price of an investment during the previous trading day (yesterday).

➤ **52 Week High and a 52 Week Low.** This represents the highest and lowest price of an investment during a 52-week period.

➤ **Close.** The price at which the investment closed yesterday.

➤ **Volume.** Sometimes shown as "VOL" in the table, the volume indicates how many shares, issues, or contracts of an investment traded for the entire previous trading day.

➤ **Net Change.** The difference in price from the previous day's close to that particular day's close. For example, if it was Wednesday morning and you were reading the financial table, the net change listed would represent the difference in price from Monday to Tuesday.

➤ **Div.** This stands for dividend, which is the sum paid to shareholders out of a company's earnings.

This is just the first part of the process in learning about the sources of performance information. Make sure you don't base your investment decisions by yesterday's closing price. There are other steps you need to complete.

Information You Can Trust

If your local newspaper does not carry all of the pricing information you need, you may also look into purchasing *The Wall Street Journal* or *Barron's*.

The Wall Street Journal is one of the world's most powerful and instrumental guides to learning about the "Who's Who" and "What's What" in Wall Street. It covers all financial markets, both national and worldwide. If you are looking for performance information (such as quotes), you can find it in the third section of the newspaper "Money & Markets," also unwittingly known as the "C-section."

This daily newspaper also provides readers with reports on economic, political, and financial news from across the country and even the world. Detailed information is listed in stories about companies making headlines, with events such as the release of a new product or a change in management. To subscribe for a 13-week trial subscription or to find out more about getting a paid subscription to their online service, call (800) 568-7625 or visit their website at **http://www.wsj.com**.

Barron's National Business and Financial Weekly is published by Dow Jones News, the same company that publishes *The Wall Street Journal*. However, Barron's provides explicit information about all the financial markets. Half of the paper is made up of articles and columns about current events—including interviews and hot news releases about companies—and the current state of the financial markets. The other half consists of pages and pages of financial tables. This publication provides extremely detailed statistical information. Barron's is also available on the Internet at **http://www.barrons.com**.

To find out more general information about companies, look into several of the following magazines. Who knows? You might find your next winner buried in a story. (Just make sure you do your homework, too!)

Business Week. The stories and reports in this magazine give a lot of information about a company, especially company profiles. Stories include performance information, business strategies, economics, personal investing, and Wall Street. Business Week updates its news on a daily basis on its forum site on America Online at keyword: **business week**.

Money. Geared more toward individual investors, this popular magazine gives much advice on personal finance issues. It also discusses information about different investment products. Money Magazine has tapped into the information superhighway through its parent company's website, TimeWarner's PathFinder, at **http://www.pathfinder.com**. Look for the Money Magazine logo, and click!

Secret
Some of the subscription prices on these magazines can add up to a small fortune. If even the trial subscription prices are too expensive for you, check out the publication's back issues in the library. Usually the library has them either in stock or on microfilm.

Getting Information Online

If you want to keep track of performance information online, there are several services available to you. These include the following:

➤ **America Online (800) 4-ONLINE.** America Online (AOL), is the fastest-growing online service in the world. AOL's Personal Finance Channel features its Market News Center, where daily financial information, economic indicators and more are found.

➤ **CompuServe (800) 848-8199.** If you want updated quotes, financial market news, and historical information about investments, CompuServe offers that and more, such as weather reports and discount shopping.

➤ **Prodigy (800) 776-3449.** It's difficult to determine the future of this company, but it certainly has been around a long time. You can get price quotes and up-to-the-minute news on thousands of individual investments and financial market news.

Careful

Be cautious about using information provided on the Internet. If you don't know the source is reliable and can't verify the information, don't let it influence your investment decisions. You should also be careful about providing personal information to unfamiliar websites and make sure you keep up with how safe your transactions are via the Net by asking the website master or technical support to explain to you in laymen's terms how your personal information is transmitted to them without Big Brother, or anyone else, watching.

Whether you use a service (such as CompuServe) or an Internet service provider (local or national Internet connection), you can access the many resources that are available on the web. Some of the most popular investment-related websites include:

➤ **The Microsoft Investor Website (http://www.investor.msn.com)** offers subscribers the ability to track your securities with a customized portfolio manager, keep up-to-date on the market with the latest financial news, research investments through its proprietary "Investment Finder" service, and even opt for a daily summary and analysis of the market via e-mail.

➤ **The American Association of Individual Investors, a non-profit trade association (http://www.aaii.org)**, offers users an archive of publication information about investing strategies, basic portfolio management, and financial planning. Also included are research tools and a community center that gives AAII Chapter updates (you join the association and become a member affiliated with a chapter in your local area) as to when meetings are forthcoming.

➤ **The Motley Fool: Finance and Folly (http://www.fool.com)** is an irreverent website with a tongue-in-cheek approach to investing in—and covering—the stock market. Their daily news reports and updates on their own portfolio(s) trades keep visitors, well, visiting again and again.

Interpreting Performance Information

Consumers' lives are filled with numbers. We rate performance on everything these days. Thumbs up or down for the latest movie release. Two or three stars for a restaurant review. Even automobiles and appliances are rated number one by magazines such as *Consumer's Digest* and *Consumer Reports*.

It doesn't stop there. Investment products are given a thumbs up or down, too. In the world of stocks, you hear about a "buy," "hold," or "sell" recommendation from investment analysts. When it comes to bond investing, companies like Standard & Poor's rate all types of bonds by giving them a credit rating in the form of a letter. As for mutual funds, futures and options, performance is rated, too.

All of the performance information is given, but how do you figure out which end is up? Here is a basic primer to understanding what performance information tells you.

➤ **Total Return.** The research reports you review are plagued with numbers. But there is only *one*—just one—number that tells you about the performance of the investment: total return.

Total return gives the sum of the price appreciation and income derived from an investment. For example, if you invested in a stock that indicates a total return of 12%, the 12 percent is what you earn from the appreciation in price of the stock (the stock price moving up) and the income that is derived from the stock (in the form of dividends that you receive).

Now, when you have stocks that don't pay any dividends, the majority of performance (total return) comes from the price appreciation. These stocks might pay a small dividend, or even no dividend at all.

Those stocks that are high-paying dividend stocks focus on income, not price appreciation. Therefore, the majority of the total return comes from the income derived from the dividends that are paid to shareholders.

➤ **Annual Return.** Annual return is the total return measured over a 12-month period. When you see an annual return of 10%, that means the investment earned ten percent—either in price appreciation, income or a combination of both—over a period of 12 months.

➤ **Cumulative Return.** The cumulative return is expressed in a period of three years, five years, ten years, and so on. The *biggest* mistake is for investors to look at the performance of a mutual fund, let's say, that states there was a 165% return over a period of five years. That *does not* mean that every year for five years you earned 165 percent a year on the investment. Rather, the cumulative return amount is the total of all the annual returns for the number of years specified.

➤ **Average Annual Return.** This return number represents the cumulative return number expressed as what you would earn for each year given. For example, if the cumulative return of a mutual fund was 30.85% for three years, the average annual return would be 9.38%, or the cumulative return divided by the number of years.

Getting a Prospectus and Attempting to Understand It

Getting your hands on a mutual fund prospectus is easy, and it's something that's required if you want to buy an investment. All you have to do is contact the fund company (the shareholder services or investor relations department) for information. It is required by law for you to receive a prospectus before you invest one cent in a mutual fund.

If you wanted a prospectus from a company regarding its stocks or bonds, the only way you can get it is if the company was having an initial offering. When a company is coming out with its very first stock or bond issue, it'll hire a large, full-service brokerage firm to sell its stocks or bonds. The announcement and sale of these securities is known as an initial public offering (IPO). If the company has already had an initial offering in the past and wanted to do it again, it would hold a *secondary offering.*

What do you do with the prospectus once you receive it? Time to pick it apart. It is possible to have a full-time job reading prospectuses and translating the "legalese." Some prospectuses have pages and pages of information that look like they were written in Swahili.

Understand that each prospectus is designed to give you the same information:

➤ Name of the company or mutual fund

➤ Purpose and policies of company or mutual fund

➤ History of company or mutual fund

➤ Investment or business objectives

➤ Costs involved with investing (such as management fees)

➤ Description of the management team

Without going into too much legal detail, here are a few basics that you should look for when you are reading a prospectus.

➤ **Before you purchase an investment, you must legally receive a prospectus.** In the case of a new stock or bond offering, this is true; otherwise, if you just wanted to buy shares of stock that "aren't new" (they've already been traded out in the marketplace) you won't receive a prospectus. However you should obtain the company's annual report. In the case of a mutual fund, you will always receive a prospectus.

➤ **If the investment pays dividends/interest payments, make sure the rate and timing are indicated.** It's important to know when your dividends and interest payments are paid out and what the rates are likely to be. These dates will help you determine when you'll be entitled to receive the dividend or interest payment and how much to expect.

➤ **Make sure a performance table is given.** By law, there must be performance information given on a prospectus. For example, a mutual fund prospectus is required to include a ten-year performance history of the fund's change in price, the dividend income earned, and the capital gains distributions paid.

➤ **Where to buy the investment.** If there is an initial stock or bond offering and you request a prospectus, the names of all the brokerage firms that you can purchase it through will be listed on the front page.

> **What?**
> The *annual report* is a formal financial statement issued by a company which shows its assets, liabilities, and earnings. This report gives an indication of how the company stood at the close of the business year and if it made any profits. A *prospectus*, on the other hand, is a legal document that describes the investment objectives, costs involved (if it was a mutual fund investment), and management.

➤ **If it is a mutual fund, make sure the investment objectives/methods are listed.** This means you should watch for any restrictions that may be given in the prospectus, such as if the mutual fund limits itself to investing in certain types of stocks or bonds. It should also tell you what kinds of stocks or bonds it will *not* buy.

➤ **If it is a mutual fund, make sure the risks are spelled out.** The prospectus should tell you how volatile the change in the price of the mutual fund is. Plus, make sure it tells you if there are any strategies that involve the use of futures, options, or derivatives (a risky, volatile form of futures and options). Fund managers use these as a way to prevent losses; however, this is an extremely risky strategy.

➤ **Read up on company business.** In the prospectus, the business should be described—does the company invest in widgets, gizmos, or thingamajigs?

➤ **What type of experience does management have?** This is key. If the management listed in the prospectus has no experience in the company or in the industry, it should be noted.

➤ **In a mutual fund prospectus, make sure you read the fine print about fund expenses and management fees.** The fund's second largest single expense is the management fee, which is the percentage of the fund's money that is paid to the fund manager for, well, managing the fund. The way the fee is calculated is stated in the prospectus.

➤ **Finally, call the company if you are having trouble understanding the prospectus.** Call the shareholder services or investor relations department of the fund or company with your questions. Many times they will provide you with the "Statement of Additional Information," which must be available to you.

Using a Financial Advisor

Secret
If you find several mutual funds with similar performance that you can't decide between, one approach is to monitor the annual expenses to make your decision. Do note that not all portfolio managers select the same positions within each fund, so you should review the manager's investment style, too.

Money managers. Stockbrokers. Trust Officers. Bankers. Certified Financial Planners. Financial Analysts.

Should you consult with one?

Creating and managing your own investment portfolio can be a full-time job, which is why these financial pros exist. Because your investment portfolio is only *part* of your overall financial picture (insurance needs, estate planning, and so on), it sometimes can be overwhelming to do it all on your own. However, the more knowledge you gain and homework you do on your own, the more you can rely on yourself for your *own* investment decisions rather than on the advice of someone else.

No matter whether or not you choose to consult with a financial advisor, you should *always* monitor your own investments. Here's a quick run-down of the types of financial professionals you may encounter.

Full-Service Brokers

Stockbrokers work for full-service brokerage firms. These firms supply clients with everything (research reports, new stock and bond offerings, client meetings, and professional

Secret
A stockbroker, no matter how much money he or she makes for you, can't promise any profits.

advice). A seasoned broker can steer you toward stock recommendations that you might not hear about, and they can give you opinions on specific investments that should be in line with your investment objectives and your financial goals.

In return for advice and services, you must pay commissions to full-service brokers. The less often you trade and the lower your volume of trading, the higher your commissions per share.

For example, if you buy just a few shares of a low-priced stock, such as $10 a share, you may pay a commission of up to 40 cents a share. But if you buy several hundred shares of a high-priced stock at $75 a share, you may pay as little as ten cents a share commission.

Those investors who need professional advice and don't mind paying for it should look into a full-service brokerage firm. The broker should be at your disposal. If you aren't sure as to when to buy or sell a particular investment, your broker can help you.

However, make sure your broker is working in your best interest. Your broker should call you at respectable hours, not make you feel pressured, and offer you advice that is in line with your financial goals and investment objectives. For example, if you are trying to invest for retirement using a moderate investment approach, and your broker is pressuring you to buy risky cattle futures, it's time to look for another broker.

How do these financial professionals get paid? They generate commissions from the trades you place. Typically, a full-service broker pockets between 30 and 40 percent of the stated commission on the trade confirmation you receive. The rest of it goes to the company's pockets. The more trades you make, the more money the broker makes.

All you need to do to place an order to buy or sell an investment is set up an account with the broker. The account can be an individual account or a joint account. Once the account has been established, you can make a trade right over the phone. Once your order has been executed, you'll receive a trade confirmation in the mail confirming what you bought, how much it cost and the commissions you paid.

Secret
If you do a lot of trading, ask for a discount on your commissions. *Don't be afraid or intimidated!* If your broker wants to keep your business, he or she should be glad to accommodate you.

Careful
Understand how a broker gets paid. If a stockbroker is making too many trades in your account—known as "churning"—just to generate commissions, call the branch manager of the firm. Understanding the method of compensation will enable you to determine if your broker is acting in your best interest or just looking to make a quick buck from your investments.

Using a Discount Broker

For those of you who do not need the professional advice of a full-service broker, check out a discount brokerage firm. You can save up to 60 percent on commissions if you trade through a discount broker rather than a full-service brokerage firm. They do this because they don't employ commissioned brokers and maintain low overheads.

You still get research reports, such as *Value Line* or *Morningstar* upon request. However, discount brokerage firms are considered no-frills operations because discount brokers do not provide you with investment advice, such as when to buy and sell a security.

The dynamic trio of full-service discount brokerage firms are:

➤ Fidelity Investments—**http://www.fidelity.com** or (800) 544-8888

➤ Quick & Reilly—**http://www.quick-reilly.com** or (800) 672-7220

➤ Charles Schwab & Co.—**http://www.schwab.com** or (800) 435-4000

These three offer everything that a full-service brokerage firm, such as Smith Barney, Merrill Lynch, or Prudential does, with the exception of the financial advice and higher commissions. In fact, you can request the same type of research reports that you would receive from the full-service brokerage firms with all of the same analyst recommendations and opinions. But it's up to you—and with no one's professional advice—to make the final decision once you've finished reading the report.

Secret
Online brokerages such as E*Trade (**http://www. etrade.com**) and Datek (**http://www.datek. com**) offer even lower commissions than the traditional discount brokers. You can trade up to 5,000 shares of stock for as little as $9.99.

You can contact a discount brokerage firm 24 hours a day, seven days a week to place trades, typically through their automated service lines. These enable you to work around the clock. So if you're tired of watching Oprah reruns at 3:00 a.m. and want to work on your investment portfolio, you can. And for what price? About 20 to 60 percent lower in commissions than their competitors.

Just like a full-service broker, all you have to do is call up your discount broker to place your trades and you receive a trade confirmation in the mail. However, because of the automated features, you can work around the clock if you want to. Plus, many discount brokers now have the ability for you to monitor and execute investment portfolio decisions right online via their Internet site. Check to see if your discount broker allows that capability. Sometimes even more discounts will apply.

Help from Your Banker

Banks offer the convenience of having all your transactions under one roof. Nowadays, working with a banker allows you a lot more freedom than it did 20 years ago. You can deposit a check into your money market account and invest in a mutual fund at the same time (see Chapter 8). The banks themselves can't sell you stock because banks are not allowed to invest and hold their customers' money in stocks, futures, options, (although you may purchase savings bonds at your bank); however, they do employ subsidiaries in their bank lobbies, affiliated with their institution, to offer you these types of investment products and services. For a fee, of course.

For those ultra-wealthies out there, banks can provide a high level of service from the trust department. These bankers (known as personal trust officers) give in-depth advice on financial and estate planning, tax preparation, and insurance. Their fees and charges are typically based on the total dollar value of your account. For example, they might charge you from 1%–3% of the value of your assets each year. If you have a total account value of $100,000, your fees could run as high as $3,000 a year just to maintain the account.

Certified Financial Planners

Sometimes considered the jack-of-all-trades investment pro, CFPs can give you a fair share of expertise. They should know about most financial subjects, including budgeting, investments, taxes, insurance, credit, real estate, estate planning, and college financing. This type of professional works with you, whether you have $10 or a million bucks to invest.

Generally, a CFP is for those investors who need an overall strategy that ties together the different aspects of your financial picture. Fee-only planners usually charge between $50 and $75 an hour, and an average visit is about three hours. Other CFPs charge, in addition to their hourly fees, a percentage or a commission on the trades that they make for you.

Money Managers

This financial whizbang is for you if you don't mind paying a little more for someone to watch over your investment portfolio and make all the decisions. You do so by giving them *power of attorney.*

Money management fees range from 4%–5% of a client's portfolio. A money manager sits down with you and discusses your financial goals in detail (as all investment pros should). This type of arrangement is for those individuals who have a lot of money and can develop enough trust in managers' abilities to let them trade as they see fit. But you should be careful because, after all, it's your money that's being controlled by someone else.

Doing It Yourself

Investors who know exactly what they are doing can do it themselves. How? Through a deep discount brokerage firm. These firms charge much, much less than their competitors. In fact, you can save up to 80 percent—sometimes more.

A deep discount brokerage firm offers the bare minimums. There aren't many offices across the country, and they mostly deal with you over the phone or through the mail. Examples of deep discount brokerage firms are:

> **Secret**
> Discount brokerage firms are the way to go once you have the knowledge and experience. You can save a lot of money—up to 80 percent—if you do it yourself.

➤ Jack White & Company—**http://pawws.com:8081/Broker/Jwc/** or (800) 233-3411

➤ Brown & Company—(800) 225-6707.

The differences between a discount brokerage firm and a deep discount brokerage firm lie in the minimum transaction fees. Typically, both types of firms charge minimum transaction fees between $20 and $40. The difference is in whether the broker charges on a per-share basis or on a value basis. Some discount brokers charge a flat $.05 to $.08 per share no matter if you buy 10,000 shares of XYZ Company Stock or only 100 shares of the same company. Other discount and deep discount firms may charge you based on how much you trade; the more shares and trading volume you incur, the lower your cost per share. Whatever the price, though, the minimum transaction fee ranges from $20 to $40.

It'll Cost You: Comparing Broker Fees and Hidden Costs

You must monitor your broker transaction fees as often as you do your investments. Why? Because not only are there commissions that you pay when you trade investment securities in your accounts, but there are also maintenance fees. These maintenance fees—which can run as high as $50 a year—are simply added to your account just for having it at any type of brokerage firm.

Other fees to watch out for are postage and handling fees. When you buy or sell an investment, you'll receive a *trade confirmation* in the mail. This is just a notice confirming the transaction you placed. Many times a postage and handling fee to mail this out to you will be added to your transaction. Some of these fees can be as high as $4.00 per transaction. Also many full-service brokerage firms will charge you an inactivity fee if you do not generate at least $100 worth in commissions to the firm. Be careful where you do your brokerage shopping.

For a sampling of what some of the largest full-service, discount, and deep-discount brokerage firms charge in commissions on transactions, check out the following scenarios. Just how much will the commissions be?

You buy 100 shares of XYZ stock at $50 a share. How much will commissions be?

Full-Commission Broker	Discount Broker	Deep-Discount Broker
$106	$49 to $55	$25

You buy 300 shares of XYZ stock at $40 a share. How much will commissions be?

Full-Commission Broker	Discount Broker	Deep-Discount Broker
$251	$89 to $116.80	$25

You buy 100 shares of XYZ stock at $30 a share. How much will commissions be?

Full-Commission Broker	Discount Broker	Deep-Discount Broker
$83	$49 to $55	$25

This is just a comparison to show you what the typical charges of particular stock trades would be, according to Mercer, Inc. The information is taken from a survey they do based on the number of shares and the price of the stock given.

Shopping for a Broker

Here's a list of additional tips to help you choose and wisely use a broker:

➤ First come, first hired, first fired. Don't hire the first broker on your list without investigating others. Interview several before choosing just one. Just like hiring that new baby-sitter for the kids, you don't want Helga the Horrible or Bubbles (no last name, of course) with no experience to watch your children. You need to find a financial professional that you feel comfortable with—and that you can afford. Collect five to ten names before you narrow the list to your final choice, and make sure you meet this person face to face. Never hire someone over the phone. After all, you will be telling this person the most intimate details of your financial life.

➤ Don't rely on cousin Mort. Make sure you know what type of broker (experienced or inexperienced) you are dealing with. Ask what professional degrees or credentials the broker has earned.

➤ Check on a professional's work history. If you want to find out if your broker has committed fraud or any other serious violations, contact the National Association of Securities Dealers (NASD) at (800) 289-9999.

The Least You Need to Know

➤ Before you invest, you need to learn as much information about a company as possible, including what type of business it's in, who its competitors are, and if it's planning to introduce any new products or services.

➤ The easiest way to remember how to decipher performance information is to think of it as the investment's track record.

➤ Getting a prospectus—and understanding it—shouldn't be difficult as long as you know you should look for key points, including any expenses or fees (if it's a mutual fund prospectus) and how long the company has been in business (if it's a prospectus from an initial stock or bond offering).

➤ Whether you choose to use a full-service, discount, or deep-discount broker is up to you. But no matter what, you should still monitor your own investment portfolio and keep up with market trends even if you opt for a financial advisor.

In the speech bubbles:
- A DRAMATIZATION...
- YOU KNOW YOU HAVE A MONKEY ON YOUR BACK.
- YES, AND HIS NAME IS OVER-SPENDING!

Chapter 6

Kick the Spending Habit!

In This Chapter

➤ Having bad habits can cost you plenty

➤ Finding that you might have more bad habits than you think

➤ Discerning between good and bad habits

So you say you're a good shopper and a smart saver. You clip coupons. You only buy the items on sale during your trips to the grocery store. And you look for that blue light at your favorite K-Mart. Those habits are honorable. You're saving money, no doubt, but there is a hidden evil that lurks inside all of us that we don't know about—the "see it and buy it" monster.

Think about when you go on a diet. You monitor your fat intake and your calorie intake. You make sure you're getting enough exercise and eating the right kinds of food. Now apply this to spending, saving, and investing. You determined what your personal financial battle plan is in Chapter 3. You know how much your net worth is and have a good idea of how much you can save and invest. However, an integral part of that plan is to monitor—and possibly cut—your spending habits. This chapter will inspire you to take a good, honest look at how you spend your money and will help you find ways to kick any overspending habits you have.

Bet You Didn't Know

Coupons are given a cash value, such as 1/20th of a cent, in order to comply with state laws. The amount is high enough to be legal, but low enough that no one will collect them. But that doesn't mean you shouldn't use them!

That Trip to the Mall Costs More Than You Think

You're at work and the clock reads high noon. It's time for lunch for most folks, but not for you. You know that it costs an average $5 per day, $25 per week, to eat your lunch out of the office. You are trying to keep your spending habits to a bare minimum. So, you take out the piece of fruit you brought from home and decide to go for a walk. Good. Not only is that nutritionally healthy, but you're also getting exercise.

On your lunch break, your walk finds you in front of your favorite Department Store, chock full of fashionable clothing at discount prices. Let's take a peek, you say to yourself. Fifteen minutes later, you're leaving the dressing room with $132.11 worth of merchandise and heading toward the cashier. Ah, but you saved money on lunch, right? Wrong! It would have been cheaper for you to eat out. It's good that you've started your personal financial battle plan, but now it's time to evaluate your financial habits.

Kick the Habit

Have an extra five bucks in your pocket? Is it burning a hole there? Do you feel compelled to spend it? The worst kind of "see it and buy it" mentality is using your credit card for unnecessary purchases. Don't rationalize that just because you have credit available on your plastic, you can (or should) buy now and pay later.

Secret
Never pay for groceries or any other perishable items with a credit card. If you only make the minimum payment amount, that bag of Mallomars, a head of lettuce, and four rolls of toilet paper could be financed for the next four months.

Let's take a $1,000 credit card purchase, for example. At an annual percentage rate of 19.8%, it takes close to 15 years to pay off that initial purchase if you only meet the minimum payments; plus, there's more than $4,100 in nondeductible finance charges tacked on. Instead, forego the $1,000 purchase, and invest the money. If you put $1,000 a year in a moderate investment paying 8% on average for ten years, guess what you'd have at the end of the decade? About $16,000. Not bad.

Individuals who spend lavishly now and count on Social Security benefits as their only source of income for later years are foolish. Many industry experts believe Social Security won't be there to help in the long run. Therefore, the burden on a successful financial future rests with *you*.

There are ways to cure bad spending habits:

➤ **First, use the power of your own mind and self-determination.** Your imagination and goal-setting can be strong motivators. Imagine how you'd feel if you had an investment account worth $25,000, or even $50,000. Picture how rewarding it is to have money that you worked so hard for grow into a substantial nest egg. Motivate your mind to believe this substantial nest egg is more profitable and rewarding than a closet full of designer clothes or a glitzy new automobile.

➤ **Second, count the number of credit cards you have in your wallet.** Five, six, maybe eight? Getting rid of the plastic (with the exception of one or two major credit cards) is imperative. Make sure you only use these during an emergency. You'll be amazed to see how not using your credit cards can help cut costs.

> **Secret**
> Consider transferring your high-rate card balances to a lower-rate card, thereby reducing some of the interest charges that are accruing.

➤ **Third, reduce some of your living expenses.** Watch your telephone and utility bills. Place your telephone calls at the times of day when rates are cheaper, if necessary. Unplug appliances that aren't used during the day. Don't leave lights on when you're not at home. Keep eating out to a minimum. These may seem like small sacrifices, but they add up.

➤ **Fourth, if you are in the market for a new automobile, consider buying a new used car— as long as you know the history behind the car—instead of a brand new car.** Why? Because a brand new car depreciates 20 percent just after you drive it out of the lot. Remember, a car *is not* an investment. In fact, you can save hundreds of dollars if you purchase a new used car instead.

> **Secret**
> If you must have a credit card, don't apply for more than two credit cards at a time. Why? Because every time you apply, the credit card company checks into your credit report, and the inquiry is recorded. If there are a lot of inquiries, then you'll be denied credit from other issuers and lenders later on.

➤ **Fifth, should you buy or should you rent? That decision really depends on your life situation.** However, if you buy rather than rent, the interest portion of your mortgage payment is 100 percent tax deductible on your tax return. And, over time, if your home's value appreciates, when it comes time to sell, you could see yourself with a tidy little profit.

Keeping Up with the Joneses

Here is one of my favorite "Gotta keep up with the Joneses" example.

Bud and Ethel Jones just bought a brand new, sporty, two-door BMW. The car is fully loaded. Their down payment was only $1,000, and they financed the rest for the next 60 months. They live a lifestyle of "bigger is better" and hee-haw at their friends who don't have sporty cars and flashy clothes. If a neighbor buys a new ten-speed for his child, Bud and Ethel seek out the most expensive mountain bike for theirs. Rather than taking the family on a camping trip to the Ozarks, the Joneses fly to Paris.

Secret
One way to track your spending habits is to keep a pocket-sized notebook with you at all times. Everytime you run to the drugstore or even the foodmart at the gas station, write down all of your purchases and tally them up at the end of the week—yes, that includes your beef jerky sticks and can of Kayo chocolate drink. Put the total into a "miscellaneous" category on your budget worksheet. You will not believe how much you spend on items on a weekly basis that are trivial.

Is it important to keep up with these Joneses? Not at all. They may be swimming in debt before long if their spending habits keep up the way they've been. Their financial future is completely destroyed. The Joneses are a status symbol family—big house, expensive car, and at least five credit cards, which I'm sure are maxed out.

Keeping up with the Joneses is the quickest way to destroy your financial future. If you try to keep up with them, how would you do it? Get another job? No, the one you have already takes 60 hours per week. You would probably have to use your credit cards, thus sinking you and your family further into debt. Don't abuse your credit cards. Using them to pay for everything—from groceries to furniture—can be bad for your financial health. All a credit card does is allow you to purchase more than you can really afford.

If I could tattoo one phrase on the inside of your eyelids it would be "Get Rid of Your Debt!" Folks, keeping up with the Joneses just digs a deeper hole for you to climb out of.

An Alternative to Spending—Investing

Creating instant wealth is not easy, unless of course, you win the lottery. We already know what the odds are with that. Creating long-term wealth is a different story, calling for patience and determination. Even if your annual salary is less than $25,000, you can afford to save money. The best solution is the 10 percent solution. You should start practicing this financial habit right away. It's a good one! Putting away 10 percent of your income into an investment vehicle that yields a pretty good total annual return makes it possible to retire quite comfortably.

Begin immediately. Don't tell yourself that you'll do it after you finish paying off the kids' dentist bills. Start today. Implementing this habit guarantees that you'll put you and your family ahead of all other obligations. It doesn't mean that you skip paying the electric bill. In fact, treat your ten percent solution as a bill. Whenever you are doing your bills, write a check out to yourself first and put it away—in a mutual fund, for instance. Or set up an automatic investment account with a mutual fund, as you'll learn in Part 3.

One way to instantly start saving 10 percent of your money is to allocate it in an automatic investment plan at a mutual fund company. This means you can take even as little as $50 a month directly from your account and invested right into the fund (which you'll learn more about in the Mutual Funds section).

Overall, once you learn more about the different types of investments that can grow over time, you will be better equipped to make a decision as to where to invest.

While it may seem impossible to have an emergency fund *and* the ability to invest 10 percent of your money each month, it is really the best way to protect yourself in the event of an emergency (and not touch the funds) while at the same time, building a financial future for you and your family.

If you are not able to fulfill both goals, initially save for the emergency fund. Then when you have about three to six months' worth of living expenses in that fund, then just re-allocate the money from the emergency fund account and begin an investment program with it, such as the monthly investment in the mutual fund of your choice.

Secret
Investing 10 percent of your money each month is *independent* of the emergency fund you have set up for you and your family. Why? Because they're two separate goals. The emergency fund should be liquid (readily available) and in a safe account, such as a money market account. The 10 percent that you are allocating to investing, in say, a mutual fund, is for your future financial goals (such as retirement, college education, a home, and so on).

The entire concept is based on the strategy of bucking the odds of living paycheck-to-paycheck—especially in the future. You know the feeling. Even before your paycheck is directly deposited to your bank account, it's already spent. You can always outspend your paycheck, but that doesn't mean you should. Get out of that rut! If you pay everybody else first and try to have fun with what's left over, you'll never get anywhere. If you have the discipline to continue building your nest egg with the 10 percent solution, you won't live paycheck-to-paycheck anymore.

Obviously, those who begin practicing this 10 percent ritual at an earlier age will find that it takes less money to create a fortune. These individuals have years to plan their work and work their plan, which puts them in a good situation because retirement comes quickly—sometimes too quickly. Americans are getting older, especially the majority of the population in our country, the baby boomers. You are a baby boomer if you were born between 1946 and 1964, and there's about 77 million of you out there. This generation has graduated from the mentality of spending everything they've earned to trying to invest for retirement. They're in their peak earning years but caught with a shorter amount of time to save for retirement.

Start as soon as you can. In fact, start *now!*

The Least You Need to Know

➤ Debt reduction is key in the '90s. If you don't stop using your credit cards to pay for everything—even nights out on the town—you'll wind up under a mountain of debt.

➤ Don't try to keep up with your neighbors financially. Status symbols are out, and getting rid of debt is in! Face it, there will always be someone who has more than you. Accept and be proud of your accomplishments.

➤ Just think 10 percent. Try and invest 10 percent of your paycheck and watch the money grow over the long haul!

Chapter 7

How to Divide Up Your Investment Pie

In This Chapter

➤ Knowing how often you should monitor your investments

➤ Using asset allocation to diversify

➤ Discovering whether your portfolio earns an A+

Should you buy stocks? Mutual funds? What about bonds? How about dabbling in options trading? Learning which investments are right for you is instrumental in building your nest egg. Determining how much of each investment should be in your portfolio is called *asset allocation*.

For you, asset allocation will mean creating the right portfolio mix based on your age and financial goals, the risk involved, and current market forces. This chapter shows you how to wisely allocate your dollars among various investments to control risk and maximize returns.

It's a Percentage Thing

Establishing the right asset allocation mix enables you to take advantage of several different types of financial markets. For example, if you have 40 percent of your portfolio invested in stocks, 35 percent in bonds, and the remaining 25 percent in cash, you've taken sufficient precautions against the possibility of stocks and bonds declining in value. (You'll learn how to set these percentages for your portfolio later in this chapter.)

Secret

Be careful of the investment pro that tells you about a "sure thing" that you should invest all your money in. Sure things are about as reliable as a plane with no wings. Remember, diversify, diversify, diversify!

Once you determine your asset allocation, it's a model that you'll follow based on the goals that you have today, your risk tolerance, and the current market environment. You might find that last year's financial strategies don't work this year. Maybe this year's financial strategies will need some fine-tuning before they'll work next year.

Why? Tax changes are always being proposed by Congress, and if put into law, would probably affect your personal finances and your investments. For example, if a capital gains tax cut is approved, that means any gains you earn on your investments will be taxed at a lower rate than previously assessed. A good historical example of how tax law changes affected Americans occurred in 1993. That year, the law imposed two new brackets on high-income Americans and reduced the number of deductions that can be claimed on a tax return.

Another reason for changing financial strategies is that your goals have changed. Maybe the kids left the nest, and it's time to sell the house and buy that condo on the golf course.

Whatever the circumstances, deciding what your asset allocation mix should be will help you achieve these goals. Whether you have $100, $1,000, or even $100,000 to invest, you should diversify your portfolio to protect you against market fluctuations and economic uncertainties.

Slicing Your Investment Pie

Once you've determined your investment profile, including your level of risk, it's time to slice up the investment pie. If you look at historical data, the most efficient portfolio would hold approximately 40 percent stocks and 60 percent bonds. By following this, you can increase your expected return without taking on any more risk, which is better than investing 100 percent in bonds that are held until maturity. The goal is to give an investor the highest return with the least amount of risk.

Does this mean that you should go out and sink 40 percent of your money into stocks and 60 percent into bonds? No, this is given as a guideline. What is involved in determining your asset allocation is based on a number of factors.

One factor in determining your asset allocation mix is risk. If the market has a problem, ask yourself how much risk you can bear. Are you going to be able to sleep at night if you see your portfolio take a 10 percent loss? That will really drive your decision. Even the professional portfolio managers use risk tolerance as a guideline in choosing the right asset allocation mix.

Secret
Base your percentage of stocks, bonds, and cash on your tolerance for risk. Look for a mix that will give you less volatility and a higher return. You want the greatest return for the least amount of risk.

Answer the following questions to help you decide how much you should invest in each category:

1. **How much of a risk-taker are you?** You already have a pretty good idea based on your answers to questions in Chapter 4. You know that the more the risk, the more the return you can expect to receive. If you are more aggressive in your investment approach, a higher percentage of your money can be allocated toward equities (stocks). However, if you are more of a conservative investor, a greater percentage can be invested in fixed-income securities (such as bonds).

2. **How old are you?** There used to be an old trick to determine what your asset allocation mix should be. "Your age should equal your percentage of fixed-income securities. The rest should be in stocks." For example, if you are 35 years old and you followed this rule, 35 percent of your money should be in fixed-income securities and 65 percent should be in stocks. The older you become, the more money you should allocate to fixed-income securities.

3. **What is your time horizon?** A long-term investment plan is a key factor when you are beginning to earmark your money. If you have a long-term investment horizon, such as a five- to ten-year time frame, you should allocate more to equities. If you have a shorter time horizon, understand that equities can give you a substantial negative return, therefore you would want to allocate a majority of your assets to fixed-income securities. Keep in mind that over the long run, equities have outperformed fixed-income securities. Because every investor is different, you need to set your own parameters and decide what the result should be—whether to invest for growth or income or both.

Diversification should be practiced by all investors because it reduces risk. The reason for the reduction in volatility is that stocks increasing in price tend to offset any negative effects of those investment securities that are decreasing in price. (For a few samples of what your investment pie might look like, check out Chapter 31.)

Timing—A Strategy Not for the Beginner

For centuries, financial gurus have theorized about what it takes to make a handsome profit. These market wizards spent their lives timing the market, but even if they hadn't and instead just let their money ride over a long period of time, they could still come out ahead.

For example, examine the stock market over the past 50 years using the Standard & Poor's 500, which is an index that's made up of 500 different stocks. Suppose you invested $1,000 50 years ago and did nothing. You didn't time the market; you just let your grand ride. That initial $1,000 investment 50 years ago would be worth almost $580,000 today. There were some pretty big bumps in the stock market along the way, but at a rate of nearly 13% compounded annually on the S&P's 500, you'd have all that dough after 50 years—without market timing.

Secret
When you are creating a sound asset allocation mix for your portfolio, all you are doing is figuring out how your money should be divided up among different investments.

Careful
It's not important for you to follow your trading patterns according to a Russian economist or track a few repetitive patterns, but rather to understand that just as there is a business cycle in economics, there are cycles in the financial markets.

Timing the market is a very involved process and should mainly be left to the graph-paper wizards, but it is interesting to read about. One ingredient to market timing includes studying the patterns of market cycles. Just notice the strange phenomenon that occurs when you get a bunch of financial Einsteins in the same room. You can count on one of them bringing up the subject of market cycles.

Why do market cycles exist? They just do. It's best to understand the basic concept of the economic and financial cycles that market watchers study. I'm not talking about how the sun moves with the moon and stars, but rather how investors make money by basing their trading decisions on the technical analysis of studying market and economic cycles.

The most interesting study is found in the *Kondratieff Wave Analyst* (P.O. Box 977, Crystal Lake, IL 60014), which is an investment newsletter that goes into great detail about our modern day economic situation and how it applies to the historical Kondratieff Wave theory. This is important because most economists and big time investors ask themselves a continuing pressing question: Where are we in the Kondratieff cycle? All you need to know is that a Russian economist named Kondratieff created this cycle. To be brief, his theory says that the cycle is expected to take from 50–54 years to be completed, and is mixed with large economic growth, war, high long-term borrowing, and inflation. Historians call it a "half-century business cycle."

The Elliott Wave system, which is described in its monthly newsletter *The Elliott Wave Theorist* (P.O. Box 1618, Gainesville, GA 30503 (404) 536-0309), uses cycle analysis to make investment predictions. This newsletter records repetitions of price patterns to predict major moves in the market.

Dollar Cost Averaging Beats Averaging Down

As you are learning the rules of investing, the language of money is quite simple. Making money will be even easier as you continue on your journey through this guide. Along the way, you will find a few warnings, too. Heed them.

One danger involves the difference between *dollar cost averaging* and *averaging down*. Dollar cost averaging is a smart investment strategy. All you do is make fixed regular investments in a stock or mutual fund—even if the market is rising or falling. This strategy works in your favor no matter what the market does. Averaging down is not the same principle. The idea is to constantly purchase shares in an investment as the price of the investment continues to spiral downward. It's a losing game.

Let me explain averaging down by using an example. If you purchase 100 shares of stock at $20 a share, your total investment is worth $2,000. If the stock drops to $15 a share, your total investment is worth only $1,500. Suppose you purchase additional shares, let's say another 100 shares at $15. Your total expense is calculated as $2,000 from your intial investment plus another $1,500 from your second purchase for a grand total expense of $3,500. By now, your average cost on the total 200 shares is $17.50 per share. Because the stock is currently trading at $15 a share, it has to rise to $17.50 per share for you to *break even* on your investment. This is an example of how averaging down can work against you.

> **Careful**
> Don't let a financial adviser talk you into this type of investment strategy. On your own, you can learn when to hold and when to sell an investment. Averaging down is a loser's game.

An A+ or an E for Effort?

Managing your investment portfolio is based on a few simple concepts: How much money should you invest? What's the best strategy for you? Can you meet your long-term financial goals? And how can you put yourself in a position to properly gauge how your stocks or stock mutual funds are faring?

The best way to determine how well your portfolio is performing is to use a benchmark. As an investor, it is important to understand how your investments are judged. A benchmark measures the standard of performance reached by other investors. Sometimes this is referred to as a market average or an index.

The most widely quoted stock indicator is the Dow Jones industrial average, but it represents only 30 blue-chip stocks. It often says surprisingly little about the day-to-day direction of the entire market. Because the Dow is so narrowly based, it's usually a poor benchmark against which to compare an entire portfolio's performance.

Market analysts have devised dozens of other stock indexes—ranging from the Standard & Poor 500, which comprises 500 stocks, to indexes that focus on just one sector, such as automobiles or restaurants. Many portfolio managers use the S&P 500 as a benchmark because it is a far broader measure of market activity than the Dow Jones industrial average. But there are other options. The Russell 2000 Index and the Wilshire Small Cap Index both track the stock performance of smaller companies. The S&P 400 MidCap Index, which tracks medium-size stocks, and the Wilshire 5000 index, which tracks all major New York Stock Exchange, American Stock Exchange, and NASDAQ stocks. These indexes exist as benchmarks against which you can compare your portfolio, depending on your investments. If you have any foreign investments, you might want to use the Morgan Stanley Capital International Europe Australia Far East (EAFE) Index. This is the most prominent index used to track foreign stocks.

If you're trying to beat the market, it's not too tough as long as you're looking at a long-term time horizon. This year, those investors, for example, who invested in an S&P 500 index fund, earned almost 21 percent during the first six months of 1997.

Secret
Index funds are sometimes based upon computer models designed and followed by fund managers. These computer models can even be so-phisticated enough to perform the trades on their own.

A number of mutual funds, called index funds, mirror how the S&P 500 performs. Your return on them will closely resemble the increases (and decreases) of the index they are based upon. In fact, you can make a lot of money with them if you invest in them over the long run.

Investing over the long run is one of the biggest secrets to making money on Wall Street. It takes a long run to average out the bull runs and bear markets. If you are investing over the long haul, hold on. You can weather it and come out ahead.

Time to Check Your Portfolio

After you create your investment portfolio, make a date with yourself the day before your birthday as a present to yourself to review your investment portfolio thoroughly every year. This review should be in addition to the regular monitoring that you do. Treat this day as a special day for yourself. Yes, you are almost one year older, and that changes many things (your health, your state of mind, and your financial affairs). Why not take advantage of this day, and thoroughly check on your investments? Your birthday is a time for reflection—thinking about what you've accomplished in the past year. Reflect on your portfolio too. See what you've done and where you want to go.

Take an hour or two to go through your records. Have you been living within your means? Are you contributing to your company's retirement plan? Have you adjusted your portfolio as you achieved your goals and your responsibilities changed?

Whatever the case, controlling your financial independence is sustained by keeping this date with yourself. It's the art of practicing self-discipline. Not only are you reviewing your portfolio on a regular basis—such as when you check your stock quotes or put your mutual fund statements in order—but this extra birthday attention that you give to your financial affairs will pay off handsomely in the future. You can also change any other pertinent financial records then. If you have made a will or bought a new piece of property, account for it during your annual review. Feel the sense of accomplishment as you check off items on your "Financial To-Do" list.

The Least You Need to Know

➤ Asset allocation is a form of diversifying your investment portfolio that protects you against market fluctuations.

➤ Learn how to properly gauge your investment portfolio by following some of the key indices. The Dow Jones industrial average, the Standard & Poor 500, and the Russell 2000 Index are just a few.

➤ Do not try to time your investments. Leave that to the professional market timers.

➤ The three main factors that'll determine your asset allocation mix include how much risk you're willing to take, your age, and your time horizon.

Part 2
Megabanks: One-Stop Shopping

The face of banking is changing. It used to be you could walk into a bank lobby and be greeted by the bank teller on a first-name basis. Not anymore. Banks have become major profit centers by focusing on transaction-based fees—all the while passing on these costs to you, Joe and Jane Consumer.

You can boot up your PC and pay bills through PC banking, online banking, and Internet banking, all from your armchair. Banks now offer Wall-Street-like products, such as mutual funds and annuities, competing with the Wall Street Big Boys.

So while you might understand the basics of what a bank can do—offering savings and checking accounts and all types of loans—as we approach the new century the banking industry will evolve into a much stiffer competitor, trying to give other financial institutions a run for their money. Your mission, should you choose to accept it, is to reduce your costs on banking services, learn more about "cyberspace" banking, and maximize your dollars with specific products tailored to your needs. Are you ready for the challenge?

Chapter 8

Banking Today—and Tomorrow

In This Chapter

➤ Discovering there are no more free toasters and lollipops

➤ Knowing what to spend on banking services

➤ Finding available bank products

Picture this. You enter your bank lobby and suddenly you're surrounded by the cutting edge of technology—fax machines, modems, PC networks, TV screens galore, and robot tellers (okay, not really robot tellers, but machines that spit out money at the touch of a few buttons). What is all this? Buck Rogers in the 21st Century?

Nope, just a modern-day bank lobby. Forget the bank brochures that you used to pick up and read for information. Bank lobbies are rigged with television monitors providing information on all bank products and services via video information channels. Everywhere you look there's a monitor. Waiting in line? Another video monitor. Want to know what's happening on Wall Street? Check the monitor.

Now imagine it's four in the morning. You are wide awake because you can't remember the amount of check number 132. (You forgot to enter it in your check register last week.) Easy enough—just dial your bank's 24-hour, seven-day-a-week hotline. Press a few buttons (don't forget your personal access code) and get your answer. Talk about technology!

This chapter takes a look at the services that today's banks provide and how those services can fit in with your investment battle plan.

You Can Take That to the Bank

Most of you already have been exposed to a bank. In fact, nine out of ten Americans have either a savings account or a checking account, according to the Consumer Bankers Association. Broken down, 79 percent of households have a checking account and 9 percent have a savings account.

Secret
In addition to the traditional checking and savings accounts, banks have money market deposit accounts (MMDAs) and certificates of deposit (CDs). These types of accounts usually earn a more competitive rate than normal checking or savings accounts, but they are still covered by FDIC insurance.

Even if you don't have a checking or savings account, you'll have to deal with a bank at some point in your life. When unexpected emergencies arise, it helps to have cash in a savings or money market account as provided by banks, even if you're earning 3% on your savings, your account can't fall in principal value, unlike stocks, bonds, and mutual funds. Cash is king when stock and bond prices are falling.

As our population ages, seniors and retired persons grow to depend on a fixed income from more conservative types of investments, and their strategy should be to keep a significant portion of their money safe from any loss. This cash on hand guarantees that the money will be there when needed.

You learned in Chapter 4 about the role liquidity plays in your investment planning. Even if you are a big-time futures player, you still need a place to park your cash for a relatively short time between your investment trading adventures. Why not in your bank? One of the best places to keep your cash on hand is in an interest-bearing account that pays competitive rates, such as an MMDA.

As investors of the '90s and the new millenium are gaining more independence regarding their finances, all financial institutions—banks, brokerage firms, financial services companies, and mutual fund companies—are competing for their cash. This has caused the banking industry to change, and you've probably witnessed a few of these changes—new bank products, higher fees, and advanced computerized services, especially online and PC banking.

Many of you have learned the essence of smart banking in the '90s, such as implementing strategies that help you *not* to incur any additional fees or charges. But what's going to take you into the year 2000 and afterward is another set of rules that relies on your ability to reduce banking fees and increase your understanding of technology.

For example, if you maintain a minimum balance in a checking or savings account, you aren't slapped with a "below minimum balance" fee. Many of you know that when you use your bank's ATM machine rather than a competitor's ATM machine, you avoid getting nicked with an ATM charge. Others have taken advantage of a bank's direct deposit feature and get that extra day's worth of interest from their paycheck.

These are all good—but the world of banking offers so much more these days.

As banks are vying for your dollars, they're trying to stay as competitive as ever. How? By paying better interest rates on your interest-bearing accounts than the next guy can. Banks also aim to provide customers with the same services as their competitors. You can bet your bottom dollar that banks are still making money, too. In fact, for the past several years, the banking industry has been enjoying record profits. How do they do this?

What?
The difference between the interest rates paid to customers on their investments and the interest rates that the bank collects on its outstanding loans from customers is called the *spread*.

Here's an example that illustrates one avenue banks use to make money. Let's say you're a bank customer at my bank and have a noninterest-bearing checking account, a savings account that pays 3% annually, and a one-year CD that pays 4.75%. You're in the process of buying a new car and need a loan. So you come to my bank, and I charge you 10% for a $15,000, 48-month loan.

Now let's do the math. If I'm paying you 3% on your savings account and 4.75% on your CD, you're getting 7.75% total on all your investments at my bank. That's what you collect from me. You are paying me 10% to borrow money. That's what I collect from you. The difference between the two is the *spread*. That means that my bank is making 2.25% on these transactions. That's how banks make money.

If the spread widens, my bank makes more money. In other words, rates that I pay my customers on their investments drop, but the rates that I charge my customers on all types of loans aren't moving as much. They're staying pretty steady, and there's more of a difference between the two. On the other hand, if the spread narrows, my bank isn't making as much money because the rates that I pay to customers' accounts and the rates that I charge on all loans fall into a pretty small range.

Banks Enter Wall Street's Turf

Wall Street contenders never really had to worry about the banking industry stepping on their toes until the emergence of bank mutual funds. As progressive banks grab more and more of the mutual fund market, mutual fund companies have been in the throes of a counterattack...but in a different form.

Wall Street players are taking a different tack in chasing consumer dollars by making deals with the banks. For example, one large mutual fund company in Chicago created a group of funds designed *only* for bank distribution. These funds are known as *nonproprietary funds* because even though the bank is offering them, there is no bank label on them. They are managed by the fund company, not the bank. All the bank does is distribute them and collect a portion of the fees generated.

About 3,500 banks sell mutual funds, and more than a third of all new mutual fund sales last year were made by banks and savings and loans. Banks have been offering mutual funds with their own label on them since the early '80s. These are known as *proprietary*

What?
Proprietary funds are mutual funds specifically designed for a bank.

funds. Several years ago, there were 110 proprietary mutual funds available to bank customers and outside investors. Today that number has increased three-fold.

To date, all bank *proprietary* mutual funds carry a load. On average, most banks are offering their mutual funds with a sales load from 4% to 6%. It's also not uncommon to see the majority of banks charging you when you first invest in the fund, called a *front-end load*, instead of when you sell,

called a *back-end load*. The maximum any mutual fund company—a bank or a mutual fund service company—can charge is 8.5%.

Here's an example of how your money might be invested in a proprietary fund at a local bank. Assuming you meet with a financial rep, you take the time to review your invest-

What?
Proprietary mutual funds are managed by affiliate bank reps and usually carry a *load*, or a commission, on top of the net asset value per share when the fund is purchased. The commission is deducted from your initial investment. Those funds offered by a bank but do not have the banking designer label on it are known as non-proprietary funds, and can be *no-load* funds, meaning, no sales fees.

ment plan, and decide to invest $5,000 in this bank fund, which carries a 5% front-end load. Here's the catch: Your entire $5,000 does *not* get invested. What happens is that $250 is taken out to accommodate the load. That means only $4,750 of your money gets invested initially in the fund. The $250 fee is for the time and service that you receive from the investment counselor at the bank. If you invest in a back-end load, the entire $5,000 goes to work for you until you sell. At that point, a fee is assessed to your account.

Bank mutual funds don't necessarily charge you a higher sales load than their mutual fund giant counterparts, but these proprietary funds do not offer you the opportunity of a no-load (no sales fee) fund. Chapter 15 explains the differences among the different types of sales loads incurred when you buy a mutual fund. Once you understand the difference between a load fund versus a no-load fund, it's up to you to choose which mutual funds you want.

Rich Cats in Blue Suits

For decades, the federal government regulated banks—specifically, how much interest the banks could pay on checking and savings accounts. Since deregulation hit in the 1980s, banks are more of a free-market business. As fees and charges have increased tenfold over the past 20 years, banks have turned into cash cows. To sum it up in three words, "More fees, please."

Unfortunately, gimmicky banking charges keep compounding these days. You've already been affected by the rise in service fees. If you bounce a check, fall below the minimum balance requirement, or stop at a foreign ATM machine (an ATM machine owned by a bank that is not yours), you are probably forced to pay a fee or surcharge. In the case of ATMs, you can be hit with an ATM fee and an ATM surcharge. An ATM fee is when you're charged a fee (nationwide average is $1.00 according to Bank Rate Monitor) by another bank when using their ATM. An ATM surcharge is when you're charged by *your* bank (can be as high as $3 per transaction) for using *another* bank's ATM.

In fact, as of this writing, several political gadflies are trying to ban ATM surcharges, but to date no legislation has been passed, although many irate consumers have voiced their opinions nationwide in various media outlets.

Here are a few classic examples of how escalating (and even ludicrous) bank charges can chip away at your savings. To be smart with your money, avoid incurring these charges whenever possible.

Secret
If you are deciding between a bank proprietary fund and a bank nonproprietary fund (such as a mutual fund offered by a bank but managed elsewhere), check to see whether the company that manages this nonproprietary fund offers a similar no-load version. If so, buy the no-load fund. Many times, mutual fund companies offer funds that are similar in investment objective and management style, but one fund charges a load and the other doesn't.

➤ **Talking to a live teller over the phone.** This one takes the cake. Your bank account could be slapped with a $2 fee if you talk to a bank service representative instead of a computer. Customers at a rather prestigious bank in Chicago were assessed a special charge for getting account information from a "live" customer service representative and avoiding their automated system. An actual person requires a salary and a lunch hour, whereas a computer doesn't, of course.

➤ **FDIC fees.** Some banks in regions of the Southeast, California, and St. Louis have added this fee to checking and savings accounts as a way of shoring up the flagging FDIC (Federal Deposit Insurance Corporation). It's not uncommon to see banks charging you about 30 cents per $100 on deposit, on up to the first $100,000 deposited in a retail checking or savings account. The fee is usually not assessed to noninterest-bearing checking accounts.

➤ **Account closing fees.** Account holders had a fit when their banks charged $10 and $15 on noninterest-bearing checking accounts when they tried to close their accounts within six months. Make sure that when you open your account, there are no fees that you'll be hit with if you decide to close it.

➤ **Bounced check fees.** These are still rising across the country, and they probably always will. According to *Bank Rate Monitor*, an industry newsletter, it costs more to bounce a check at a bank than at a savings and loan or credit union. In 1997, the average cost of a bounced check charge was well over $22.00 at your local bank.

➤ **Foreign ATM fees and ATM surcharges.** These are ATM transactions that you make at a rival cash station across town. ATM fees range from 50 cents to $2. Who has control of these fees? You do. Don't use your ATM card at a foreign ATM station and you won't get nicked with any more charges. 25 percent of bank customers don't know what it costs to use an ATM card.

➤ **Loss of interest below a particular balance.** Get this. Some banks tell you that they won't pay you any interest on your savings account if the balance falls below a certain level, such as $50. Avoid stashing your cash in these types of accounts.

➤ **Overdraft fees.** Not only can you get charged a possible $20 bounced check fee, some institutions charge you additional moneys—the average is $3—for each day you're overdrawn.

➤ **Online banking fees.** Many banks, aiming to capture your dollars through your computer and a simple modem hook up, charge a variety of fees, depending on whether or not you must utilize proprietary software, or, if you can just log onto their website and then perform transactions. Typical charges for monthly account maintenance on *both* types of setups average $4.95 per month.

Careful

Online banking fees for performing transactions over the Internet don't include the cost incurred by using an Internet Service Provider, such as America Online, NetComm, Netscape or Earthlink, for example.

Start paying more attention to the steady rise in bank fees and charges—*always*. Find out what your account really costs you, because virtually all fees are going up, up, and up. You can use the following techniques to bank wisely:

➤ **Review all fine print that your financial institution gives you when you open your account.** By law, according to the Consumer Bankers Association, banks must post advance notice before increasing fees on checking and savings accounts. Read everything!

➤ **If your banking habits don't fit your institution's fee schedule, start shopping around.** For example, look for lower minimum balance requirements and reduced or non-existent ATM fees as you check out the competition. The savings can really add up.

➤ **Establish relationship accounts.** By keeping high balances in a combination of checking and savings accounts, CDs, and so on, you can qualify for benefits, such as discounts on bounced-check charges and waived annual fees on bank credit cards.

Choosing the Bank Product for Your Needs

The following are the basic products that are offered by banks today, some of which have been discussed earlier in this chapter:

➤ Passbook savings accounts.

➤ Checking accounts.

➤ MMDAs (money market deposit accounts).

➤ CDs (certificates of deposit).

➤ U.S. savings bonds.

➤ Proprietary mutual funds.

Before deregulation hit, banks were allowed to pay a maximum of 5.25% on passbook savings accounts. In fact, it was about the only account that a bank offered that paid interest. They were called passbook savings accounts because when you opened up an account you would receive a little book (the passbook). Every time you made a deposit or withdrawal, your transaction was posted in the passbook, which acted as your statement.

Today, it's anybody's ballgame. Banks are free to pay what they choose on these savings accounts. In fact, they don't even come with little passbooks anymore and are now just called savings accounts. If you are going to keep some money in a savings account, make sure you meet the minimum balance requirements because bank fees can eat up a lot of your interest earnings.

Savings accounts are good for temporary cash havens when you are in the process of determining where you're going to invest your money. They are also a good place to stash some cash while the financial markets are volatile or when Aunt Gert leaves you $100,000 and you haven't figured out how to spend it yet.

Checking accounts come in all shapes and sizes these days. Unlimited check writing, overdraft protection, free ATM use up to ten transactions per month—you name it, it's out there. But all for a price. Chapter 10 explains the basics of a checking account and how to find the best deals.

If you just want to pay a few monthly bills, it's best to check out an MMDA. This offers the best combination of liquidity and better-than-average interest rates. Rates paid on these accounts usually change on a weekly basis. These types of accounts offer check writing features, but you are usually limited to three checks per month. Typically, the minimum investment required is $1,000 to get the account going.

CDs usually pay the highest interest rates of any bank product. Touted as a safe investment, CDs enable you to lock into a specific interest rate for a certain period of time. Here's the kicker. If you withdraw any of your money from the CD—even a penny—you are faced with pretty stiff penalties (about three month's worth of interest).

Remember when you were little and instead of getting a toy for a birthday present, you got a piece of paper with your name on it that looked like a check? It was probably a savings bond. I know two little boys out there who have made a killing at their birthday parties because relatives buy them these bonds. Savings bonds offer market rates of interest, and you don't have to pay taxes on the gains until the bond matures. Plus, you can buy them with as little as $25. You'll learn about these in Chapter 24.

Remember, proprietary mutual funds are the ones with a bank's wrapper, but be careful with these. Many of them sport high loads and don't have substantial track records. If they do carry a longer history—something like three years—many of the returns are quite conservative.

The Least You Need to Know

➤ Banks have captured a share of Wall Street's target market. The introduction of bank mutual funds has forced some Wall Street competitors to take a second look at their new neighbor. Consider banks as an alternative for your mutual fund investing, but make sure to review the fine print regarding "loads," also known as sales charges.

➤ You'll have to deal with a bank at some point in your life. As part of your investment planning, make sure that you allocate a portion of your investment portfolio to cash for emergency purposes. The percentage depends upon you and your situation.

➤ Bank fees are so fat these days that banks are livin' high on the hog. Rather than a general fee that covers everything, there are different fees attached to different transactions, such as charges for transactions at foreign ATMs. Be sure to pay more attention to the steady rise in fees and charges. Look for lower minimum balance requirements and reduced ATM fees. And don't pay for those ATM surcharges if at all possible! Instead, plan your ATM visits as much as possible on a weekly basis and use your bank's ATM.

➤ Know and understand the different services that your bank offers you. Savings accounts, checking accounts, money market deposit accounts, and certificates of deposit are common products you'll see at your bank. Proprietary bank mutual funds usually carry a fee—which is a load—and average from 4% to 6%, with an 8.5% maximum. Be careful.

➤ Start out with a savings account if you can't meet the minimum on a money market deposit account. Once you have enough money, switch over to an MMDA.

Chapter 9

Should You Consider a Savings Account?

In This Chapter

➤ Savings account evolution

➤ Knowing when you should have a savings account

➤ Savings accounts in your future

When I was a little girl, my idea of fun was to make as many bank deposits as I could and watch the interest accrue in my passbook savings account. Even if I only had two bucks to deposit, I'd stand in line for a teller window, anxiously waiting for the teller to stamp my new bigger and better balance in my little passbook. Boy, I thought I was rich as I watched the money grow.

It wasn't until I deposited a check from a relative that I understood how the banking industry really worked. The check bounced. Boing! is an understatement. My little passbook savings account was hit like a torpedo gone astray. I didn't get the money from the deposit, of course, because the check bounced. Reluctantly, I took my passbook to the teller and she made the adjustment. It was a horrible scene, but I think I've recovered.

Except for the bounced-check tragedy, watching my savings account grow was a great learning experience for me. I learned the concept of depositing money and earning interest on my deposits. This chapter covers the basics of how savings accounts work and how to use them (or not use them) wisely as part of an overall investment plan.

The First Savings Accounts

What?
You can open up a savings account at a *bank* or a *savings and loan*. The difference between the two is that historically banks, also known as commercial banks, were in business to provide services to commercial or institutional customers (the big guys). Savings and loans provided services (such as mortgage lending and CD investing) to the average Joe. Today, it's anybody's ballgame.

Actually, the world of banking began many, many years ago. In about 4 B.C. the Greeks invented the bill of exchange. This was for merchants only and was the equivalent of today's savings accounts or an ATM machine. A merchant could deposit a sum of money (coins in those days) with his banker. The banker would then give him a letter in exchange for the coin deposit. When the merchant had to make a road trip—for vacation, to shop at outlet stores (just kidding), or a business trip—he would take the letter to another banker in another city and collect money. This was how the bill of exchange worked.

Savings accounts have evolved since the old letter of credit. For a number of years, the initial deposit required to open a passbook savings account was minimal—only $25. Plus, the interest that banks and savings and loans (S&Ls, which are also known as *thrifts*) paid on passbook savings accounts was regulated at a maximum 5.5% for S&Ls and 5.25% for banks.

Since the early 1980s, when the banking industry became fully deregulated, fewer and fewer banks offered the old-fashioned passbook savings account to their new customers. Most—if not all—banks today offer a statement savings account, which provides a monthly or quarterly update of transaction activity.

What type of impact did deregulation have upon initial deposits and the interest rates paid on these accounts? Most banks, S&Ls, and credit unions require at least a $100 initial deposit. Today, banks and savings and loans are free to choose how much—or how little—to pay in interest on customer deposits.

Bet You Didn't Know

One important type of bank is the money center bank. These banks are located in the major financial centers of the world, such as New York, Los Angeles, Chicago, San Francisco, London, Paris, and Tokyo. Money center banks play a major role in the world's banking industry because they are large lenders and have a lot of customer deposits.

How little, indeed. According to *Bank Rate Monitor*, an industry newsletter, the average rate paid on a savings account was a little over 2.26% in 1997, much less than yesteryear's rate of 5.25%. The interest that accrues in your savings account is based on two principles, the method of compounding and the starting date set by the bank. In the banking industry, compounding is set on a daily, monthly, quarterly, and annual basis. Table 9.1 shows how the method of compounding works.

Table 9.1   How Much Bang for Your $1,000?

Rate	Annual	Quarterly	Monthly	Daily
3.00%	$1,030.00	$1,030.34	$1,030.42	$1,030.45
4.00%	$1,040.00	$1,040.60	$1,040.74	$1,040.81
5.00%	$1,050.00	$1,050.95	$1,051.16	$1,051.27
6.00%	$1,060.00	$1,061.36	$1,061.68	$1,061.83
7.00%	$1,070.00	$1,071.86	$1,072.29	$1,072.50
8.00%	$1,080.00	$1,082.43	$1,083.00	$1,083.28

If you understand the methods of compounding, you'll come to this conclusion: The faster the reinvestment, the more money you'll earn in the end. Look at how much more money you have if you earn 4% on $1,000 compounded daily versus having it compounded annually! This principle applies to all investments that use compounding, such as CDs, money market deposit accounts, and so on.

Depositing your money into a savings account keeps it safe from loss of principal and can stabilize your investment portfolio. Safety is an integral part of investing, and a savings account can provide that. However, safety shouldn't be the only requirement you look for in an investment.

Secret
When you sign up for a bank account, see what type of compounding method is offered. The more frequent the compounding the more you will earn.

Keeping It Liquid

During your investment planning—and actually for the rest of your life—you need to have a portion of your investment portfolio kept liquid, that is, readily available. Another name for it? Cash, and you keep that in a savings account. These liquid accounts should be some type of interest-bearing account that provides income and preservation of capital. If an unexpected emergency arises, this account provides the safety net, but it also provides a good parking place when you're trying to decide which investment to purchase.

In the past, investors kept this portion in a savings account. Today, savings accounts offer rates that are much lower than in the past, and have difficulty in keeping up with inflation. The yields that are paid on savings accounts are typically about 2%–3% below those of quality bonds.

The bottom line? Unless you have a very small amount of money to save, it may be wiser to open an account that pays higher interest rates and returns. Skip the bank sweepstakes that seem to be permeating the newspaper ads these days, and instead search for a better source of returns on your liquid account. Perhaps an MMDA (money market deposit account) is right for you.

When to Choose an MMDA

Banks, thrifts, and credit unions have been offering this type of account since the early 1980s when deregulation hit. The banking industry has been competing against other types of interest-bearing accounts by paying whatever they wish on an MMDA. When the MMDA first appeared, banks were paying interest on them in double digits. With the 1990s, those double-digit rates hit the skids, and it wasn't uncommon to see only a 3% or 4% rate on these accounts.

What?
Always look for an account that provides a *day of deposit to day of withdrawal* compounding method. This way, your money earns interest the day it is deposited and will continue to do so until you withdraw it.

Daily collected balance is another method where cash and checks that you deposit from your bank earn interest immediately, but checks from other banks do not earn any interest until they've cleared.

There's also a method called *low balance compounding*. With this one, the interest is paid only on the lowest balance during the time period. Try to avoid low balance compounding if you can.

MMDA rates will always be higher than those on today's savings accounts, usually by .25% to .50%. The average yield on an MMDA in the first half of 1997 was 2.48%—still lower than the previous decade, but a slightly better return than a savings account. These rates are adjusted weekly, based on what the competition is doing and the general direction of interest rates. Because these rates change weekly, they are known as short-term rates; you can't lock in a specific rate on them, as you can on a CD.

Originally, depositors needed $2,500 to open an MMDA. However, since 1986, there has been no legal minimum deposit requirement. Typically, though, banks have the option to set their own requirements. Today, when you open an MMDA, you'll find most banks require a minimum investment of $1,000 before you earn the better-than-savings-account interest rates that are paid. Many money market accounts offer checking privileges. Therefore, you'd receive a checkbook—similar to a checking account—and are allowed to write up to three checks per month, according to federal banking law. This way, you can withdraw some or all of your cash at any time. You also are allowed to make three electronic transfers a month, so you can withdraw money—either by check or via electronic transfer—six times a month.

Here are some hints for effectively using an MMDA:

➤ Because you're limited to writing only three checks per month, use an MMDA for your "fixed" bills, such as the mortgage/rent, car payment, and insurance payments. Don't use one of your three opportunities to write a check by paying the dry-cleaner or your daughter's Girl Scouts monthly dues.

➤ Using the electronic transfer feature is handy because you also can make three large transfers a month into your regular checking account, which should offer unlimited check writing. The benefit is that most of your money will be earning higher interest for a longer period of time than if you let it sit in a savings or noninterest-bearing checking account.

➤ There are penalties if you fall below a certain minimum balance, and these penalties vary from bank to bank. Find out if your bank does not pay any interest on your MMDA if the balance falls below the minimum requirement.

Secret
Some financial institutions offer higher rates and yields on MMDAs if you keep a higher balance in them. These types of accounts have what are called *tiered rates*.

As with savings accounts, checking accounts, and CDs, MMDAs are covered by FDIC insurance. Under current law, each depositor with an account registered at a bank or savings and loan is insured up to $100,000. You don't get FDIC insurance with a mutual fund or a bond. We'll discuss more about safety concerns while planning your investments in Chapter 12.

One of the best strategies that I've seen is to consolidate most of your cash—the safety portion of your investment portfolio—into one liquid account, like the MMDA. It pays the highest yields of the bank products and offers a relatively high degree of liquidity. Make sure you utilize the allowable three checks per month and the electronic transfer feature. That's smart money talkin'!

Secret
Make sure that you shop around for a money market account that has check-writing features. One of the best ways to chase higher rates and yields on MMDAs is to subscribe to *100 Highest Yields*. Call (800) 327-7717 for subscription rate information.

Fitting an MMDA into Your Portfolio

You're always going to need some cash on hand. One of the best ways to obtain liquidity while continuing to receive a return is to keep a portion of your portfolio in a money market account.

The percentage really depends on your needs. Most financial advisers recommend that you keep between three and six months' worth of living expenses in an "emergency fund." This does not mean in a shoe box! In the past, consumers would keep their emergency money in a savings account. However, why not take advantage of the slightly higher yields paid on a money market account and still have the same liquidity in case of an emergency?

There is no rule of thumb. If you keep the majority of your investment portfolio in a money market account, you do miss out on the opportunity to have your money grow while invested in stocks, bonds, or mutual funds. However, if you don't allocate a dime to an emergency fund, when the emergency arises and you need money fast, there won't be any.

The Least You Need to Know

➤ Gone are the days when you could earn 5.25% on a passbook savings account. Banks are free to pay whatever rate they want on savings accounts. That's why it pays to search for the highest savings rates and yields around. If you have access to the Internet, visit **http://www.bankrate.com**, Bank Rate Monitor's website, which posts the highest rates and yields nationwide based on its weekly surveys of more than 2,500 financial institutions.

➤ A good alternative to savings accounts is the money market deposit account. It still carries FDIC insurance, pays better rates than a savings account and provides just as much liquidity.

➤ Once you open an MMDA, make sure you understand the penalties for falling below the minimum balance. For example, if your bank does not pay interest on your account when your balance drops below a certain minimum level, find another bank. Penalties vary from bank to bank, so shop around!

Checking Out Checking Accounts

I'll never forget the time during my freshman year of college when a friend of mine and I were in the grocery store, and she wanted to buy a candy bar. She didn't have any money on her and wouldn't take a loan from me, so she wrote a check for 50 cents.

She got her candy bar, but it cost her more than 50 cents—the check bounced. Her parents were furious. "What's the matter? Don't you have two quarters?" they screamed at her. I wanted to laugh, but that 50 cent candy bar cost her an extra $16 because she didn't have available funds in her checking account to cover it. Today, that bounced check would've cost her more than $22. I hope she savored every last morsel.

Bouncing a 50 cent check is not, obviously, a smart use of a checking account. This chapter identifies other checking account faux pas, and explains how you can avoid them.

You'll Always Need One

Despite how expensive checking accounts have become, you always need some type of checking account to pay bills. For example, when you pay the rent, are you going to send $700 in cash to your landlord? I don't think so.

A checking account is part of your investment plan for several reasons. First, you need it to *buy* other investment securities. For example, let's say you open an investment account at a discount brokerage firm. You want to buy 100 shares of stock in an up-and-coming health care company, so you purchase 100 shares at $27 a share and you *owe* your discount broker $2,700 plus commissions. How are you going to pay for it? In cash? No. You write a check to the brokerage firm (not to the broker) and it is deposited into your account.

The second is convenience. The average household grocery bill is about $150 or more these days. It isn't convenient (or safe) to carry that kind of cash around with you. Most grocery stores offer check cashing cards that enable you to write a check to the grocer for the amount of the purchase plus additional moneys, usually up to $50, which in this day of paperless transactions, is definitely convenient.

Third, having a checking account helps you keep track of your expenses. You can follow your budget closely if you itemize your transaction record in your checkbook. Keeping track of your expenses is a big part of your investment plan because it details whether you should cut certain spending habits.

Now that we've established good, solid reasons for having a checking account, let's take a look at the different types that exist.

Interest-Bearing Checking Accounts

Checking accounts never paid interest on deposits prior to 1974. Once the money market mutual fund was born—which is different than an MMDA and discussed in greater detail in Chapter 9—banks were forced to offer a negotiable order of withdrawal account, which used to be known as NOW or Super-NOW accounts. Today these are commonly referred to as "interest-bearing checking accounts."

Deregulation wiped out the maximum 5.25% interest customers could earn on their checking accounts. Similar to the savings account scenario, banks today are free to pay whatever they choose on a checking account or not pay any interest at all. It's their call!

Unlike an MMDA, you can write as many checks as you want with an interest-bearing account; but many banks have a per-check charge plus a monthly maintenance charge, which is sometimes eliminated if you keep your balance above their minimum requirements.

The rate of return is the same as with savings accounts. Most require a minimum balance, set by the bank, to earn interest. If you fall below the minimum balance, bounce a check, or use your ATM card elsewhere, some banks assess you a zillion service charges. Better watch out—an interest-bearing checking account can be quite costly if you don't follow your bank's rules.

Managing Your Cash

Wall Street contenders are now cozying up to banker's corners and offering alternatives to your bank's basic checking account. It seems that everybody in the financial services industry wants to help you manage your money.

Known as asset management accounts, or sometimes cash management accounts (CMAs), these types of accounts offer everything under the sun. The concept behind this account is to consolidate all your financial operations into one account. Before you determine if it is worth it, you should understand the rules.

First, an asset management account can be opened only through a full-service or discount brokerage firm. You can buy stock, sell bonds, and write a check to the telephone company from just one account. This sounds appealing because it appears to have less paperwork, but is it less confusing? Maybe, but not less costly.

For example, Merrill Lynch, a full-service brokerage firm, offers a CMA account. Opening up the account requires an initial deposit of $20,000 in cash or securities. You can have a combination of $10,000 cash and $10,000 worth of securities. Whatever you leave in cash in the account earns competitive money market rates.

Fees to maintain the typical asset management account range from $25 to $100 a year. That's just for having the account—it doesn't include any commissions you incur for trades. Many firms offer credit cards as part of these accounts. With the Merrill Lynch CMA, you can apply for a VISA Gold debit card, although it'll cost you an additional $25 a year just to have the card. If you don't want to pay the extra $25, you can apply for the free VISA debit card—it won't cost anything extra.

Another example? Smith Barney offers the American Express Gold card—with a $100 annual fee—in its

Secret

Don't keep a lot of money in an interest-bearing checking account that's loaded with fees. You can earn more interest with an MMDA. Use a an interest-bearing account as much as needed to keep from incurring any additional service charges, or look for a lower-cost, noninterest-bearing checking account with fewer fees.

What?

Asset management accounts, offered by many full-service and some discount brokerage firms, usually require a large initial deposit—between $5,000 and $25,000—from a combination of cash and/or securities. With asset management accounts, you can write checks and invest in stocks, bonds, mutual funds, and other investment securities all from one account. Unlimited checking privileges usually are offered, although sometimes with a minimum check size of $100 to $500.

Financial Management Account (FMA). It also requires a large initial deposit to activate the account—$10,000 in cash and/or securities.

Secret
Assets in a cash management account—cash, stocks, bonds, mutual funds, whatever—are insured up to $500,000, including $100,000 in cash, by the Securities Investor Protection Corporation (SIPC).

For those of you who write a lot of checks, asset management accounts do offer a plus—unlimited check writing, although some firms require a minimum check size of $100 to $500. Many asset management accounts offer ATM cards. You'll pay as much as $1 for each ATM transaction, however, and ATM stations are limited because of the type of network they run on.

If you have enough money to open an asset management account, more power to you. However, remember that fees and charges are higher with an asset management account than a bank. If you like to keep all your money management services under one roof (trade stocks, invest in bonds, pay bills and opt for mutual funds that don't charge a load), consider an asset management account.

Credit Union Checking

Credit unions offer one of my favorite alternatives to bank checking accounts. Unlike a bank or a brokerage firm that works in the best interest of the stockholders, a credit union works for the benefit of its members. You have to join a credit union before you open an account. For example, many teachers can belong to a credit union because of a common affiliation—they're all teachers. The company that you work for might have a credit union. Perhaps your church can provide some information about a credit union that's available for you because you're a member of that church.

The advantages to opening up an account at a credit union include lower transaction fees and better rates on loans. Most credit unions also require lower minimum balances on their checking accounts, which are known as *share draft accounts*.

Credit unions don't take just anyone; you have to join through a group. To find a credit union near you that you're eligible to join, contact the Credit Union National Association (CUNA) at (800) 358-5710 or write to them at P.O. Box 431, Madison, WI 53701. You can also reach them online at **http://www.cuna.org**.

Finding the Best Checking Deals

Getting a great deal on a checking account is almost like trying to find that needle in a haystack. It seems impossible.

For example, in New York, a bank might offer a low-cost checking account that doesn't pay any interest and allows customers to write up to four or five checks per month for free. That might be low-cost in New York, but not in Fairfax, Virginia or Boise, Idaho. In other regions where there's more competition among banks to get your dollars, banks offer better low-cost checking accounts to customers.

Bet You Didn't Know

How affordable a checking account is differs from bank to bank. Maintaining a checking account used to be very expensive; today it's just moderately expensive—as long as you do your homework!

Take your time when shopping for a checking account, and look for the following features:

➤ **Free checking.** Not all banks offer this type of account, but when they do, check it out.

➤ **Low bounced check fees.** Even if you don't bounce any checks, there are times when you may deposit someone else's check and it will bounce—and you'll get hit with the $20 charge. (Trust me, I know from experience!)

➤ **No foreign ATM transaction fees.** Make sure your checking account allows you to perform ATM transactions at rival teller machines without charging you a penny for doing so—including avoiding ATM surcharges.

What?
A *free checking account* is one that has no monthly maintenance fee, no penalty fee if your balance drops below a certain level, and no transaction fee no matter how many checks you write.

➤ **Only buy the basic checks offered if you have to buy them at the bank.** Checks ordered through a bank are expensive, so limit yourself to the basic blue or yellow.

➤ **Avoid those checking accounts that charge you an inactivity fee.** If you don't write any checks, you'll get nicked with a fee. Don't bank on this feature.

There are a host of other fees that can be charged. Finding the best deal in a checking account requires patience. You need to take time, do your homework, and read the fine print from the brochures the bankers give you.

Avoiding Fee Freaks

Banks are super fee freaks and have to be in order to make money, but you don't have to make them any wealthier by paying for charges that you could avoid if you do your homework. The following guidelines will give you an indication of what strategies you can implement:

➤ You might be better off having a noninterest-bearing checking account, a savings account, or an MMDA than an interest-paying checking

Secret
Start looking for accounts that *charge the least* rather than those that *pay the most*.

account. Many of the banks that offer interest-bearing checking accounts carry extra fees and charges with them. Compare the interest you earned on your checking account to the fees you paid. Those nasty little fees could have gobbled up what you earned in interest.

➤ Don't fall below the minimum balance. If you fall below the minimum even six times a year, at an average $5 fee per time, you're paying an extra $30 a year.

➤ If you maintain low balances, choose a checking account with a "no minimum balance" requirement. This account won't pay any interest, but you won't have any additional charges.

Buy Your Own Checks

Another way you can save money is by not ordering your checks from your bank. Instead, use an outside check distributor. The following companies offer checks fully imprinted with your name, address, bank, and account number:

➤ Checks in the Mail—(800) 733-4443

➤ Current Inc.—(800) 533-3973

➤ Image Checks—(800) 562-8768

The introductory cost is $4.95 for the first 200 single checks and $5.95 for 150 checks with carbon copies—plus $1 for shipping and handling. This is around half of what banks typically charge—$10 to $18.50 for 200 basic checks. Shop around!

The Least You Need to Know

➤ Just because you have checks left in your checkbook doesn't mean you have money left to burn in your checking account. Make sure you balance your checkbook once a month when you receive your bank statement. Watch for any hidden fees and charges and cross-reference them with your bank statement.

➤ Asset management accounts do provide fewer paperwork hassles, consider them if you like to keep all your money management transactions under one roof, but be prepared to pony up an initial deposit from $5,000 to $25,000.

➤ Don't get a checking account just for convenience. It'll cost you in the long run. In fact, skip the interest-bearing checking account if you tend to fall below the minimum balance requirement often.

➤ I know I sound like a broken record, but watch those fees and charges, especially if you bank at a foreign ATM station or bounce a check. Foreign ATM transactions run as high as $2.50 per transaction and bounced check fees average around $18. Even stop payment fees are up there—$15 on average.

Chapter 11

Investing in Certificates of Deposit

In This Chapter

➤ Deciding whether it is worth investing in CDs

➤ Knowing where to buy CDs

➤ Picking the best deals on CDs

➤ Chasing higher CD yields—on the Internet

Want a safe, surefire way of knowing how much profit you'll get when your investment matures? Invest in a Certificate of Deposit (CD).

Considered a safe, one-decision investment, a CD is an interest-bearing investment offered primarily by banks that lock you in for a specific period of time. They won't keep you up at night, either. (Recheck the investment pyramid in Chapter 4.) This chapter explains whether or not you should invest in CDs, the pluses and minuses of CD investing and gives you some solid advice for picking the right CD for your investment portfolio.

CD Primer

A CD is a pretty cut and dried investment. Pick your time period, verify the rate and yield you'll receive, and invest your money. That's it. You'll know ahead of time how much you'll get even before the CD matures. For example, if you invest $10,000 at 7% for one year, you will earn $700 in simple interest.

Certificates of deposit are one of the most common types of investments for investors who don't want to carry a lot of risk. In fact, they are one of the safest money strategies around. Since banking deregulation in the 1980s, banks have been able to offer whatever interest they want to pay on CDs.

Times have changed, though. It's not uncommon to see single-digit CD yields these days—even on terms as high as five years. According to 100 Highest Yields ($124/year, (800) 327-7717), the national average yield on a one-year CD in the beginning of September 1997 was 5.17%.

Many CD investors have been hard hit by these lower rates in the past decade, especially those who had enjoyed double-digit rates paid on their CDs in prior years. If they wanted to roll over (reinvest) their CD into a new CD upon maturity, rates have been practically cut in half, because of the new market rates of interest.

Bet You Didn't Know

Remember the rules of compounding from Part 1? The more frequent the compounding, the more interest you earn on your investment. When chasing higher yields on your certificates of deposit, look for the most frequent compounding method available to earn as much interest as possible.

Many fixed-income investors who shop for high rates have been attracted to bank ads promoting "the best rates in town." The rate is the stated interest you will be paid on the CD. If it's stated as simple interest, the interest will not compound at all. And remember the benefits of compounding? The method of compounding on a CD varies; it can be compounded daily, monthly, or quarterly.

Understanding CD Terms

The period of time you have your money in a CD can be as short as one month and as long as ten years, but CDs generally come with the following maturities: one-month, three-month, six-month, one-year, two-and-a-half-year, five-year, and ten-year. Seven-year CDs are cropping up these days, too. Keep this philosophy in mind: The longer you invest your money, the better the rate.

Watch out for those publications or financial advisers that say certificates of deposit are tied to a Treasury bill or fluctuate based on market conditions. Some banks offer these types of CDs, but a bank can offer whatever rate it wants. There is no index that a CD is tied to unless it is specified by the financial institution offering it, and there is no federally imposed ceiling or floor that banks are supposed to follow. They are free to set their own numbers.

Rates Versus Yields

The most important thing to remember when shopping for a CD: Learn how rates and yields impact your CD buying decisions.

You'll notice that there's a difference between the rate and the yield that is paid on a CD. This is always the case with any interest-earning investment, such as a savings account, a certificate of deposit, and even many types of bond securities.

The difference between the rate on a CD and its yield is explained this way: The *rate* is what you earn from your investment and is determined at the initial time of investing. The *yield* is what you receive when the investment matures.

Bet You Didn't Know

More certificates of deposit mature in April and October than at any other time of year.

Should You Invest in a CD?

A CD may be the all-time investment for the risk-averse, but they may not be the all-time investment *all the time*. Why? Because, just like investing in the stock, bond, and mutual fund markets, you need to implement timing strategies when it comes to your CD investing.

Even though many financial planners and investment advisers religiously preach the following safe money strategy, that is, only invest in CDs on a short-term basis, usually under a two-year maturity, as a way to keep your money short-term, you could lose out in the end. Why? Because if the two-year CD you bought only earns 6% (that's a fixed rate, mind you), and one year into your two-year CD, a two-year CD is paying 7%, you've just lost out on earning 100 basis points more by locking in a lower rate the year before. So, in a rising interest rate environment, you want to time your CD investments on a shorter time-horizon. Here's what your strategy would look like:

1. In 1997, you buy a $5,000 two-year CD with a rate of 6%. Your $5,000 plus interest, will mature in 1999.

2. In 1998, however, a two-year CD is earning 7%—a full 100 basis points *higher* than the two-year CD you bought last year.

3. You still "own" that two-year CD earning 6%, and your $5,000 is locked in that rate. You cannot switch to the higher rate because you are locked in, or, if you did, you will face withdrawal and tax penalties that, in the end, wouldn't be worth it.

4. Moral of the story: In a rising interest rate environment, stay short on your CD investing.

Here's another example. Suppose you bought a $10,000 five-year CD in 1985 when the average rate was near 10%. That's not a bad rate to lock into. You were a happy camper because you basically knew what type of yield you'd receive at maturity in five years.

When the CD matured in 1990, you were faced with the dilemma of what to do with your $10,000—known as your principal—plus the interest you received. You wanted to roll it over into another CD, but the same five-year certificate was only paying 6% because rates fell dramatically since your first investment. That's the *reinvestment risk* in certificates of deposit. When you tie up your money for a longer period of time, you aren't guaranteed a better rate once the CD matures.

Secret

When interest rates are expected to rise, your best bet is to invest in a CD for a very short time frame, so you can take advantage of higher rates when it matures. You could wait until rates have peaked and lock in your rate but only if you know for sure that interest rates are definitely on the upswing.

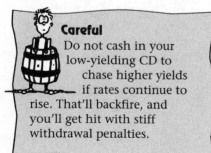

Careful

Do not cash in your low-yielding CD to chase higher yields if rates continue to rise. That'll backfire, and you'll get hit with stiff withdrawal penalties.

I'd like to add one caveat: If rates are dropping, then it wouldn't pay to stay short on your CD investing, but rather opt for longer-term CDs. Why?

Here's a real-life example: If you purchased a ten-year CD in the mid-to-late 1970s when rates were really low, you would have missed the opportunity to earn a better yield during the interest rate boom of the early 1980s. Your money would have been locked in for those ten years, and you couldn't have taken advantage of the higher rates.

Anybody can invest in a certificate of deposit provided they understand the rules and penalties that apply when money is withdrawn before maturity. Here are some guidelines to keep in mind:

➤ You know that a portion of your nest egg should be allocated to safe investments. A CD may be a good choice, depending on market conditions, but don't forget the stiff penalties involved—usually taken from interest income—when you withdraw even one cent before the CD matures.

➤ The banks set interest rates on CDs and this determines where the general level of interest rates are headed. If a bank wants to attract more customers, it may raise its rates on the CDs it offers.

➤ Remember that the interest you earn on a CD is fully taxable at the federal, state, and local levels even if the interest is reinvested.

➤ Although CDs are a safe investment, inflation inevitably plays a part in reducing your purchasing power. In fact, your after-tax, after-inflation return could leave you with less than what you started with. Your goal is to earn an interest rate higher than inflation—and taxes, if possible—when you're deciding how to allocate the nest egg portion of your investment portfolio. Table 11.1 shows how inflation can harm this nest egg investment.

Table 11.1   The Effects of Inflation on an Investment Yield

	3% Inflation	4% Inflation
Initial investment (one-year CD)	$10,000	$10,000
Interest earned (at 5%)	$500	$500
Total investment at maturity	$10,500	$10,500
Taxes paid (at 28%)	$140	$140
Total after taxes	$10,360	$10,360
Less inflation	$311	$414
Purchasing power at maturity	$10,049	$ 9,946

➤ Consider investing in a rising rate CD. As long as interest rates are rising, the rate on these CDs rise, too—usually every six months.

➤ Also available is a stock-index CD, which is based on the S&P 500 index rather than interest income. Here's how it works. The CD takes the average level of the S&P 500 during its specified time period. If it is a two-and-a-half-year CD, the average level taken from the S&P 500 is two-and-a-half years. The CD pays interest equal to twice the average percentage increase. This means that if you have a $10,000 two-and-a-half-year CD and during that time period the S&P 500 gains an average 4.8%, you receive more than 9.5% interest on your CD. This does not mean you earn more investing in a stock-index CD, because you aren't able to reinvest dividends or get compounded earnings as you would with another index investment or CD that compounded frequently.

If You Have $100k, Here's How to Play

Once you have worked hard enough to accumulate $100,000 as part of your safe money strategies (independent of a stock or mutual fund portfolio) you do have another deposit account option available to you, a Jumbo CD.

Rates and yields on Jumbo CDs could pay as much as 1% more than a regular CD. Keep in mind that even though you may be able to earn a better rate on a Jumbo CD, your account is only insured up to $100,000 through FDIC insurance. In essence, you are moving above the FDIC limit.

Secret

If you invest in a Jumbo CD for $100,000 or more, remove the interest from your account every month and place it elsewhere—such as in an MMDA at your bank. This way your initial investment is protected under FDIC insurance. And, still implement your smart money strategy of seeking frequent compounding to earn as much interest as possible, and not forsake that just because the additional dollars and cents aren't covered by FDIC insurance until you get your monies transferred. Remember: Not one dollar has ever been lost by a bank that failed that was covered by the $100,000 FDIC insurance. In the day and age of electronic transactions, check to see if your financial institution can do this automatically for you through an electronic funds transfer. It'll save you the time—and hassle—of having to do it yourself.

Attention Jumbo CD investors! Available to you is *Jumbo Flash Report*, a weekly publication that surveys the top yields for one-month, two-month, three-month, six-month, one-year, two-and-a-half-year, and five-year Jumbo CDs. The subscription price is as follows: 13 weeks, $118; 26 weeks, $154; one year, $245; two years, $398. All the banks listed in Jumbo Flash Report are nationwide and rated by Veribanc, an independent bank safety rating firm that has established a three-star rating system to grade the financial strength of banks.

In addition to receiving the weekly publication, you can sign up for a one-year subscription, and for another $130, you can also receive a special fax service. Every Thursday prior to Monday's publication date, you'll receive your subscription via fax. This service is advantageous for those of you who need to know the rates immediately. Call (800) 327-7717 to order a subscription, or write to Editor, *Jumbo Flash Report*, P.O. Box 088888, N. Palm Beach, FL 33408. You can search for Jumbo CD yields at **http://www.bankrate.com**.

Bank or Brokerage Firm?

Not only can you purchase a CD directly from your bank, but you can also buy one at a brokerage firm. Most brokerage firms sell bank CDs directly to their customers.

There's a catch. Even though a broker may promise that your CD is insured, it may not carry a federal deposit guarantee, like FDIC insurance that covers deposits up to $100,000 in your bank account. Deposits at a brokerage firm are covered by the Securities Investor Protection Company (SIPC), which is not the same thing as FDIC insurance.

Bet You Didn't Know

FDIC insurance guarantees coverage for its account holder deposits up to $100,000. SIPC, which stands for Securities Investors Protection Corporation, protects assets up to $500,000. However, not one dollar has ever been lost by a customer with $100,000 FDIC insurance of a bank that failed. So, should you buy a CD and pay the extra money to a broker for that extra piece of insurance? I wouldn't.

Some might argue that buying a CD from your broker enables you to receive a higher yield than if you were to purchase it at a bank. In most situations, the broker will find the highest-yielding certificate of deposit among participating banks and savings and loans nationwide. The broker gets a fee—usually about 1% of the CD's yield—from the bank in exchange for increasing the number of deposits at the issuing bank. But you can do this yourself, simply by visiting Bank Rate Monitor's website at **http://www.bankrate.com**.

It might look as a viable way to purchase a CD until you calculate what fees are charged to you. What a broker doesn't tell you is that his fee usually reduces your yield, so you don't earn as much as you can if you purchase your CD at your bank. Brokerage fees are an average $2.50 per $1,000 face value amount, and they are built into the transaction. Brokers definitely make money by offering certificates of deposit to clients. If they don't get a fee from the institution, they'll take it out of your yield—as much as .5%. Shop for the best rates yourself. You can get a better yield at another place.

> **Secret**
> Bank Rate Monitor offers the national averages on certificates of deposit, as well as CDs offered by local lenders. You can visit them online at **http://www.bankrate.com**. In fact, for BRM visitors, special Internet banking deals are available through links to bank websites offering higher-than-average CD rates and yields.

Stiff Penalties

You'll understand the full ramifications of "penalty for early withdrawal" if you ever try to liquidate a CD halfway through its elected time period.

There is no way around it. If you withdraw any of your money—$100, $10, or even $1— from the CD before it matures, you are slapped with an early withdrawal penalty, which is set by each bank and differs nationwide. Generally, it's often three to six months' worth of interest.

If you withdraw your money early and are under 59 1/2 years old, your account will also be hit with a 10% penalty. Do the math. Three to six months' worth of interest plus an extra 10% can really add up.

Chasing Higher CD Yields—Out of Town and Online

Guess what, folks? You don't have to stick to your local bank down the street to have access to high-yielding CD rates. You don't even have to stay within your time zone. Many banks accept out-of-state deposits by wire transfer or through the mail if you invest in one of their CDs. The highest-yielding CDs are published in various newspapers across the country, and probably include your hometown newspaper if you are from a large metropolitan area.

My favorite way to chase higher CD rates is by subscribing to *100 Highest Yields*, a weekly publication that tracks which bank or S&L is offering the highest rates on CDs—and MMDAs—nationwide. This publication lists the 20 highest-yielding bank MMDAs and six-month, one-year, two-and-a-half-year, and five-year CDs across the country. These listings give Veribanc's bank safety rating—from three stars (the best) down to no stars (didn't even make their list). By subscribing to *100 Highest Yields*, you also have access to research and topics (which include best credit card rates and top auto loan rates) from its sister publication, *Bank Rate Monitor*.

To subscribe to this service, call (800) 327-7717 anywhere in the United States for a subscription. Subscription rates are as follows: eight-week trial subscription, $48; one-year subscription, $124; and a two-year subscription, $210. Add $55 per year for surface mail to all foreign countries.

If you're plugged in, you can also chase higher yields online. Internet banking deals are flourishing, sometimes offering a full-percentage point higher on typical long-term CDs.

Some examples, as of mid-summer 1997: First National Bank and Trust posted a one-year CD yield of 6.35%—115 basis points higher than the national average of 5.20% in mid-July. This yield, at that time, was available to First National Bank and Trust customers who opened up an account with them right online. How? The user would simply complete a form with his or her information, such as name, city, state, ZIP, and amount of CD (how much) and the term. You would have to most likely have your originating bank's routing number from, for example, your checking account, to transfer the monies into FNBT to purchase your certificate of deposit. Note: Rates and yields on CDs listed do change. Contact the financial institution for updated information.

Other banks that are pioneering the move to all-electronic banking include Capital One, Falls Church, Va., which gives savers who open up their account online and deposit $25,000 into its Money Market Account a 5.75% annual percentage yield—more than double the national average of 2.64%, as of mid-July 1997. Note: Rates and yields on CDs listed do change. Contact the financial institution for updated information.

Are these higher yielding savings products here to stay? Most likely, as "cyberbanks" don't require a lot of operational costs as other banks do, thereby passing the savings onto customers. But one thing is for sure—these cyberbank products carry the $100,000 FDIC insurance.

Of course, if you haven't tried cyberbanking, the issue of safety and security can be a concern. Many institutions use a type of encryption, meaning that it is virtually impossible for anyone using current technology to steal information. Simply put, it is like sending your mail inside of a steel safe. So, typically, the types of encryption used in Internet banking allow only you and the bank to see your account information. Ask your banker to explain the details in laymen's terms just how it works.

Here are some key questions you can ask your banker about online banking:

1. Find out if your financial institution offers or plans to offer an online banking service. You will want to find out all the charges and fees involved and what types of transactions you can and cannot do online.

2. When you sign up for online banking, ask your banker how long it takes for each transaction to take place. Does a funds transfer take place immediately? If you pay your mortgage on a Monday, when will the payment be debited from your account and credited to the recipient on time?

   Example: You pay your electric bill electronically on Tuesday; however, once your financial institution's processing department receives your "electronic request," many financial institutions may still have to print out a check and mail the payment to the electric company. The result? Your electronic bill payment might not get paid until five business days later. Find out the details from your financial institution. (Note: For BankNOW banks, money is debited on the day the check clears.)

3. Ask your banker about the security of online banking. Typically, the types of encryption used in online banking allow only you and the bank to see your account information. Ask your banker to explain the details in laymen's terms just how it works.

4. Online banking has been around for ten years yet that does not mean mistakes can't happen. In the event of a technical problem, or a duplicated transaction, ask your banker what steps you will need to take to rectify any situation—be it your error or not. If you inadvertently duplicate a transaction or send money to the wrong creditor, you need to know how to correct the error and not pay substantial bank fees in the process.

5. Find out what the process is if you wanted to close the account. It may be easy to open an online banking account, but how difficult is it to close it? Is there a charge? Your banker should tell you what is involved from a financial as well as technical perspective.

The Least You Need to Know

➤ When you invest in a CD, you are locking your money in at a specific rate for a specific time period.

➤ If you withdraw your money at any point during that time period, you face stiff penalties—sometimes up to six months' worth of interest could be lost. If you are under the age of 59 1/2, you also get slapped with an additional 10% penalty.

➤ To chase higher yielding CD rates—and money market deposit account rates—subscribe to *100 Highest Yields*. For subscription information, call (800) 327-7717 or write to *100 Highest Yields*, P.O. Box 088888, N. Palm Beach, FL 33408.

What About Safety?

Safety. The mere word conjures up synonyms such as "protection," "shield," and "defense." But where does the safety of money fit in?

Let me give you an analogy. In order for us as homeowners, for example, to protect ourselves against fire loss or us as people to guard against high medical bills, we secure some type of insurance. We should also consider protecting another commodity—our money.

You must have insurance to protect yourself from loss, even in your investment portfolio.

Financial catastrophes have blown many investment plans to smithereens. To avoid this, you should have some type of insurance to cover your deposits and investments. This chapter explains how you can ensure that your bank deposits are safe.

Promises, Promises

You're at your local bank ready to make a deposit. As you stand in the line for the teller window, you notice a sign out of the corner of your eye that says, "Deposits Insured Up To $100,000." "So what," you say to yourself. You hand your deposit to the teller and feel confident that nothing can go wrong. Your money will be there when you need it. Plus, it's backed by the government, so you assume your money is safe. Or is it?

What?

FDIC stands for Federal Deposit Insurance Corporation. This organization was created in 1933 after thousands of bank depositors were wiped out during the stock market crash of 1929 and the Great Depression.

Government efforts to bail out savings and loans and shore up failed banks splashed headlines a few years ago, leaving depositors uneasy about the safety of their insured accounts. For your protection, the Federal Deposit Insurance Corporation (FDIC) was created.

The FDIC is the federal agency established in 1933 that guarantees—within limits—funds on deposit in member banks and savings and loans, which are also called thrifts. Deposits in a credit union are insured by the National Credit Union Association (NCUA). The FDIC also performs other functions, such as making loans or buying the assets of other banks to help mergers or prevent failure. It isn't necessary to know how many banks have failed or the specific number of mergers and loans the FDIC has made. All you need to understand are the limitations on the insurance coverage for your bank accounts.

For any deposit account—be it a retirement account (one of the several Individual Retirement Accounts (IRAs) now offered as a result of the new tax laws of 1997), a self-employed retirement plan (for self-employed persons), a 401(k) plan established by a corporation; checking accounts, savings accounts, money market deposit accounts (MMDAs), or certificates of deposit—the maximum amount of coverage the FDIC provides a depositor is $100,000.

And for Your Protection

Over the past several years, more banks and savings and loans have been liquidated than in any time since the Great Depression, and that's caused even more concern for consumers who rely heavily on the safety of their bank deposits. Bank deposits—like a savings or checking account, a CD, or even an MMDA—are known to be the safest investments around. But there are limits to the safety you can expect.

As you learned in Chapter 11, when you invest in a Jumbo certificate of deposit, any amount above $100,000 is not insured by the Federal Deposit Insurance Corporation. Take a closer look at how shocking the numbers can be. In the nation's entire banking system, (including commercial banks, retail banks, savings and loans, and savings banks) there are currently more than $6 trillion in deposits, with over $672 billion in deposits above the $100,000 insured limit. Any amount above the insured limit is liable to be lost in case of a bank failure.

Several years ago, in December of 1993, the federal government changed the maximum insurance coverage that individual depositors can get for self-directed retirement accounts—such as an Individual Retirement Account (IRA)—held in one bank. This is important because 35 percent of all retirement assets are held in banks or savings and loans. Before, accounts up to a $400,000 maximum were fully covered. The maximum is now $100,000.

> **Secret**
> When you think of a bank's safety, consider more than just your insured deposits. If a bank fails or is going through major cost-cutting, any type of account you have will be affected. This includes your mortgage, your auto loan, and even your credit card.

Can you bank on insured and even uninsured deposits? What if you invest in a mutual fund at a bank? Is it covered by insurance? The rule of thumb is that each depositor is covered up to $100,000 (including principal *and interest*) at the same institution, but if you invest your money in a bank mutual fund, none of your money in the mutual fund is covered by FDIC insurance.

To protect money you invest in banks and savings and loans, you need to follow these guidelines:

➤ Make sure you bank at a federally insured institution. Look for the FDIC seal shown below or ask your customer service representative whether the institution is an FDIC member.

Each depositor insured to $100,000

The FDIC logo.

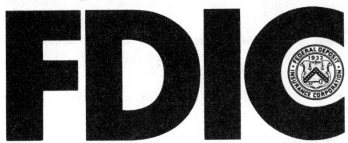

FEDERAL DEPOSIT INSURANCE CORPORATION

➤ Keep in mind that depositors, not the accounts, are insured up to $100,000 including interest and principal. If you have three accounts at one bank worth $100,000 each for a total of $300,000, you are only insured up to $100,000—not the full $300,000.

➤ If you have an IRA at a bank that accumulates to more than $100,000 over time, the only way to get more than the $100,000 coverage will be to spread the accounts

Secret
When you see the FDIC logo, rest assured that your money is safe. Despite bank runs and the savings & loan debacle, nobody with insured deposits of $100,000 or less ever lost a penny in the event of a bank or S&L failure.

among different banks. If you maintain your IRA at a brokerage firm, your assets are insured up to $500,000 by the Securities Investors Protection Corporation, known as SIPC.

➤ If you invest in a mutual fund—proprietary or non-proprietary—at a bank or savings and loan, understand that it is not (and I repeat NOT) covered by FDIC insurance. Many customers mistakenly think that these mutual funds are backed by the FDIC because they're sold by banks. Not true. Make sure your banker is professional enough to disclose the difference between insured deposits and uninsured investments.

➤ If you still want to keep more than $100,000 in deposits at a bank, check your bank's safety. It should have a solid financial track record, no bad loans, and astute management. I'll tell you where to go for bank safety information later on in this chapter.

A Word About Brokerage Accounts

Not only can a bank fail, but consumers are aware of the scandal that occurs in the brokerage industry. The 1980s saw a lot of hoopla over liquidated brokerage firms. In the past, the nature of the brokerage business was founded on reliable partnerships—then greed came into play. Today, these firms are large, impersonal corporations, but they do provide insurance!

The 1970 Securities Investors Protection Act covers investors through its non-profit SIPC, the Securities Investors Protection Corporation. Keep in mind that the SIPC is not a state, government, or even a federal agency. The group that funds it is made up of dealer members, such as Merrill Lynch or Prudential brokerage firms.

Your brokerage account is covered up to $500,000 per customer, including $100,000 in cash. Note that not everything is covered by SIPC, only cash and securities. Securities include stocks, bonds, certificates of deposit (if you bought your CD through your broker), and warrants on securities Futures and options aren't covered at all.

The SIPC insures your brokerage account in the event a brokerage firm fails. If a firm does fail, your accounts are usually transferred to another brokerage firm or your investment certificates (such as stock or bond certificates) are sent directly to you. Speak with your broker or an investment representative to clarify the nitty-gritty details of how the coverage works, especially if the certificates are sent to you to ensure that all paperwork is correct. Find out what kind of fees are involved with the new firm holding onto your certificates if you want to "re-deposit" your certificates with the new firm. This is known as a "safekeeping" charge.

The only other things SIPC does not cover are any losses that you incur because of a bad investment decision. If you invested in a stock and it hits the skids, that's your loss.

How's Your Bank Doin'?

Learning about the safety of your bank or savings and loan is just as important as learning about investing. After all, when you buy an insurance policy for your automobile, do you just sign the dotted line and drive away? No! You take time to understand what type of coverage would help you in a particular situation.

If (and when—let's think positively!) you'll be placing any of your money above the maximum insured limit of $100,000 at a bank or savings and loan, it pays to find out about the financial health of the institution.

Contact Veribanc toll-free at (800) 44-BANKS or write to P.O. Box 461, Wakefield, MA 01880. Ask for their bank safety rating on your particular institution. Veribanc assigns a star rating system to financial institutions. Three stars is the highest rating a bank can receive. This service isn't free—the cost is $10 for information about the first bank, and $5 for each additional bank processed during the one request. All requests can be charged to your credit card. The bank safety rating is given to you right over the phone. Plus, Veribanc also mails you a confirmation of your order, a one-page financial data sheet complete with explanations of what the data means and how to interpret it.

Secret
If you have more than $500,000 in your account, you should immediately transfer the amount over $500,000 to another firm so that all of your investments are covered by SIPC. You cannot obtain additional coverage from SIPC. If, however, you have several accounts at various brokerage firms, each with $500,000, as long as only one brokerage firm goes "belly up" at a time, each account will be covered.

In addition, Veribanc publishes a quarterly newsletter, *The Bank News Release*, which costs $20 and explains a synopsis of what's happened within the most recent reporting quarter in the industry.

Another organization that offers information about bank safety ratings is *Weiss Safety Ratings*, Inc., 3300 Burns Road, Palm Beach Gardens, Florida 33410 (800) 289-9222. For $15, you receive a verbal safety rating of your financial institution, with ratings ranging from A+ to F. The $15 fee can be charged to your MasterCard, Visa, American Express, or Discover credit card.

The Least You Need to Know

➤ The Federal Deposit Insurance Corporation (FDIC) insures customer deposits of up to $100,000 in the same institution in federal banks and savings loans. Any amount over $100,000 is not covered by FDIC insurance in the event of a bank failure.

➤ The insurance that protects customer accounts at member brokerage firms is Securities Investor Protection Company (SIPC) insurance. The coverage limit is $500,000, which may include $100,000 cash.

➤ You can find out how safe your bank is by contacting Veribanc at (800) 44-BANKS. They'll provide you with information and a safety rating of your financial institution. However, there is a fee for this service: $10 for the first request, and $5 for each additional request. Or, for $15, you can call Weiss Safety Ratings, Inc., at (800) 289-9222 and get a verbal report about your bank's safety. Both Veribanc and Weiss Safety Ratings, Inc. accept all major credit cards.

Part 3
Mutual Fund Mania

If you have a million dollars to invest or even half a mil, any broker or investment adviser would love to have you as a client. You'll get the best advice money can buy and pay for it, too!

So what do you do if you're like most people who don't have a million bucks? Or even $100,000? Well, you still need to get the best advice that your money can buy. But where?

There's a near-perfect answer—a mutual fund. There are more than 7,000 types of mutual funds that exist today. As you read through this section on mutual funds, you will discover one of the biggest secrets on Wall Street that may help you realize many of your financial dreams, such as a child's college education, a new home, or retirement. The secret? It is…well, I can't reveal that on the first page now, can I? But you'll soon find out.

Chapter 13

Simple Mutual Fund Strategies

In This Chapter

➤ Knowing one of the biggest money-making strategies on Wall Street

➤ Understanding what a mutual fund is

➤ Selecting mutual funds that are the best for you

My, how the world of mutual funds has changed.

Although the very first mutual fund was created somewhere in Europe during the 1800s, the mutual fund industry hasn't even been around for a century in America. A few years before the stock market crash in 1929, the very first mutual fund was born on the East Coast. Twenty years later, after the "big one" (World War II), there weren't even 100 mutual funds around.

Today there are more than 8,000 mutual funds—and the industry is booming! Mutual funds are one of the most common vehicles and best alternatives for average Americans to own different types of securities like stocks and bonds and diversify their portfolio.

And, with mutual funds, it doesn't matter how wealthy you are to invest. There are simple mutual fund strategies that enable you to begin with as little as $50. Either way, you're rich enough to invest in one of the most talked-about investment products around, as you'll discover in this chapter.

Basic Training

Imagine an investment that doesn't require a large initial investment, has barely any fees (if any), allows you access to your money all the time, and is as safe or as risky as you want it to be. It sounds too perfect, huh? You're probably asking yourself "So what's the catch?" Guess what, folks. There really isn't one.

In a mutual fund, many investors (whether they have a lot of money or only a little bit) pool their money into a large fund organized by investment professionals. In this pool, investors own shares, depending on how much money they put in. The more money you invest, the more shares you can buy. What do these shares represent? All kinds of stocks and bonds from some of the best-run companies in the world.

What?

Diversification is the concept of not putting all of your eggs in one basket, for example, spreading the risk by purchasing several types of investments. Mutual funds offer this strategy for investors because each fund purchases so many different types of stocks or bonds.

A mutual fund—especially a no-load mutual fund—is as close as you can get to a perfect investment product. You can cash them in whenever you need the money; therefore, mutual funds are extremely liquid. They tend to keep your risks down, too, because they implement the strategy of *diversification*. Mutual funds don't completely eliminate risk, but they can bring the risks down to a comfortable level, depending on what fund you invest in and what your investment objectives are.

Those are just the basics. As you continue to develop further knowledge about making money in mutual funds, you'll find they may be a great way to get your feet wet in the investment world.

One of the biggest determinants in selecting a mutual fund is your age. Why? Most financial planners advise that the more time you have on your side, the more aggressive you can be in your approach. For example, some financial planners will advise younger clients to invest 80 percent of their dollars in aggressive mutual funds, while advising older clients and retirees to allocate only 20 percent of their dollars to the same category. The longer you invest, the more you can temper risk.

Some mutual fund companies are getting in on the lifestage bandwagon. Vanguard Funds, for example, tailors specific funds to age groups incorporating risk levels in its Vanguard LifeStrategy Portfolios. They offer four portfolios—moderate, conservative, growth, income—all which fall under the balanced fund category. Each fund invests in a combination of Vanguard Funds to achieve a mix of stocks and bonds. The percentage allocated to each asset class, again, depends on age.

How Do I Buy Mutual Fund Shares?

Investing in a mutual fund is quite simple. You can purchase both load and no-load funds from a full-service and discount broker or a financial planner, or directly from the mutual fund company. *Load funds* are those mutual funds that charge you a sales fee.

No-load funds do not charge their shareholders any sales fees. There are strong cases made for selecting no-load funds, and, as long as you or your financial adviser understand the elements of the fund (objectives, holdings, other fees), choosing a no-load fund is a more cost-effective strategy.

All of the mutual fund companies listed in Appendix B will send you information about their families of funds at your request. Call their toll-free numbers listed to receive information. You can complete the application and send it in along with your check directly to the mutual fund company. When you want to make an additional contribution to your mutual fund, you just send in a check, along with your account number and the name of the fund. You can also have money automatically debited from your checking or money market account and electronically transferred to the fund.

Many fund companies have websites that offer a plethora of information on their fund investments. Consider doing a search online of these companies to have as much information as possible before investing or meeting with your financial adviser.

Once you invest, you will receive a monthly statement detailing information about your mutual fund, including how many shares you own and how much your portfolio is worth. Plus, you'll receive a statement every single time you make a purchase or sales transaction.

Secret
Whether or not you are using a broker to invest in a mutual fund, make sure that you read the application, prospectus, and performance information (refer to Chapter 5) and follow up on an ongoing basis.

Secret
If you are going to invest a lot of money, check with the shareholder services department about the procedure for a bank wire-transfer. This eliminates the possibility of losing a very large check in the mail. Find out what the mutual fund company and your bank charge for this.

How Do I Sell My Mutual Fund Shares?

Selling your mutual fund shares is known as redeeming your shares or a *redemption*. Usually, all you need to do is contact the shareholder services department over the phone and let them know how much money you need from your investment. It usually takes about five business days for the transaction to clear. At that point, a check will be sent to you.

There are load mutual funds with a back-end load. This means that when you sell your shares (within a certain period of time of initially buying them), you will be charged a sales fee.

Secret

Find out how much it costs to have your proceeds (the money from the redemption) wired to your bank account. This saves a step in paperwork, and you'll have access to your funds immediately because you won't have to wait the required two to three days for the deposited check to clear.

The Whole Kit 'N' Kaboodle

For those of you who are developing long-term financial plans, mutual funds offer one of the best ways to keep those plans in line and reach your financial goals. If you invest in a mutual fund over the long haul, you don't have to worry about timing your investment. The guesswork is eliminated for two reasons. First, because you are practicing diversification, your portfolio is positioned to protect you against the ups and downs of the financial markets. Second, you have access to professional management. How? The investment professionals who make all of the buy and sell decisions in the mutual fund are known as *portfolio managers*, and make the buy/sell decisions for you.

Are They Any Good?

Portfolio managers of some mutual funds are good, and some are not so good. How can you pick the best from the rest?

You have to know how to study their track records and pick a good-quality fund that is in line with your investment objectives. If not, make sure you are dealing with a broker or salesperson who knows enough about the mutual fund to help you choose the right one for you.

Bet You Didn't Know

Years ago, the majority of funds charged a load of 8.5% as a way to induce the salespeople to sell their own funds instead of somebody else's. Investors have caught on, though, and are much smarter these days about avoiding excessive fees. Average loads hover around 4% now.

What?

Portfolio managers are the people who decide what types of securities to buy and sell in a specific mutual fund, keeping in line with the fund's objectives. The fund's collection of securities, typically stocks or bonds, is known as a *portfolio*.

The performance of a mutual fund isn't necessarily or entirely based on the skill of its portfolio manager. True, the final decision about whether to buy or sell a stock or bond for the fund rests with the portfolio manager, but he or she has access to some of the best research reports around that you might not be able to get your hands on as quickly as they can. However, fund research reports, such as Morningstar and Value Line's Mutual Fund Investment Survey, are available at no charge at your local library. Many portfolio managers utilize the same information.

Portfolio managers typically have their own research staff to provide them with the information they need to make better buying and selling decisions.

If you want to monitor the performance of your mutual fund, a few companies are listed in Chapter 5 that survey the performance of thousands of mutual funds. For a complete listing, refer to Chapter 17.

Learning the Differences Between Open-End and Closed-End Mutual Funds

Two kinds of mutual funds exist: *open-end funds* and *closed-end funds*. They both offer the advantages of professional management and skill, the comfort that you don't have to put all of your eggs in one basket (diversification), and the fact that you don't need a lot of money to start investing.

But there are differences, mainly in the way the shares in each fund are sold. Following are the distinctions between the two:

> ➤ **Open-end mutual funds.** These types of funds create new shares all the time as more money is invested in them (although many open-end mutual funds are "closing," not becoming closed-end, because of the enormous amount of assets held in the fund). Check with the fund company to see when it closed, and, if there are any possibilities of a fund re-opening in the foreseeable future. There have been situations where funds, right after closing its doors to new investors, experience lackluster performance; however, this is not *always* the norm).

When you invest in an open-end mutual fund, the number of outstanding shares increases because not only do the other investors own their fair shares, but you do, too. The portfolio manager of the fund is constantly working with millions of dollars coming in and out of the fund practically every day.

Typically, when a mutual fund is on a really hot streak (its performance is incredible and returns are high), a ton of money will be dumped into the fund. Wannabe investors chase this fund for higher returns. Unfortunately, this leaves the portfolio manager with the problem of buying the stocks or bonds in the fund at higher prices, because the money *must* be invested when the fund shares are purchased. This forces the portfolio manager to butt into cardinal investment rule #1: Buy low and sell high.

Secret
Before you invest in a mutual fund, make sure you understand the fees involved. A load fund, as you recall, is a fund that charges a sales fee. A no-load fund does not charge you a sales fee. Both of these have other expenses involved that are passed onto shareholders. You will learn more about these—and what to watch out for—in the next chapter.

➤ **Closed-end mutual funds.** These mutual funds issue a limited and fixed number of shares in order to avoid the previously mentioned problem of wannabe investors chasing hot mutual funds. Portfolio managers in a closed-end fund are not stuck with the potential problem of one month having millions of dollars pumped into the fund and the next month barely a penny.

The shares that are issued by a closed-end fund are listed on the New York Stock Exchange (NYSE), the American Stock Exchange (AMEX), or the NASDAQ. You don't deal with a mutual fund company when you buy or sell shares; because they are traded like a stock, you buy and sell them just like publicly traded stock, with other investors. You purchase them from a brokerage firm and pay regular brokerage commissions, unless of course, you buy them at a discount or deep discount brokerage firm.

What Else Do They Offer?

To sum it up here, if you invest in a mutual fund, you benefit in several of the following ways:

Secret
If you invest in a mutual fund and your needs change (for example, if you are retiring), see if your mutual fund company offers telephone switching. Why? Because you can switch some of your fund shares to a high-paying dividend stock fund or even a bond fund (so you'll get income from the interest payments). However, make sure there are no transaction costs involved with telephone switching.

➤ **Instant Diversification.** If you have $1,000, you could buy stock, but you won't get a lot of shares, obviously depending upon the trading price of the stock at that time. Mutual funds offer you the chance to get your feet wet in the stock (also known as "equity market") and bond markets without putting up a lot of money. If you invest that $1,000 in a fund holding 25 different stocks, you reduce your risk.

➤ **Lower fees and charges from no-load and low-load funds.** Because mutual funds are made up of hundreds of different stocks and bonds, the portfolio manager pays reduced commission rates when buying the securities (as low as two cents a share). This way there are no exorbitant fees to pass on to you, the investor/shareholder. Over time, you have more of your money going to work for you instead of having fees or charges eating up your principal.

➤ **Telephone switching.** Here's how it works. If you own a common stock mutual fund from T. Rowe Price, for example, but you're not happy with the performance over the past several years or you've met your financial objective with that particular fund, you can switch to another one of their funds. All you do is place a telephone call. This is known as *telephone switching*. Exchanging or swapping one fund for another isn't limited to just stock mutual funds; if you want to switch from a stock mutual fund to a bond mutual fund, most telephone switching agreements allow you to do so.

➤ **Dividends and capital gains are reinvested automatically.** When you evaluate performance of a mutual fund, you should look for payment of dividends and capital gain distributions. Before you tackle this one, understand the difference between the two.

Dividends are the investment income that come from the stocks or bonds the fund owns. You receive income dividends (after the fund deducts its management fees, which are different than loads or commissions) in proportion to the number of shares you own. These are distributed on a monthly, quarterly, or annual basis.

Capital gains are different. The meat of a mutual fund is stocks or bonds. Now, when you buy low and sell high, what do you get? A profit. That's what these portfolio managers are trying to do (usually, depending on the objective of the fund): buy the securities in the fund low and sell them for a higher price. When this happens, a profit is realized. That profit is passed on to you as a *capital gain distribution* only once or twice a year. You are taxed on these capital gains at your income tax bracket. Due to the changes in the tax laws in 1997, discuss with your tax adviser or accountant how these new laws will affect you, if at all, regarding capital gains.

Unless you elect otherwise, the monies you receive from dividends and capital gains go to buy more shares in the fund, even if they only buy a fraction of a share. This is known as "reinvesting dividends." Over time, reinvested dividends and capital gains work for you because they continue to buy more shares—and these fractional shares will add up!

➤ **Automatic payment system.** When you read Chapter 16, you'll discover another advantage to buying mutual funds. You can set up automatic payment systems from your bank account to your mutual fund—without lifting a finger. Convenience. Consider it. I certainly do.

NAV—What Does It Mean to Me?

NAV stands for *Net Asset Value*. This is how a mutual fund is priced. If you can comprehend how a mutual fund is priced, you will understand one of the ways to buy a mutual fund.

Each trading day, usually in the afternoon, the total market value of the securities (stocks, bonds, and so on) the fund owns are added up. For example, if the fund owns 1000 shares of common stock of Reebok, and Reebok stock closed at $45 1/2 per share, the calculation looks like this: $1,000 \times 45\ 1/2 = \$45,500$. The fund does this for each individual security. It then adds up the value of its other assets, such as any cash (dollars and cents) it has or that is owed to it. The entire total provides a figure from which the fund subtracts all of its liabilities, as well as any other fees it owes elsewhere.

The result is the total net assets. This figure is then divided by the number of shares outstanding (the total number of shares that you and all the other investors own in the fund), which ultimately gives the net asset value (NAV) for each share.

What does all this mean? When the market value of the securities goes up, the NAV goes up. On the other hand, when the market value of the securities goes down, so does the NAV. When you invest in a mutual fund, you buy it at its NAV. Simply put, if you have $5,000 to invest in Founder's Worldwide Growth Fund, and, hypothetically, its NAV is at 10, you can buy 500 shares in the fund.

Secret
The exception to this rule is for money market funds. The share price of a money market fund is a constant $1.00 per share, so the NAV is always known.

However, in the real world, if you want to invest in a mutual fund you do so by buying new shares from the fund at the NAV that's calculated at the end of the day. This means you never know at *exactly* what price you get your order—whether it's a buy or a sell. (A sell is known as a *redemption*.) This is mutual fund pricing rule number one: All orders received by the fund before the trading day comes to an end (9:30 a.m. to 4:00 p.m. EST) are executed at whatever NAV price is calculated that day. Therefore, the execution price (the price at which you'll buy your shares) is only figured after the close.

That's how the NAV works for an open-end mutual fund. For a closed-end mutual fund, it still trades at a net asset value (NAV), but it can sell for more or less than the value of its portfolio.

Many different newsletters exist that cover the mutual fund industry. Here's a list of a few newsletters that will help get you started:

➤ *Fidelity Insight* is a newsletter about all of Fidelity's mutual funds (**http:// www.fidelity.com**). This publication gives hints and tips about mutual fund investing. To subscribe, call (800) 444-6342 or write to Mutual Fund Investors Association, 20 William Street, Suite G70, Wellesley Hills, MA 02181.

➤ *Morningstar Mutual Funds* (**http://www.morningstar.net**) provides subscribers with detailed information about all different types of mutual funds, including performance. For further information, call (800) 876-5005 or write to Morningstar, Inc., 225 W. Wacker Drive, Chicago, IL 60606.

➤ *Mutual Fund Forecaster* written by the folks at the Institute for Econometric Research, gives a blow-by-blow account of what's currently happening in the mutual fund industry along with information about specific funds. Call (800) 327-6720 or write to 3471 N. Federal Highway, Ft. Lauderdale, FL 33306.

➤ *No-Load Fund Investor* is one of my favorite monthlies. Sheldon Jacobs, the editor, gives solid performance information in the tables listed in the newsletter. For subscription information, call (800) 252-2042 or write to P.O. Box 318, Irvington-on-Hudson, NY 10533.

Also available are online newsletters and magazines covering the mutual fund market. When doing a search on the Internet, using one of the search engines (such as InfoSeek, Excite or Lycos), simply type in the words **mutual fund** at the keyword prompt and select **search**. Keep in mind that many times a brokerage firm or fund company's website may appear. Some of their content explains the basic how-to's of mutual fund investing, but many times these are strictly online brochures for their own wares.

Trading Closed-End Mutuals

When a stock trades, you have a bid, ask, and closing price, as you'll learn in Part 4 on investing in the stock market. The same thing goes for closed-end fund trading. If the closed-end fund price—its current trading price—is higher than what the portfolio is worth, it is said to be trading at a premium. When it is selling for less than what the portfolio is worth, it is said to be trading at a discount, which is analogous to bond investing.

When does it sell at a premium and when does it sell at a discount? It will usually sell at a premium when investors find the closed-end fund to be extremely popular. Then investors don't mind paying such a high price for it. For example, if the only way to invest in Bangladesh was through the Bangladesh closed-end fund and investor demand was high, the fund would grow to be extremely popular. This may push up the price on the fund, causing it to trade at a premium. Investors may still be hot after the fund and be willing to pay twice as much as it's worth. Don't laugh. It's happened quite often with many different closed-end funds that invest in foreign countries. (You'll learn about "Going Global" with closed-end funds in the next chapter.)

> **What?**
> In *money market funds*, your money is invested in safe and liquid securities, including short-term government securities and repurchase agreements (repos). This fund pays money market rates of interest, like an MMDA and offers check writing privileges. *Repurchase agreements*, also known as REPOs, are agreements between a buyer and a seller of securities, usually government securities (like a T-bill), where the seller agrees to repurchase the securities at a certain price and time. Banks and financial institutions use repos as a way to park their cash on a short-term, temporary basis.

To follow closed-end funds, check out one of the following newsletters that provide regular insight into the closed-end fund industry, listing winners—and sometimes losers, too.

➤ *Morningstar Closed-End Fund Survey*, (800) 876-5005, gives a complete listing of nearly all closed-end funds. The listing includes a description about the fund, its investment objective, and an analysis, too. If the price is out of your range ($195 for a bi-weekly annual subscription), your local public library should have this information updated on a timely basis. Most often it is found in the business reference section at the circulation/periodical department.

137

➤ Tom Herzfeld's *Investor's Guide to Closed-End Funds*, (305) 271-1900, is a definite must-read if you want more information on closed-end funds. On a monthly basis, Herzfeld provides you with easy-to-grasp concepts of the closed-end fund world, including those closed-end funds that invest in domestic stock and bonds plus foreign stocks and bonds, too. They do send out sample copies if you request one. Otherwise, a two-month trial subscription is $60 and an annual subscription is $325.

One Final Note

If you're among the gazillion consumers dazzled by some of the high investment returns that mutual funds are reporting in your local and national media these days, you're not alone.

Secret
Closed-end funds tend to skyrocket to premium prices right after they issue shares. Check to see which closed-end funds are investing in an unpopular category of stocks—those that aren't necessarily on a broker's recommended list. Those funds will probably be trading at a pretty steep discount and pro-vide the potential opportunity to invest at a very low price.

Just getting your feet wet is a bit easier with a mutual fund than if you were to sink all of your cash into just stocks, or only bonds. Building an investment portfolio of more than just one mutual fund is even a good investment strategy—for anyone. If you're hot on a trail of last year's winner and blindly decide to write a check, well, that's not a smart money move at all. Here are some hints for getting started in mutual fund investing.

➤ **If you're just starting out in mutual funds, pick a mutual fund company that offers a variety of different types of funds, such as various stock and bond funds.** This way, you can learn as much as you can about all the different types of funds in your "fund family." Another important point: Make sure that you can switch from one fund to another at no additional charge.

➤ **Keep things simple.** A conservative investor needs to start somewhere but start slowly. Don't jump in too quickly. Start out by buying only one or two funds that are in line with your investment expectations and financial goals.

➤ **Although mutual funds offer conveniences, do not simply invest in a fund and then forget about it.** You must be able to monitor your mutual fund and your entire investment portfolio on an ongoing basis. Your risk-comfort level may change, and the financial markets may change—they usually do, don't they?

➤ **To find the right mix of what you should do, incorporate specific asset alloca-tion strategies in your investment philosophy.** Mutual funds offer the best way to implement asset allocation. (Chapter 31 provides a good review of asset allocation strategies.) How? Because whether you have $100 or $100,000 to invest, you can protect yourself against market fluctuations and economic uncertainties by deter-mining the right investment mix specifically designed for you.

➤ **Proceed with caution, because if you don't do your homework, you will get burned.** True, mutual funds offer one of the best investment alternatives around. But the responsibility lies in understanding what they can and cannot do for your investment portfolio. Make sure you understand how much risk you are taking.

The Least You Need to Know

➤ Open-end mutual funds pool all investor money into one fund that is designed to have a specific objective (which you'll learn more about in the following chapters) and continually offer new shares. Closed-end mutual funds issue a fixed and limited number of shares and are traded like publicly traded stock on a financial exchange.

➤ Mutual funds offer many advantages, including convenience, small minimum investment requirements, diversification, and professional management.

➤ The best way to choose a mutual fund is to look at your whole investment picture and decide what you're trying to accomplish. Are you saving for retirement? A house? A month-long vacation for your golden anniversary? Ask yourself how much risk you can tolerate, and make sure you understand the relationship between risk and reward. The more risk, the more reward.

➤ When searching online for mutual fund information, you may come across fund company or brokerage firm websites. Some of the information is basic how-to investing on mutual funds, however, note that the focus of the how-to articles are marketing-brochure oriented to entice you to invest.

➤ Your future comfort depends on how wisely you pick today. Don't blindly write out a check to last year's winner. Do your homework!

Chapter 14

Meeting Your Mutual Fund Objectives

> **In This Chapter**
>
> ➤ Knowing when you can invest in a mutual fund
>
> ➤ Learning the different types of mutual fund objectives
>
> ➤ Going "global" and reap the rewards of foreign investing

"Is now as good a time as any to invest?"

When people find out that I write about investments, that's the question they'll ask me nine times out of ten. The others usually want to know what I would invest in given current market conditions. Well, I don't mean to disappoint anyone, but I never give recommendations. My goal is to give you enough information to make your own decisions and help you understand what your financial adviser is advising. So what I can tell you, at least from this chapter, is that you will learn about the different types of mutual funds you can invest in and the potential for making money in them over time.

Jumping In

Markets go up and down like two ten-year-olds on a teeter-totter, leaving small investors wondering when they should begin their investment plan. My answer? When it comes to mutual funds, it's basically any time you're ready, especially if you're investing on a long-term basis.

How can this be?

Unlike investing in stocks or bonds, mutual funds often take the guesswork out of trying to time market fluctuations. You have professional portfolio managers to do that. And it can be difficult for them, too; if it wasn't, all mutual funds would be winners. But as long as you invest in a mutual fund, which represents a diversified portfolio of stocks or bonds, the movement in any one of these securities is likely to be offset by movements in the others.

Unfortunately, most investors respond to the changing market conditions completely opposite of the way they should; they purchase securities when prices are really high because everybody and his brothers are gangbusters over the rise in prices. Then these same investors will turn around and sell near the end of a decline because they panic. The best advice I've heard has been passed down through the years. It comes from legendary market watcher (and ultimately a millionaire) Bernard Baruch. His theory is based on the contrary approach. "Buy straw hats in the winter time and your snowsuits in July." Think about it. How expensive is a snow suit in July? Not very. And when was the last time you needed a straw hat in the dead, cold, blustery days of winter? Probably never—unless you live in Hawaii and don't have to deal with five-foot snow drifts. The moral of the story: Don't follow the crowd.

My favorite "you're investing and don't even know it" strategy and one of the best ways to deal with market fluctuations is through *dollar-cost* averaging. Using this technique, you space your purchases out on a regular basis. You get more than an average cost here. You develop a habit of making regular purchases, thus building a lifetime savings program that may ensure a rather comfortable lifestyle in the long run.

You Don't Have to Suffer from Fund Paralysis

There are more than 7,000 funds out there, representing $6 trillion in assets (or probably more by the time this goes to press). Short of throwing your hands up in frustration, which way do you turn?

You might already be familiar with some of the big fund families out there, such as Fidelity, Dreyfus, and American Century. Good. But what if you're not, and you don't have a clue about how to find a good fund?

You learned in the last chapter about open- and closed-ended funds. Within each of those types of funds, there are three fund categories: stock, bond, and money-market funds. The slight confusion comes from the different types of investment objectives found in each category. In the following sections, you will learn to identify the type of mutual fund you need to match up with your investment objectives and financial goals. For a listing of mutual fund companies, their types of mutual funds, and their addresses and phone numbers, check out Appendix B. Good luck!

The Mutual Fund Mission

No matter what the fund invests in, it is classified according to the risk levels it takes. Here's a sketch of each.

➤ **Aggressive growth.** Funds with this objective invest in companies or securities that usually achieve the greatest growth records over the longest haul. In fact, some of their long-term records are quite phenomenal, boasting as high as a 56% *average annual* return over a five-year period. These funds do extremely well in bull markets. In bear markets, though, their shares are likely to suffer pretty sharp price drops. Out of all of the stock funds, these are the most risky.

Secret
Both aggressive growth and growth stock funds offer young families and singles a good investment strategy. Why? Because they have a longer investment time frame, spreading the risks over time.

➤ **Growth.** Go down a few levels on the investment pyramid for this one. Growth funds don't carry as much risk as aggressive growth funds do—but that doesn't mean they're 100% risk-free. The name of the game is the same, though: Long-term growth is where it's at. Portfolio managers of growth funds tend to look into companies and securities with good, steady track records instead of putting emphasis on some fancy aggressive trading techniques. This kind of fund invests in large growth companies and blue-chip stocks.

➤ **Growth and income.** Growth is the key in these funds, too, but emphasis is also put on investing in stable companies and securities that pay dividends. So you have the best of both worlds— long-term growth and dividend income. These are also sometimes referred to as "equity-income funds." An investor who is unsure about getting his feet wet and can only risk getting his big toe damp should look into a growth and income mutual fund. There is less risk involved here than with an aggressive growth or growth fund.

Secret
Growth and income funds are good investment choices for older families and empty-nesters. They offer reduced risk when compared to a straight growth fund, yet they provide a steady level of income.

You still get the best of both worlds with long-term growth and the potential for price appreciation and dividend income.

➤ **Income.** Generally considered a bond fund (you'll learn about them as you keep reading), income funds are mostly made up of bond funds. However, high-paying dividend stocks, such as utility companies, round out the category. These funds fall in the low to moderate risk level on the investment pyramid (unless the income fund is a risky junk bond fund!).

Stock Jocks

Stock funds, sometimes known as common stock funds, or equity funds, typically seek growth, usually over a long period of time through investments in the stock market. In a common stock fund, the value of your investment can fluctuate more on a month-to-month basis than in many other types of fund investments. Because of the fluctuation, you take on more risk. There are no guarantees that your investment will perform well. However, as you might already know, in exchange for more risk you have the potential to reap great rewards.

So why should you take these risks? Because those great rewards could mean quite a bit more money in your portfolio. That is why common stock funds typically have a growth objective. They give investors the opportunity for much greater growth than any other type of fund does. Because common stock represents ownership in a corporation (refer to Chapter 19), when the corporation makes more profits and sales, who benefits? The owners—meaning you, the shareholder. Thus, the value of the stock goes up, and so does the value of your mutual fund shares.

Not all stocks in a common stock fund rise at the same time, though. Many times, when a mutual fund is investing in different business *sectors*, one sector might be performing quite well, and the other might not be doing so hot. That's how a mutual fund provides a cushion to these bumps in the road, so to speak. Because a common stock fund offers diversification, the bumps in the road are a bit milder, therefore reducing the risk a bit.

Careful

Don't strive to constantly hit a home run with aggressive growth mutual funds. Make sure you choose a fund that will meet your investment objectives and that comes close to doing well over a longer period of time.

What?

Sectors are specific areas that a mutual fund will concentrate on. If the fund wants to diversify, it invests in many different sectors. However, there are mutual funds—known as *sector funds*—that specifically invest in companies in just one industry, such as biotechnology, real estate, and transportation.

Bond Investing Through Mutual Funds

The bond securities in bond funds range from short-term to long-term, just like bond maturities do. The bond fund portfolio manager buys bonds, aiming to achieve both a high yield and stability. That is hard to do because of the see-saw with bond prices and interest rate changes. When bond prices go up, their rates go down, and vice versa: when bond prices fall, their rates rise.

The biggest component of a bond fund is income, which is why they are often called income funds. In a bond fund, your money is used to buy bonds. Easy enough. As with bond investing, each bond in the fund carries a specific interest rate and a maturity date. The bond fund portfolio manager buys and sells bond securities that fit with the investment objective of the fund. These portfolio managers have to follow the bond market and interest rate fluctuations to the letter. As interest rates rise and fall, the value of the bond securities owned by the bond fund rise and fall, causing the bond fund share prices to rise and fall.

When choosing a bond fund, you need to consider both the maturity dates of the bonds purchased by the fund (short-term, intermediate-term, and long-term bond funds) and the different kinds of bonds the fund invests in. They include Treasury funds, municipal bond funds and corporate bond funds. Table 14.1 describes different kinds of bond funds and the bonds each kind seeks.

Secret

Many small company stocks (which tend to be more risky) and international stocks are found in an aggressive growth fund. The risks are more intense, but the payoff is more rewarding if you can hold on for the ride.

Table 14.1   Bond Funds and the Types of Bonds They Hold

Type	Invests in
U.S. Government Bond Funds	Long-term U.S. Government bonds and some government agency bonds.
High-Yield Bond Funds	Low investment-grade corporate (a.k.a. "Junk Bond Funds") bonds.
Corporate Bond Funds	Less risky IOUs from corporations.
Municipal Bond Funds	Federally tax-free bonds issued by cities, which usually have long-term maturities.
Ginnie Mae Funds	Mortgage-backed securities issued by government agencies.
International Bond Funds	IOUs from foreign corporations in the form of a bond.

All bond funds are taxable bond funds, with the exception of municipal bond funds. The interest on municipal bonds is exempt from federal taxes.

Don't Overlook This One

Balanced funds split their investments equally between stocks and bonds. When one market zigs, the other zags. The main theory is to balance the two with the objective of reducing risk. Consider it diversification at its best. It's a conservative approach, and the allocation strategies in each of the funds are usually determined by which category of assets the portfolio manager thinks will do better in the current market.

Secret

How many mutual funds do you need to diversify your portfolio? It really depends on how much money you have to invest. Mutual fund experts give the following guideline: If you invest $10,000 or less, you only need two or three funds. For each additional $10,000 you invest, add three more funds to your portfolio.

Balanced funds are for those investors who need to take a conservative approach and who don't want to assume the 100 percent risk associated with a mutual fund that invests only in stocks. Fortunately, because there are some stocks in the fund, you do get price appreciation in addition to the income you receive from the fixed-income investments (bonds, that is) in the portfolio.

Now for the Money Markets

When you need liquidity and preservation of your capital, look into a money market fund. It is an open-end mutual fund that invests in highly liquid and safe securities such as repurchase agreements, short-term government securities, and certificates of deposit. Many investors choose money market funds as a way to temporarily park their cash until situations change, using it as an emergency fund or as a safe haven during a rough market environment. You can also simply keep your money in money market funds until you decide which stock or bond fund investment you want.

Secret

If you live in New York or California, there are specialized muni-bond funds that invest in bonds only in that state. Often, the interest from these funds is exempt from state and local taxes in addition to federal income taxes. These bond funds are known as "double-tax-exempt" or "triple-tax-exempt." Because of the exorbitant state income tax rates in these two states, it could pay off to get more information about these from some of the large mutual fund families listed in Appendix B.

One advantage to using a money market fund is that you have check writing privileges. Much like a money market deposit account offered by a bank, a money market fund allows you to write up to three checks per month, with a minimum check size usually around $500.

The most common type of money market fund is a taxable money market fund. Anytime you receive any interest from the fund, it is taxable on all levels. Other money market funds include government money funds (which invest in Treasury bills and government agency securities) and tax-exempt money funds (which invest in short-term municipal securities).

Here's what you need to look for in a money market fund:

➤ **Convenience.** Make sure your money market fund has a check writing feature. This will be convenient in times of emergency or when you need to send in a check for your other investments.

➤ **Minimum investment amounts.** What type of initial purchase is required? Minimum investments usually range from $1,000 to $2,500, although you can get started through an automatic investment plan with as little as $50 a month. You'll see how in Chapter 16.

➤ **How fast your cash goes to work.** How quickly is your money invested once the check is received? Find out.

Bet You Didn't Know

The first money market fund was designed only 22 years ago, yet today the industry boasts more than $600 billion in assets.

Being "P.C." with Your Fund Investing

Just a brief mention about another kind of fund objective. If you have an inkling to save the rain forest or to invest specifically in those funds that boycott companies that perform unethical, environmentally damaging, or immoral acts, you can invest in Socially Responsible Investment Funds. This is political correctness of the '90s in its truest form.

The idea behind these funds is not so much the potential gain in growth or income, but the idea that the companies you invest in are following not only your investment philosophy, but also your ethical and moral beliefs. Some of the mutual fund companies listed in Appendix B offer socially responsible mutual funds. Call their toll-free shareholder services numbers for further information.

How to Buy 500 Stocks for Under $1,000

Index investing is a strategy that savvy mutual fund managers have been using for years. Obviously, you can't buy shares of every single stock in the S&P 500 or the Russell 2000—your commissions alone would be hundreds of thousands of dollars! There is one way around this dilemma—index fund investing.

Each index fund maintains stocks that are chosen to mirror the index it represents. You would invest in an index fund for the long-term rewards; they maximize the potential for long-term gains. Therefore, you should invest in an index for the long haul in order to take advantage of the long upward track record. Here are some examples. Keep in mind these are not recommendations, just examples to get the point across.

For example, there's United Services' U.S. All American Equity Fund (800) US-FUNDS, a no-load fund (no commissions or sales charges) that allows investors to track the S&P 500. With this fund, you don't even need a lot of start-up money—only $1,000. Dreyfus and Vanguard, two of the largest fund companies available, also offer index funds to investors that mimic the S&P 500.

Secret

If you have invested with a mutual fund company that offers many different funds, consider opening a money market fund in addition to your other fund investments. If you do, you can conveniently have your money automatically transferred from your money market fund to another fund without having to send in a check.

Secret

For those of you concerned about preservation of capital, invest in money market funds that invest 100% in Treasury bills. Three funds available are Capital Preservation Fund (800) 4-SAFETY, T. Rowe Price U.S. Treasury Money Market Fund (800) 638-5660, and Dreyfus 100% U.S. Treasury Fund (800) DREYFUS.

Many mutual fund companies have taken the cyberplunge and created websites, giving investors the opportunity to learn more about specific funds, the chance to get up-to-the-minute quotes, and even the ability to place fund trades right online. You can find out if your fund company has a website by simply calling the shareholder services department toll-free number (many are listed in Appendix B), or, using one of the search engines, such as Excite, Lycos, or Infoseek, do a Net search using the fund company as a keyword. Tip: If you are an AOL subscriber, use the keyword **Mutual Fund**, which will take you to the Mutual Fund Resource Center, located in AOL's Personal Finance Channel. Here, you can learn about basic mutual fund information, as well as place trades with the dozen or so fund companies, such as Dreyfus, Scudder, and Kaufmann funds, available on AOL.

Or, check out the Gateway family of funds at (800) GATEWAY. Gateway has three index funds available: the Index Plus Fund, which mirrors the S&P 100, a basket of 100 stocks; the Capital Fund, similar to the Index Plus Fund, but designed for the more aggressive investor; and the Small Cap Index Fund, made up of the 250 small company stocks that make up the Wilshire Small Cap Index. This minimum initial investment is low too—only $1,000.

The leader in index funds is Vanguard, **http://www.vanguard.com**, (800) 662-7447, boasting seven domestic (that's United States) stock index funds and six international stock index funds (plus a few bond index funds to boot). Its most popular fund, the Vanguard Index Trust 500, mirrors the S&P 500. Some of the other funds it offers are the Vanguard Value Index Fund, Vanguard Growth Index Fund, Vanguard Total Stock Market Fund, Vanguard Extended Stock Market Fund, and Vanguard Small Cap Index Fund. (The first three are no-load funds. The others charge a fee ranging from 1%–2.5%. That means it is a load fund. More on this in the next chapter.)

Here's a further look at some of the market indexes a mutual fund might try to mirror:

➤ *The DJIA (Dow Jones Industrial Average).* This index tracks the movement of 30 of the largest blue-chip stocks, such as AT&T and Coca-Cola, which are traded on the New York Stock Exchange. It is most affected by movement of higher-priced shares, like IBM, for example. Known as a Dow "look-a-like," the ASM Fund tracks the DJIA.

➤ *The S&P 500 (Standard & Poor 500).* This index tracks 500 blue-chip stocks, mostly traded on the NYSE. It's the benchmark to which most portfolio managers compare themselves. No small stocks are included. Some mutual funds include Fidelity Market Index, T. Rowe Price Equity Index, and Vanguard Index 500.

➤ *The Russell 2000.* (Sounds like a snowblower, huh?) This index tracks 2,000 stocks from companies with an average of $250 million in market cap (the price of the stock multiplied by the number of shares outstanding). It's considered the best barometer for small stocks. Mutual funds specializing in small cap indices would include Gateway Small Cap Index and Vanguard Small Cap Stock Fund.

➤ *The S&P 400.* This is an index of medium-sized stocks, those with a median market capitalization of $1.6 billion. (S&P's 500 requires $13 billion.) Formed in 1991, S&P 400 is considered another good benchmark for a typical growth stock mutual fund that tends to invest in medium-sized companies. One example is Dreyfus Peoples MidCap Stock Mutual Fund.

➤ *The Wilshire 5000.* No, this index doesn't count the number of rooms at the Beverly Wilshire Hotel in Beverly Hills. Rather it tracks all of the stocks listed on the NYSE, the AMEX, and the NASDAQ. Dreyfus Wilshire Small Company Value Fund and Vanguard Index Extended Market follow the Wilshire 5000.

➤ *The Morgan Stanley Capital International Europe Australia Far East (EAFE) Index.* If you want to track almost 1,100 foreign stocks in 20 different countries, check this one out. It's considered the most prominent index for investing in foreign countries. Vanguard has two funds, Vanguard International Index Europe and Vanguard International Index Pacific.

➤ *The Lehman Brothers Aggregate Bond Index.* This index represents the bond market in general, composed of Treasuries, agencies, corporates, mortgage-backed, and asset-backed securities. One mutual fund that mirrors this index is Vanguard Bond Index (total bond market).

Odds are if you contact a mutual fund company and ask them if they have an index fund that mirrors any of the above-mentioned indices, they'll have one. Go for it!

Going Global

If you have a yen for investing in Japan or a strong desire to put your pesos in Latin America, you might want to invest abroad. But save that plane ticket. You can spread your investment all over the globe simply by choosing a mutual fund that invests in foreign companies.

What about the risks? Well, there are many, but the returns can pay off handsomely. When I wrote the first edition of this book, the average annual return of an international stock fund was 40.2%. And for 1996? Down to single-digits, my friend: 6.05% according to the Morgan Stanely EAFE Index. How could this be? As you may know, past performance does not indicate future performance, and the past several years have been a classic example. Many investors who parked their cash overseas in international stock funds in 1993 celebrated with double-digit returns due to booming foreign economies. But in 1994? Not-so-hot, as the average annual return on an international equity fund hovered around a *negative* 10%. Just goes to show you the risks involved on a yearly basis in investing.

Careful

Investors beware. Figure out your risk tolerance before jumping into just one fund. More conservative investors might want to pick a broad-based fund (one that invests in several countries in a region like the Pacific Rim) as a way to reduce risk because foreign markets are choppy.

Careful

Because many of these international funds are new, you might have a difficult time comparing one-, three-, and five-year returns because of a lack of data. Some investors might want to wait until an adequate return period is established.

You can invest internationally in either open-end or closed-end mutual funds; if you choose closed-end funds, you can invest in specific country funds, such as India.

Are the distance, the language barrier, and currency differences a concern for investors? Not at all. Just pick a country and read up on current events in that company (in your local paper, *The Wall Street Journal*, or a magazine like *Business Week*) on an ongoing basis.

For example, if you keep up on what's going on in the Far East either through reading material or through business contacts there, you can invest in this region through a mutual fund. It's easy. You don't have to research foreign companies and run up your international calling card. Professional portfolio managers do it for you.

If you want to diversify your international mutual funds, you could, for example, pick a Japanese fund and a non-Japanese fund (those funds that eliminate Japanese investments from their portfolio) to balance the act.

For more adventurous investors, international bond funds are also available, though many financial experts forewarn, "Proceed with caution!" because of the currency fluctuations. This has to do with the rise and fall of a specific country's monetary unit—like the dollar in the U.S., the franc in France, the Deutschemark in Germany, and the yen in Japan. Investors interested in a bond fund should be aware that currency fluctuations (the ups and downs of the monetary unit) can affect the yield of their investment.

For example, you wouldn't want to invest in a fund that invests in German debt instruments if you think Germany's currency will weaken, because in the end you will lose money when you switch back to the dollar. There are other ways to invest in the currency of a foreign country, but those are for the more savvy investor.

You can invest in an international currency mutual fund, too, although they are quite risky and do carry sales charges. If you want to try to profit from the ups and downs in the currency market, look into Huntington International Currency Portfolio (800) 354-4111, which has a high-income fund, a global currency fund, and a hard currency fund.

Huntington Bank does make available on its Internet site information about foreign countries and global trading. For more information, visit them at **http://www. huntington.com**.

Or play the currency game. Here's how it's played. Say you think the franc, the French currency, is going to strengthen against the dollar in the near future. Walk into any international bank and exchange your dollars for francs at the current exchange rate. Then, when the franc does strengthen, you return to the bank and turn your francs back into dollars, making a profit on the deal. Buy low and sell high, you know?

But be careful. Investors should be aware of the *spread*, which is the difference between the bid and ask prices of the currencies. For example, if the bank has an asking price of $3 per franc but a bidding price of $1 per franc, and you have to get rid of your foreign currency in a hurry, you'll wind up losing money.

Careful
Keep it under lock and key—it's better stow your foreign currency away in a fireproof safe in the event of theft or fire since you're not able to deposit your currency in a savings account and must take physical possession of it.

Another disadvantage is that you won't be able to earn any interest on the foreign currency after the initial exchange; you can't deposit your French francs or Japanese yen into your savings or money market account. And, of course, there's always the danger that, in the case cited, the currency will weaken.

Chasing Big Returns Overseas

Another way to invest in an international mutual fund is through a closed-end fund. These funds contain about $79 billion in assets, but are a tiny part of the mutual fund universe. Some closed-end funds are dubbed "country funds," such as the Growth Fund of Spain, the Indonesia Fund, and the Korea Equity Fund, which invest in companies from the same country or region.

These funds, also known as *emerging markets funds*, returned an average of 4.14% in 1996. This is another sector that, since the first edition of this book, has seen a dramatic drop in its average annual return. In 1993, when foreign and emerging markets were celebrating sky-high returns—67%—investors rejoiced. Today? You can do better at a high-yielding money marketing account—*and* have FDIC insurance! Note, however, that today's average annual return is no indication of the future.

Some investment experts say that a good way to get involved in the rapid economic growth in foreign countries is through closed-end funds, although investors should note that on the risk pyramid closed-end emerging market funds rank right up at the top.

Remember though, as with all closed-end funds, emerging market funds trade either above the NAV or below it. This is the premium or the discount, as determined by supply and demand in the marketplace. A steep premium, again, is a sign that a fund is over-priced and poised for a correction (a drop in price). Conversely, deep discounts suggest that the fund is undervalued and that share prices may be set to rise.

Another factor to consider when you invest in a country fund is whether the investment is diversified enough. Most financial planners advise not to invest too heavily in one sector or one type of stock. So does investing in country funds mean less diversification and therefore more volatility? Not at all. A fund might invest in only one country, but it

151

may invest in so many different business sectors that you aren't putting all of your eggs in one basket.

For further information about closed-end country funds, contact the closed-end fund newsletters listed in Chapter 17, or subscribe to one of the following publications or send for sample copies:

➤ For a free pamphlet offered by the Investment Company Institute (the trade organization for lobbying and providing public education on mutual funds) call (202) 326-5800 and ask for the brochure "A Close Look at Closed-End Funds."

➤ *Closed-End Fund Digest* is published monthly and costs $150 for an annual subscription or $85 for a six-month trial offer. For a free sample copy, call (800) 356-3508.

➤ *Internet Closed-End Fund Investor* is an online research tool that allows you to check closed-end fund performance, gives weekly and daily charts of closed-end funds and a snapshot of recent data specific to the closed-end fund industry. Log on to their website at **http://www.icefi.com**.

Reading the Fine Print

Beginning to research a mutual fund is as easy as learning to read a mutual fund quote in a newspaper. Table 14.2 lists a few mutual fund quotes.

Table 14.2 Reading the Fine Print on Hypothetical Mutual Fund, "The Sky's the Limit"

SKY'S THE LIMIT FUND CO.*	NAV	Offer Price	NAV Change
Sky Aggr Grwth Fd	26.75	N.L.	+ .22
Sky Growth Fund	15.50	N.L.	+ .06
Sky High Yield Bond Fund	6.75	N.L.	– .11
Sky Long-Term Gov't Bd Fund	8.25	N.L.	– .09
Sky Income Fund	21.00	N.L.	– .10
[a]	[b]	[c]	[d]

The above quotes are fictitious and used only for example purposes.

The following list describes the columns in Table 14.2:

[a] These are the different funds. Usually because there is not enough room in the columns of the financial section of your paper, many of the funds are abbreviated. If you don't know where to find the fund, get the toll-free number for the fund company to call customer service and ask!

[b] NAV stands for net asset value. This is the price per share you would pay if you were to invest.

[c] This is the offer price, but in the case of a no-load fund, the NAV is both the bid and offer (ask), or the purchase and redemption price of the fund. For a fund that has a sales charge, known as a load, the purchase price is the NAV plus the load. At redemption, it is only the NAV. N.L. stands for no-load.

[d] This is a change that measures the previous day's close to this trading day's close (just like a stock quote).

Reading the fine print also entails knowing what to look for in a *prospectus*, which is about 30 pages of legal mumbo jumbo that contains the investment policy and guidelines of the fund. It is quite necessary to understand this document, because all portfolio managers must keep their investment practices in line with the prospectus.

Without going into too much detail (because a whole book can be written on how to read a mutual fund prospectus), here's a brief list of what you should look for:

> **What?**
> A *prospectus* is a legal document that contains the basic description of a mutual fund and its investment guidelines and policies. By law, the mutual fund company must send one to you before you invest.

➤ Understand the management fees and fund expenses. These are the fees paid to the fund management company and are independent of the mutual fund sales charge, which is known as a load. Management fees are generally the largest single expense in the fund. The prospectus will tell you how the fee is calculated. Generally, management fees range from 0.5% to 1.0% annually based on total net assets of the fund.

Fund expenses are also known as the expense ratio and generally range from 0.6% to 1.5% (and sometimes higher) on the total net assets of the fund. This fee is taken out of the dividend income that shareholders would get. For example, if a fund receives dividends and interest with a total of 10% in a year, and fund expenses are 2%, there is 8% left to distribute to investors as income dividends.

> **Secret**
> Any decisions you make regarding your portfolio should be re-evaluated periodically as the time horizon on your investments changes. For example, retirement investing for a 20-year-old is clearly a long-term concern, so such a portfolio can emphasize many aggressive funds. As retirement draws near, however, it would be prudent to shift into more-conservative funds or into a guaranteed savings account.

➤ Check out who the management is. The prospectus usually lists who the portfolio manager(s) are, their affiliations, and some general information about them.

153

➤ Make sure the prospectus tells you how much of an initial minimum investment is required, and how much subsequent investments must be. On the flip side, make sure you understand the redemption procedures you must follow to sell your shares.

➤ Make sure an annual prospectus or annual report will be sent to you. By law, most funds are required to send you, the shareholder, a new annual prospectus.

The Least You Need to Know

➤ When you invest in a mutual fund, you are investing for the long haul. Therefore, if you are wondering when is the best time to begin, you may want to start thinking about it today. The more time you have on your side, the better.

➤ There are three different types of mutual funds: stock funds, (known as equity funds, too), bond funds, and money market mutual funds. If you understand the different types of investment objectives in each, such as growth, growth and income, and income, you can pattern your investment plan accordingly.

➤ One of the best ways to invest in a growing foreign market and diversify your portfolio to include worldwide exposure is through investment in a mutual fund.

➤ Learning how to read a mutual fund quote in the financial section of your newspaper is easy. All you need to know is the company name and the fund(s) you have invested in, and you'll find the NAV (net asset value) or share price, the offering price (unless it's a no-load, in which case "N.L." will appear), and the NAV change, which is the change between the closing price of the previous trading day and the day listed in the paper.

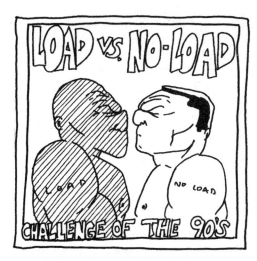

Chapter 15

Load Versus No-Load: Which to Choose?

In This Chapter

➤ Learning whether to choose a load or no-load fund

➤ Understanding how no-load funds make money

➤ Finding handbooks and resources about no-load mutual funds

I could sum up this chapter in one easy sentence: If you had your choice between load and no-load funds, opt for the no-load fund. The explanation as to why, however, takes a few more paragraphs. To learn more about load and no-load funds, let's move on.

Load Versus No-Load—Does It Really Matter?

The way in which mutual funds are marketed determines whether or not they're a load fund or a no-load fund. As you will recall from previous chapters, a *load fund* is a mutual fund that carries a sales charge. In the past, most load funds used to charge up to 8.5%. Nowadays, as mutual fund investors are becoming more sophisticated, the average loads have dropped to around 4.5%—although they range from 2%–6%.

So what's the advantage of investing in a load fund? Professional advice, for one. You don't have to wade through the more than 7,000 funds in existence to make your choice. If you tell a broker your investment objectives and financial goals, that financial professional will help you by identifying funds to consider, telling you when to buy the fund, and also advising you when to sell it and get into an even better fund, if possible.

What?

With a *load fund*, you buy shares with the help and investment advice of a broker. Therefore, the broker or salesperson is compensated for his or her time, effort, and expertise. That's where the load comes in.

Secret

Although you can purchase no-load funds from a broker, it doesn't make any sense to because the idea is to avoid paying any sales charges.

Here's how a load fund works. If you invest $1,000 in a mutual fund that has a 5% load, that entire $1,000 doesn't go to work for you—only $950 does. The remaining $50 is broker compensation. Thus, only 95 cents for every dollar is invested in the fund. That's the disadvantage to investing in a load fund.

So what about *no-load funds*? These are sold directly by the mutual fund company; no salesperson is involved. However, there are some money managers and financial advisers that do offer you the ability to invest in no-load funds with them (their means of compensation are calculated on a percentage of your asset basis, not through fund fees).

Considering the previous example, the entire $1,000 that you invested—and not a cent less—would go to work for you if you invested in a no-load fund instead of a fund with a load. When you purchase a no-load mutual fund, your total investment goes directly into the fund without any deductions.

The down side to no-load funds is that you do not receive any advice on which fund to buy, as you would with a load fund. All of the buying and selling decisions are left up to you. That's why doing your homework and consistently monitoring your investments can pay off—but only if you keep it up.

Let's see how your own research might pay off. Table 15.1 compares making similar investments in load and no-load funds. Assuming an annual return of 12% and that you reinvest all of the dividends and capital gains for the next 20 years, Table 15.1 shows you how far ahead you'd come out by investing in a no-load fund instead of one charging an 8.5% load.

Table 15.1   Payoff Comparison on a $1,000 Investment with a 12% Return in a No-load Fund Versus a Fund with an 8.5% Load

Timing	No-load	Load	Difference
Investment less load	$1,000	$915	$85
Value at one year	$1,120	$1,025	$95
Value at five years	$1,762	$1,613	$149
Value at ten years	$3,106	$2,842	$264
Value at twenty years	$9,646	$8,826	$820

The total difference between having all of your money go to work for you (buying a no-load fund) versus paying for investment advice in the situation illustrated in Table 15.1 equates to almost 1,000 bucks.

It is up to you to make the load versus no-load decision. There are some excellent performance load funds just as there are some really bad no-load funds. Again, you make the call. If you want expert advice and don't mind paying for it, you may choose a load fund. However, if you want to save money (which I always recommend) and do the work yourself (you should know the information yourself to begin with) it pays to research no-load funds.

Wait! There's More!

More fees, that is. Some mutual funds add other fees, too. They don't do this haughtily or inadvertently. The following types of fees should be reported in the mutual fund prospectus.

Funds with *back-end loads* are set up to compete with no-load funds. All of your money goes to work for you in the beginning when you invest, but if you redeem your shares before a certain period of time, you will get nicked with a back-end load fee (like when you are "backing out" of something). Typically, this fee is adjusted on a sliding scale. The longer you stay invested in the fund, the more the fee is reduced. For example, if you sell the fund within the first year, you might get hit with a 5% back-end load. If you sell in the second year, you could wind up paying 4%, and in the third year 3%, and so on. Usually, if you stay invested in the fund for at least four years, you won't be charged any back-end load fees when you sell.

12b-1 fees, also known as 12b-1 plans, are those charges that cover the costs of the mutual fund company's advertising and promotional efforts. These fees range anywhere from .25% to 1.50% of the fund's total assets each year. The name of this fee comes from an SEC rule (12b-1).

Exchange fees, as discussed earlier, may be charged when you move your investment from one fund to another in the same fund family. Try to find a fund that does not charge for this, although in your research you might come across exchange fees as high as $5 per transaction just to make the switch. The mutual fund prospectus highlights the details.

Secret
Find out if a *back-end load* is charged when you invest in a mutual fund. Many times a mutual fund will require that you remain invested in the fund and not redeem any shares for a year or two to avoid paying this sales charge.

Secret
If a fund in which you are interested states on its prospectus that it has 12b-1 fees in excess of .25%, shop around for another fund. Why? Because you're simply paying the fund company for advertising its information. Consider it a "marketing expense."

Secret
When you are shopping around for a no-load mutual fund, look for funds that do not charge for telephone switching privileges. Even though the idea is to invest for the long-term and not switch in and out of funds constantly, you still need to avoid any fees that just aren't necessary.

Show Me the Way

Throughout this book, I hope to help you learn how to crawl, to walk, and then to run, all the while holding your hand as you go through your journey about learning how to make money on Wall Street. I can't give you secrets, but I hope to share some simple step-by-step strategies to point you in the right direction. As such, here are some simple mutual fund strategies that may help you save money when you buy and sell them, and teach you where to go for very detailed information that will not overwhelm you. You are definitely on your way.

Smart Money Move #1: If you want to buy a no-load fund, buy it directly from the company.

You shouldn't go through a broker to buy a no-load fund. Instead, purchase a mutual fund straight from the company that offers them as a way to reduce "the middle man." Contact any of the no-load fund companies listed in Appendix B.

After you call one of the companies for information, they will send you a prospectus, a marketing brochure (usually), and an application in case you should want to invest. Fill out this application, attach your check for your initial investment, and mail it back to the company.

Decide if you want to open up an individual account or a joint account. If it's just you, you are the only one authorized to do any trading. If it's a joint account, both parties need to sign the application form.

Smart Money Move #2: Look at past performance but consider other factors too.

Choosing the best no-load mutual fund is crucial. The best way is to define your investment objectives, match up funds with the same objectives, analyze the past performance on three or four different mutual funds over a ten- to fifteen-year period, and then track the performance of each fund in both up and down markets. You can track the performance of mutual funds from the rating services listed in Chapter 17.

What you want to do is select a mutual fund that has made its shareholders money in a variety of environments (when interest rates were high or low, when the stock market was up or down, and when our economy was in an inflationary period or in a recession).

Smart Money Move #3: If you want to do as well as the market, consider an index fund.

You'll remember index funds from the last chapter. An index fund is a mutual fund that mirrors an index. There are usually very low costs associated with index funds, and they are a good way to get your feet wet without spending the effort and time of doing the homework necessary to beat the market. But don't get lazy with this type of investment; you still need to monitor performance.

Smart Money Move #4: If you have an account at a discount or deep discount brokerage firm, you may have access to no-load funds without having to contact the no-load fund company.

For example, if you have an account at Charles Schwab & Co., you have access to and can elect to buy almost 200 mutual funds that Schwab has affiliated in its OneSource network at no additional charge. You can opt to invest in their mutual funds via e.schwab, its online trading service that offers a 10% discount on trades for using its proprietary software (call (800) 435-4000 for information on its software), or research the OneSource service—among getting quotes and financial news information—via its website at **http://www.schwab.com** or keyword: **Charles Schwab** on America Online. Its website offers a 20% discount to those investors who trade securities in their Schwab account online. For more information, contact the Charles Schwab discount brokerage firm closest to you, or call (800) 435-4000 for information about these funds.

Another discount brokerage firm is Fidelity, mostly known for its ubiquitous no-load Fidelity funds, but also makes available other funds for investors. Its website, at **http://www.fidelity.com**, gives visitors real-time quotes using the Fidelity WebExpress (SM) function, and an easy step-by-step approach to opening up an account right online.

Smart Money Move #5: Consider subscribing to a mutual fund newsletter.

Investing requires ongoing discipline and research, and a good newsletter reporting on mutual fund performance can help make your job easier. There is a list of a few of the more comprehensive (and credible) newsletters in Chapter 13, and there is a guide to the rating agencies that evaluate all of the four thousand plus mutual funds in Chapter 17. Some rating services will provide you with a sample copy or trial subscription of their information, which should give you an idea of how mutual funds are rated for performance.

You can also check the business reference section of your local library. It won't require you to wade through stacks of information for weeks at a time, but time is required. If you don't want to spend the time, you might as well say adios to your dime. For a list of other mutual fund newsletters, see Appendix B.

Smart Money Move #6: Set up an IRA account at a no-load mutual fund company.

Since the strategy of putting your money into an Individual Retirement Account (IRA) is to let your money grow tax-deferred until you take it out at retirement, take advantage of long-term mutual funds by investing in your IRA. All you need to do is ask the mutual fund company for an IRA application to set up the account. It's as easy as setting up a regular mutual fund account. The advantage here is that the capital gains and dividends you receive are tax-deferred. It's a great way to plan and invest for the long-term. Remember, however, that not all IRA contributions are tax-deductible. Check with your tax adviser.

The Least You Need to Know

> ➤ Whether you pick a load or a no-load fund is completely up to you. A load fund is a mutual fund with a sales charge added to it. This sales charge goes to pay the broker or salesperson who gave you the help and advice in choosing the fund. A no-load fund has no sales charges. Therefore, you do your own research and make the decision about which fund to buy.

> ➤ There can be other fees associated with purchasing or selling a mutual fund: a back-end load, which is the charge you pay if you redeem your shares before a certain period of time; a 12b-1 fee, which is incorporated into the fund and pays for the fund's marketing and promotional expenses; and an exchange fee, which you get slapped with should you choose a fund that charges you when you switch from one fund to another in the same fund family.

Chapter 16

Investing in a Mutual Fund with $50

In This Chapter

➤ Understanding that you don't need a lot of money to buy mutual fund shares

➤ Finding mutual funds that offer this type of program

➤ Choosing on your own: yes or no

Think about what $50 buys these days—one pair of designer jeans, one-quarter of a week's worth of groceries for the family, or an initial investment in a mutual fund.

Trust me, your jeans will someday have holes in them, and last week's groceries will be long gone next week. The $50 mutual fund investment is here to stay.

Many mutual fund companies, such as Putnam, Franklin, T. Rowe Price and American Century, offer strategic plans designed specifically with you, the small investor, in mind. In fact...

It's as Easy as A-B-C

Learning the alphabet was easy. It's just as easy to use this simple mutual fund investment strategy created for the small individual investor. It's the automatic investment plan.

Here's what you do. Before you even sign up to invest in the mutual fund of your choice (even before you receive a prospectus), whether you are calling or sending away for information, ask if the mutual fund company offers an automatic investment plan. If so...

➤ You have the option to invest in the fund for as little as $50 a month.

➤ Many fund families waive the $1,000, $500, or even $200 minimums, thereby allowing you to start with a small amount of money.

➤ You are automatically building your investment portfolio without having the added burden of writing a check once a month. The monies are electronically transferred, typically between your bank checking account and your mutual fund account.

After you contact the shareholder services department and when you receive the prospectus and application form, many times you have the option of enrolling right off the bat in this type of program. Complete the application form with the necessary information—name, address, Social Security Number, and so on. In the section marked "Automatic Investments," indicate how much you want to have automatically invested in the mutual fund. Some funds allow you to start their program with as little as $50 to $100 a month. You can have them automatically invest more, though, if you want.

How does it work? You give the mutual fund company the authority to electronically transfer the money from an account you specify in the application. This account can be a savings account, checking account, or even a money market account. In fact, if you already have a money market mutual fund account (which is basically cash) at the same fund company, you can have the money automatically transferred from the money market fund.

Should the monthly investments come from one of your bank accounts, you need to provide the fund company with your bank's nine- or ten-digit ABA number (also known as the routing number), the account number from which the monies will be electronically transferred, and the amount of money you want automatically invested each month. And if you want to set it up so the mutual fund company makes automatic deductions from your checking account, you usually have to attach a voided check.

What does this plan do? For little money to start with, you are practicing the investment strategy of dollar cost averaging.

Just as a recap, look at what dollar cost averaging can do for you. Remember that it is simply a system of making regular, fixed investments into a stock, or stock or bond mutual fund. You do this all at a predetermined time, for example on the 15th of every month (you get to pick the date). In fact, you can time it right after you receive your paycheck to ensure you will have the money in your bank account. In addition, you can make additional deposits at any time you want.

Secret
If at all possible, do not touch the money you invest through an automatic investment plan. It's a tool to help you be disciplined, so don't give in to temptation.

Because you are doing this on a regular basis, you get to take advantage of any dips in the share price. Therefore, if the share price drops from $15 a share to $12, that same $100 monthly investment will buy more shares. And, when the share price rises after you purchase these shares, the value of your mutual fund portfolio rises as well. How can you figure this out? Simply multiply the number of shares you own by the current share price to calculate the value of your portfolio.

By implementing the dollar cost averaging strategy, you take out the guesswork of when to buy low and sell high.

When you implement dollar cost averaging, time becomes your best friend. Just $100 a month invested over a period of ten years in a growth stock mutual fund, reinvesting all dividends and capital gains, can yield you almost $32,000.

Folks, I can't stress this enough. *It is never too late to sign up and get an automatic investment program underway.* Sure, there is always tomorrow, but you have opportunity on your side today. Make the best of it by starting a program like this one.

So Who's Got the Goods?

You can start your automatic program in various ways, by dealing directly with a mutual fund company or by going through a discount brokerage firm. Usually, you should deal directly with the fund to avoid any fees or additional charges. However, some discount brokerage firms are waiving the fees on their automatic investment plans.

Consider this example of an automatic investment program. United Services All-American Equity Fund is an index fund that mirrors the S&P's 500. You only need a $100 minimum investment and subsequent investments of $50 a month. This is called their ABC plan, which stands for "automatically building capital." Personally, I think it means it's as easy as ABC, because it is a simple means of building wealth through the years. This is a no-load fund.

A list of a few mutual fund companies that provide easy-to-use automatic investment plans can be found by contacting some of the largest fund companies listed in Appendix B.

Strategies to Use So You Can Do-It-Yourself

If you follow some of these investment principles, you'll be off to a great start:

➤ **Think long-term.** Many successful fund investors allocate their monies in long-term growth equity funds after consulting research publications such as what Value Line and Morningstar publish.

Secret

If you are going to enroll in an automatic investment plan through a discount brokerage firm, make sure you choose a fund without any transaction fees. Because you are investing on a monthly basis, brokerage firm charges would add up. Instead, check out those funds in their "network system." Charles Schwab & Co., for example, does not charge additional fees for those funds which provide an automatic investment program.

➤ **Look at past performance, but don't count on it for the future.**

➤ **Decide before you buy, when to sell.** At the beginning of this book, you determined what your financial goals were. As such, you should have a "goal price" in mind before you invest, and, when the goal price or account value grows to your target price, re-evaluate your position to see if you should continue holding. Sometimes your goals may have changed, which will affect your decision whether to sell or not.

Investment Clubs: Your Own Fund (Sort of)

An *investment club* is a group of people, it could be as few as five or as many as 30, who pool their money together, kind of like creating their own fund. Although all of the people decide together which stocks to buy or sell, one person usually functions as a

Secret
You may end up paying less in commissions if you tell the discount brokerage firm you're buying shares for an investment club account. Why? Because you are generally buying more shares in each transaction than the average small individual investor.

Secret
Make sure you have a club treasurer who is responsible for keeping track of all of the financial records, such as deposit and withdrawal amounts and dates, so your group can stay organized when it comes tax time.

leader. Make sure you pick someone whom you trust and whom you think can be objective. Minimum investment? You pick it! Usually, though, minimums start around $100 with monthly deposits in increments of $50 each.

Everyone shares in the wealth, but not just in the profits you may make. You might learn a lot about investment products that you never heard of before; maybe there's a financial professional in the group who has access to research reports or a doctor who knows a lot about health-care stocks. Plus, you are practicing the art of diversification and dollar cost averaging when investing through an investment club.

The easiest way to get started is to contact the National Association of Investors Corporation, the NAIC, at (248) 583-NAIC. You may also write to them at P.O. Box 220, Royal Oak, Michigan 48068 to get a guide about how to start an investment club. In an easy, step-by-step approach, this guide gives you the financial know-how to open up a brokerage account, apply for a federal tax ID number (different than a social security number), and create a near-perfect record-keeping system.

Can you make money in an investment club? Sure. In fact the NAIC reports that more than half of all investment clubs have a better average annual return than the S&P 500 every year. Some of the professional portfolio managers can't even do that!

The Least You Need to Know

➤ Start investing in a fund's automatic investment plan as soon as you can, provided that you are comfortable with the mutual fund's investment objectives and guidelines. With as little as $100 a month, in ten years you could make up to $32,000—nearly triple your investment!

➤ Dollar cost averaging is one of the best investment strategies around. You consistently invest money into a mutual fund—for example, on a regular basis at regular intervals.

➤ If you have the inkling and a few friends who want to join you, you may consider starting an investment club. You don't need as much money to start—about $30 to $100 a month. For further information, contact the NAIC at (248) 583-NAIC.

Chapter 17

The Rating Service War

In This Chapter

➤ Understanding how a mutual fund rating service helps investors

➤ Finding the top bananas that are available to you

➤ Knowing what to look for in a mutual fund rating service

Now that you know what types of mutual funds exist—and believe me, there are many—it's time to determine which mutual fund rating service you need to help you make better educated decisions about investing in a mutual fund.

Do you want funds that invest in companies that are poised for strong growth over the next three to five years? Maybe you want a fund that seeks out companies that are socially responsible and environmentally or politically correct. Perhaps a fund that requires a low minimum initial investment is what you're looking for so you can dollar cost average your way into long-term wealth.

Whatever the case, today's 50 million plus mutual fund investors need report-like information that will assist them in making their strategic investment decisions in mutual fund buying. This chapter helps you figure out where to turn for information.

> **Bet You Didn't Know**
>
> Mutual funds have been around since the 1920s, but survey companies have only rated them for the past 30 years.

On a Scale of 1 to 10

When I was a little girl, my mother and father would play the "On a scale of 1 to 10" game with me, my sister, and my brothers. Every time we went to a restaurant for dinner, they would ask, "Okay, kids, on a scale of 1 to 10, how would you rate the food?" Whenever we saw a movie it was, "On a scale of 1 to 10, children, whaddaya think?" Even before my youngest brother was born, when we were picking names for him, "Okay, you three, on a scale of 1 to 10, do you like the name 'Matthew'?" My childhood was a constant rating service. I'd give it an 8 1/2.

Mutual funds are given their own version of "On a scale of 1 to 10" by more than a few contenders. You briefly learned about them in Chapter 5, but here's more information to help you choose the best mutual fund for you.

Separating the Best from the Rest

You can pick a fund that has a winning record today according to any of the mutual fund surveys and rating companies that exist. But that doesn't mean that same fund will be tomorrow's winner. What you can do is pick a relatively good mutual fund rating service or even subscribe to a few newsletters that cover the mutual fund industry (see Chapter 13). The advice given in most surveys and newsletters comes from financial analysts, investment advisers, or even financial planners. Remember that none of these survey reports or newsletters is predictive in nature; they just give the facts.

Here are a few ways you can get advice and cut through the murk on the 8,000 mutual funds that exist today.

The most informative and user-friendly survey of mutual fund performance—and one of the most popular—is Morningstar, which offers a number of print and software products that offer data and analysis on more than 7,500 open- and closed-end funds.

Its twice-monthly newsletter *Morningstar Mutual Funds*, is the engine that drives the company Morningstar, Inc. The surveys are compiled into full-page reports, and there is commentary on each fund by mutual fund analysts.

Morningstar rates each fund with a star rating system on a scale of 0 to 5; five stars is the highest honor given to a mutual fund. Each fund receives a star (or no stars) depending on a combination of its past performance and the risks involved. According to Morningstar information, "the rating is a measure of performance based on risk and gives investors a way to narrow down the group of funds that they want to look at more in depth."

These reports are updated on a twice-monthly basis. The *Morningstar Mutual Funds* newsletter costs $395 per year. But it is also available on a trial-subscription basis that runs $55 for a three-month trial. If that price is still a little out of your range, *Morningstar Mutual Funds* is available free of charge at your local library.

The company also publishes the newsletter *Morningstar No-Load Mutual Funds*, lists 600 no-load and low-load mutual funds based on the same criteria as its predecessor. For $145 for one year, subscribers receive a binder with five issues; every four weeks a new, updated issue is sent.

Morningstar is also available via cyberspace—keyword: **Morningstar** on America Online, as well as its own website at **http://www.morningstar.net**. Both sites offer free mutual fund performance information, giving you the latest data on the top 25 performing funds by asset class (growth, internation, corporate bond, and so on), as well as detailed performance numbers, star rating and fund fees on 8,000 mutual funds in existence. And, your search is easy:

1. Determine whether you want to search your funds by star rating or investment objective (growth, income, and so on).

2. If, for example, you are looking for an equity-income fund, you'll find a screen that offers the top contenders based on best performance (total return) in the past year. Annualized three-year returns are posted as well. Fees, such as loads, are given, in a column format, along with a star rating.

3. You can get more information by clicking on the fund of your choice and pulling up a performance sheet listing the fund's ticker symbol, a brief description about the fund's investment objective, as well as year-by-year return information. Also included? The portfolio manager's name and tenure, minimum amount required to invest, and contact phone and address.

Also helpful is Morningstar's search function, which allows you to reduce your time online by entering specific fund information you are seeking. Also available online—Morningstar's Editor's Choice articles and commentary, written by the company's top mutual fund analysts.

To subscribe to either publication, call toll-free anywhere in the U.S. (800) 876-5005 or write to Morningstar, Inc., 225 W. Wacker Drive, Chicago, IL 60606.

> ## Bet You Didn't Know
>
> Morningstar also publishes information on variable annuities, variable life, variable universal life, and U.S. stocks. These products, published biweekly, monthly, quarterly, and annually, are tailored to meet the needs of specific groups of investors—from novices selecting their first funds to financial professionals who need the most comprehensive information and the quick screening, graphing, and ranking capabilities of CD-ROM software.
>
> If you have questions about any of the Morningstar information available through America OnLine, or visit its website at **http://www.morningstar.net**, or if you'd like to more information about Morningstar's products, please contact our product support department at 800-735-0700.

Also available to you is *Lipper Mutual Fund Profiles*, a quarterly survey for both institutional and retail investors (that's you and me) via its company, Lipper Analytical Services.

Lipper Mutual Fund Profiles includes an evaluation of past performance of the 800 largest load and no-load mutual funds. Each profile tells you how well or how poorly a fund has done during a certain market cycle. You can subscribe to this quarterly report by calling (212) 208-8000. The cost is $132 for an annual subscription.

Or, if you're an online junkie like me, check out Lipper and CNNfn, CNN's financial news channel, at **http://cnnfn.com/yourmoney/lipper**. The two joined forces in mid-1997 to provide *The CNNfn Lipper Mutual Fund* report. This service gives you updated prices and profiles on thousands of mutual funds as tracked by Lipper Analytical Services, Inc.

Secret
If you can't afford to subscribe to these rating services, find out if they offer a trial subscription. If not, they are free of charge at your local library. Check the business reference section or ask your favorite librarian for help!

The site offers information on any individual U.S. mutual fund, and the ten largest U.S. funds, the ten hottest and coldest funds, depending on the time period and asset class you request in your search.

The Value Line Mutual Fund Investment Survey is a report that analyzes a total of 1,500 open-end mutual funds and gives a full-page analysis every other week to subscribers on specific funds. The comprehensive report is published three times per year.

For a three-month trial subscription, Value Line charges $49; six-month trial subscription is $155, and an annual subscription is $295. For subscription information, call (800) 284-7607.

Another service that provides mutual fund investors with the possibility of picking a winner happens to be the most cost-effective: it's only $19.95 for the guide. *The Mutual Fund Almanac* by Dr. Gerald Perritt contains profiles and performance ratings and records of more than 3,000 load and no-load mutual funds. However, since it is published annually, it is only updated once a year instead of once or twice a month, unlike other rating services. To order, call (800) 326-6941 or write 12514 Starkey Road, Largo, Florida 33773. Also available is the *Mutual Fund Letter*, a monthly publication that includes the latest news about the mutual fund industry, as well as in-depth profiles on specific funds in all sectors. The cost: $89 per year. Call (800) 326-6941 for additional information.

Also available are a group of publications from CDA/Wiesenberger, the country's first mutual fund tracking service. Three publications, *Mutual Funds Update*, *Mutual Fund Report* and the *Investment Companies Yearbook* are available depending on your needs.

Mutual Funds Update is a monthly publication reporting on Wiesenberger's entire database of funds each month—more than 9,000 mutual funds as of August 1997. The book lists funds information alphabetically and fund performance by objective. This way it is easy to compare return information among similar funds. The *Update* includes expert analysis on industry trends and events, and is also the only publication in the industry that reports on fund mergers, name changes, liquidations, and splits.

The *Mutual Fund Report* is also published monthly, but in a loose-leaf format that is pre-punched for a three hole binder. The *Report* offers a quick reference when you just want the numbers. Funds are grouped by more broad categories than in the *Update*, and while there is not commentary or industry information, many investors turn to the *Report* for its clear tabular reports.

Their most well-known publication *Investment Companies Yearbook*, Wiesenberger's flagship publication, is published once annually in April. This 1,700-page book is the ultimate reference tool for every investor. It summarizes all of the information found in the *Update*, includes full-page profiles on 700 of the most widely-held funds and also covers facts and figures which shaped the investment industry over the past year.

The *Mutual Fund Report* is sold for $275 for a one-year subscription. The *Update* is available in a three-month trial subscription for $50 or in a one-year subscription for $295. The *Investment Companies Yearbook* sells for $295 per book, or you can combine it with a *Mutual Funds Update* one-year subscription for a package price of $395. If you are interested in subscribing to any of these publications, or if you would like further information, call Wiesenberger's product support lines at (800) 232-2285, or write to CDA/Wiesenberger Publications, 1355 Piccard Drive, Rockville, MD 20850.

Tidbits to Keep in Mind Before Subscribing or Investing

No matter what type of service or mutual fund survey report you choose when investigating mutual fund(s), here are a few tips to keep in mind.

➤ **Remember to remain objective.** You have to have an objective source that focuses on the continuity of the mutual fund manager, and the report must evaluate that portfolio manager's performance. If the report says "This fund stinks because the portfolio manager stinks," consider choosing another service. Look for objectivity, not a panacea.

➤ **If you're coming into mutual funds for the very first time ever, look at all of the analyses out there—not just the promotional material that both load and no-load fund companies send to you.** If you've kept all of your money either under your mattress or in a savings account, you'll want to do as much research as possible prior to investing your money as a way to familiarize yourself with what you're investing in, as well as establish your objectives and understand the different levels of risk involved with each mutual fund. Mutual fund investing is a different ball game. These reports are there to help you hit a home run.

➤ **Make sure you stick with tracking a fund's performance over the past one-, three-, and five-year periods.** Check to see if there's even a ten-year fund history. A fund that's been around longer doesn't necessarily make it a better investment, but you can see how the fund performs during *both* bull and bear markets.

➤ **Mutual fund investors should not focus solely on which fund is really hot right now.** If a really hot aggressive equity fund is gracing the front covers of all the top financial magazines, that doesn't mean you should go out and invest. *Remember, past performance does not indicate future performance.*

➤ **Do your research and don't just read a financial magazine for your bottom line investment decisions.** Understand why a fund is top banana or a rotten apple. Many magazines and newspapers report the winners, but today's winner could be tomorrow's loser—just as today's loser could be tomorrow's winner.

➤ **Check out the track record of the fund's portfolio manager.** Contact the fund company to find out how long the portfolio manager has been there. Why? Because each manager has his or her own trading style. Plus, if he or she has a solid history with the fund, great. If the fund has been a winner but has a brand new manager, the same performance might not be repeated.

Careful
Keep in mind that those funds that haven't been around all that long obviously don't have any past performance history. Be careful when considering one of them.

➤ **Not only should you consider the performance ratings and the safety of the fund, but you should make sure the fund company offers other features (which should be noted on the survey).** These features include telephone switching, where you can call up and switch from one fund to another with no additional service charges; monthly newsletters published by a fund family, which provide great research information and educational material for you to read on an ongoing basis; and automatic investments, where the fund automatically debits your checking or savings account for as little as $30 to $50 a month and invests the monies into the mutual fund.

The Least You Need to Know

➤ On a scale of 1–10, subscribing to a mutual fund survey report or service scores a definite 11. Make sure you know the different types of services that are available to you, and that you are comfortable with the language in their reports.

➤ Past performance is not indicative of future performance. When you pick a mutual fund from a survey report, don't choose it just because it was last year's big cheese. It could really be sour grapes next year, and you'll be left with nothin'!

➤ Be sure to read other information sent to you by mutual fund companies, including their monthly newsletters and investment information. But *don't* invest based solely on this promotional material—do your homework first!

Part 4
Stock Market 101

If you think about the stock market, what types of images do you conjure up? A ticker tape running across a screen with numbers and fractions? Anxious traders flailing their arms, making hand gestures (all kinds, I'm sure), screaming at each other, and trying to buy or sell shares of stock in the pits of a financial exchange?

Is it financial wizardry in the making? Not really—there's nothing mysterious about the stock market. Trading dates back to the times when people used to barter their goods. Farmers would stand in the middle of their fields, bickering about how many cows one farmer would get in exchange for the other farmer's chickens.

Today, with all the trading floors on all of the fourteen major financial exchanges in the United States and the computer whizbang trading programs, you can find many opportunities to make money in the stock market. This part explains how you can get in on the stock market action and gives you basic strategies for maximizing your stock market profits.

Chapter 18

Getting Your Feet Wet in the Stock Market

In This Chapter

➤ Learning the stock market jargon—first

➤ Figuring out how the stock market works and trades

➤ Knowing how and when to buy and sell stock—easily

Civilization and profits go hand in hand.

—Calvin Coolidge, speech, New York City, November 27, 1920.

Ah, the stock market. The raison d'être for many investors. Why? Consider the following.

From 1926 through 1996, the average annual return on small-cap common stocks was 13.76%, not counting dividends being reinvested. Even a $10,000 investment on January 1, 1926, would have grown to $482,872 as of December the previous year.

Buying stock can be lucrative for your investment portfolio, and note that it's also good for the country, too, for it provides industry with the capital it needs to build business, which creates jobs. But owning stocks is risky, as many of your elders can attest.

Your grandparents' or parents' conversations about how they lost all of their money during the Great Crash of '29 remain vivid in your brain. Even the 508 point plunge in the Dow Jones Industrial Average on October 19, 1987 frightened regular, average Joe people—like you and me—into thinking that the stock market is a dangerous, hectic, and volatile place. But it doesn't have to be—as long as you know what you're getting into.

This chapter explains how you can get on the road to being a successful stock investor. If you stay in the stock market for a longer period of time, you can lower your chance of losing money. That's why many financial advisers promote the "buy-and-hold" strategy rather than market timing. You can make money investing in stocks if you give the stock market—and yourself—enough time! After you read this chapter, you'll know *what* a stock is and *how* to buy and sell one.

Taking Stock of Stocks

When you hear the word "stock," most of you will think of *common stock*. Common stock is a *security* that represents ownership in a corporation or company. A *share* of common stock represents a portion of ownership in a particular corporation. For you to own a share of common stock, a company has to offer common stock to the public, which they do in an *initial public offering*. At the point the company sells stock to the public, the company becomes a publicly traded company. (If it were a privately held company, no shares of any type of stock would be issued to anybody.)

After the great stock market crash in 1929, investors were worried, and so was Congress. In an effort to supervise the registration of new securities, Congress passed the Securities Act of 1933 and the Securities Exchange Act of 1934 and then created the Securities and Exchange Commission (SEC).

The SEC's responsible for overseeing any new securities that are ready to be traded, disclosing any pertinent information about an investment to the public, and enforcing trade regulation, but you already know who the SEC is and how powerful it can be if you saw the movie, "Wall Street." Remember when Charlie Sheen, hot-shot broker, got busted? He received inside information about a company and tried to profit from the increase in the company's stock price by investing in the stock before it took off. The SEC came down on him because using inside information in an investment transaction, whether you profit from it or not, is illegal. Off to the hoosegow.

WHAT?

What?
Another name for an investment product is *security*. You'll see the terms *security, investment security*, and *investment product* used interchangeably in this book. *Common stock* shares are securities that represent an ownership interest in a company.

Understanding how the ownership part of common stock comes about is important. For example, if I own a telephone company called Bells and Whistles and need to raise more money, I would issue shares of ownership—common stock—to the public. Why would I want to do this? To raise more money for business operations. If you wanted to invest in my company, then you would buy these shares from a brokerage firm that is associated with the offering.

Bet You Didn't Know

Often, you'll see "tombstone ads" in newspapers like the *Wall Street Journal* advertising a company's initial stock offering. The reason they're called "tombstone ads" is because there are no frills in the advertising, just information about the who, what, where, and when—like a tombstone.

The money that is raised for my company is done through an *initial stock offering*. The company would then hire several brokerage firms to handle this stock offering, and you, the investor, would buy the shares from one of these brokerage firms in this initial sale. The money that's raised goes to the company. When the company sells these shares to the public through the initial stock offering, it is said to be offered in the *primary market*. Once the initial offering is completed, the company doesn't receive any additional monies (unless it has another stock offering, which would then be called a *secondary offering*).

Here's a basic idea of how the initial stock offering process works:

1. All the initial investors who purchased the stock at the initial offering own the stock at the price they bought it. For example, let's say the initial offering was to sell 1,000,000 shares of XYZ Company stock at $10 a share so the company could raise $10,000,000. The offering was successful, and all 1,000,000 shares were sold.

2. You, as the investor, bought 100 shares for $10 each. You control $1,000 worth of XYZ Company stock *until the stock starts trading in the financial markets*. When it does that, the stock is said to be trading in the secondary market, when the price will rise and fall.

3. When a stock trades in the secondary market, it is bought and sold by other investors. Typically, the transaction (the buy or the sell) takes place on the floor of an exchange.

The price at which you buy the shares is determined by one thing—the company. After the initial stock offering, the company has the money it raised and needed. The company doesn't receive anything from

WHAT?

What?
An *initial stock offering* (sometimes called an *initial public offering*) is the first time a company issues its stock. A *secondary offering* is any stock offering made after the initial offering—be it the second offering, the third, or the tenth.

WHAT?

What?
Declared by a company's board of directors, *dividends* are quarterly cash payments made to stockholders. It's a way for a company to share its profits with you. Think of it as a profit distribution.

any trades afterwards. Even if all 1,000,000 shares were bought and sold by other investors in one day, the company does not receive a dime.

Bet You Didn't Know

When banks pay income, it's called interest. When stocks pay income, it's called a dividend.

Whether the price of the stock (and therefore its value) rises or falls depends on what the company does internally with the money it raised in the offering. If, for example, the XYZ Company used the $10 million to increase the production of their goods and services, then the value of the stock would increase because if production is up and sales are increasing, the company may have a profit at the end of the year. In this case, the company will sometimes pay *dividends* to its stockholders (usually on a quarterly basis).

Why buy common stock? The biggest reason is to achieve a profit. When you earn a profit, you incur *capital gains*, which is the profit you receive when you buy low and sell high. The difference in price at which you buy and sell the stock, expressed as a percentage, is your *return*. All investors hope that a company's sales and earnings will grow so they can sell their shares for more than they bought them.

What?
Capital gains is a profit from the sale of an asset. If you buy low and sell high, you'll make a profit, which is reported to the IRS as your capital gains. Capital gains are now taxed at a maximum of 28% when the new tax laws of 1997 were established. If you were to have a loss, it would be called a *capital* loss. A *return* on a stock is expressed as the percentage increase (or decrease) in the price of the security since purchase. For example, if you bought 100 shares of stock at $10 a share and sold all of your shares five years down the road for $20 a share, your return would be 100%.

The second reason is to receive dividends. Investors who buy common stock are hoping the company will generate profits so these profits can be distributed to the shareholders.

Last but not least, the tax benefit comes into play. You do not incur a tax situation until you sell the stock. For example, even if you bought 100 shares of the XYZ Company at $10 a share and the current trading price is $50 a share, you don't have a profit (or a tax situation to report to the IRS on your tax return) until you sell it. Until you do so, it is known as a *paper profit*.

What happens if I didn't raise enough money for my company the first time around? I would then conduct a secondary offering by issuing more shares. More shares of my company stock would be outstanding, and that would reduce the portion of ownership (or *equity*) you have in my company. For example, if you own 100 shares of ABC Company when there are 10,000 shares outstanding and I sell ten thousand more shares, a total of 20,000 shares are outstanding. Your ownership is reduced by 50%.

People invest in common stock for many different reasons. If you're a risk-taker you might want to make a large return on an initial investment, in which case you'd look for stocks that appreciate in price. Or you may want to keep a steady, safe flow of income, in which case you'd go after dividend-paying stocks because they provide income. Either way, you can get both forms of income return from investing in common stock, as explained in the next few sections.

Mo' Money Through Dividends

As a shareholder (or part owner of my company), you might receive a dividend, which comes from my company's *earnings*. Companies report their earnings in an earnings report table on a quarterly basis. However, my company doesn't always have to declare a dividend. In fact, if my company falls on hard times and the earnings drop, the first thing to go will usually be the dividends that are paid to shareholders.

When discussing company earnings, you should be familiar with the following terms:

What?
The interest or value that you have in an investment is your *equity*. For example, owning one 1/100 of my company is your equity in my company. Stocks are sometimes synonymously called equities.

➤ **Revenues.** The total gross sales figure of a company before any expenses are deducted.

➤ **Net Income.** The amount of profit earned during the time reported (a quarter). Many times companies will compare their net income figures on a quarter-by-quarter basis.

➤ **Earnings per share.** Indicates how much of the profit from net income is attributed to each common share of stock that is outstanding.

After reviewing their earnings, corporations make dividend payments to common stock shareholders on a quarterly basis. The following four dates determine who gets paid and when in this process:

Declaration date. This is the day that the board of directors announces the dividend, how much it's going to be, and when it'll be paid to common stock shareholders.

Record date. On this day, the company examines its list of shareholders. To receive the dividend, you must be on the list on this day. If not, sorry Charlie, you don't get the dividend.

Ex-dividend date. This day comes four business days before the record date. Investors who buy the stock aren't entitled to receive the dividend if they purchase the stock after this date because it takes three days to settle (finalize) the trade. This trading procedure is known as the regular way (three-day) settlement. Hang in there. This'll make more sense in a minute.

Payment date. This is the day when the company actually cuts the dividend checks. Usually, it's about two weeks after the record date.

Bet You Didn't Know

When you buy or sell a stock, it takes three business days from the initial transaction date for the trade to settle. This is known as the *regular way (three-day) settlement*. For example, if you were to sell 100 shares of stock at $10 on Tuesday, you'd receive $1,000 less commissions (your net proceeds), but not until three business days later on Friday.

Using an illustration will help. By looking at the following figure, you can determine when you should buy the stock in time to receive the dividend.

October

Sunday	Monday	Tuesday	Wednesday	Thursday	Friday	Saturday
	1	2	3	4	5	6
7	8	9	10 Declaration date	11 Ex-dividend date	12	13
14	15	16	17 Record date	18	19	20
21	22	23	24	25 Payment date	26	27
28	29	30	31			

An example of key dates leading up to the payment of a common stock dividend.

Secret
Take the dividend that was paid to you, and add it to the rise in price of your stock. Now divide that by your beginning price, and you have the total return on your investment, which includes your dividend income and price appreciation.

The board of directors declares a $.50 dividend on Wednesday, October 10th. This dividend will be paid to the owners of record as of October 17th, and the company will mail out the checks on October 25th. For you to receive this dividend, you need to be on the list as a shareholder as of October 17th. That means the last day you can purchase the stock, get on the company's list, and be eligible to receive the dividend is October 10th. If you purchase the stock on October 11th (the ex-dividend date), you won't be entitled to the dividend.

How much are dividend payments? Whatever the board of directors says they are. To determine the amount of dividend you'll receive, multiply the number of shares you own by the amount of the dividend. For example, if you own 200 shares of a stock and the dividend is $.75, your dividend payment will be $150. Keep in mind that a company doesn't have to declare a dividend and that the amount of the dividend is not fixed. One quarter it can be 50 cents, for example, and the next quarter it can be ten cents.

Go Figure!

Stock prices typically trade in sixteenths of a point these days due to the New York Stock Exchange's new rules in the summer of 1997. For stocks, each point is equal to $1; 1/16 of $1 is 6.25 cents, 1/8 of $1 is 12.5¢. The easiest way to remember how stocks are priced is by making a little chart that looks something like the following:

1/16 =	.0625 =	6.25¢
1/8 =	.125 =	12.5¢
3/16 =	.1875 =	18.75¢
1/4 =	.25 =	25.00¢
5/16 =	.3125 =	31.25¢
3/8 =	.375 =	37.50¢
7/16 =	.4375 =	43.75¢
1/2 =	.50 =	50.00¢
9/16 =	.5625 =	56.25¢
5/8 =	.625 =	62.50¢
11/16 =	.6875 =	68.75¢
3/4 =	.75 =	75.00¢
13/16 =	.8125 =	81.25¢
7/8 =	.875 =	87.50¢
15/16 =	.9375 =	93.75¢

When a stock price starts to rise, it'll move up in varying increments. If the current price is $50 a share, it may trade at $50 1/16, 50 1/8, 50 3/16, $50 1/4, $50 5/16, $50 3/8, and so on. If the stock is rising rather quickly, it may trade from $50 1/8 and jump to $51, for a rise in price of 7/8ths of a point. To determine the market value of your stock, you'd multiply the number of shares that you own by the current price of the stock. If you own 100 shares and the stock is at $50 1/2, your market value is $5,050. Got it?

Let's get your noggin working. Pop quiz! Get your pencils ready. If you own 100 shares of the EFG Company and the current price is $20, the market value of this stock is $2,000. Let's say the price jumps to $21 3/8. What is the new market value of your stock portfolio?

a. $2037.50

b. $2137.50

c. $2317.50

d. $2371.50

If you did the math, the correct answer is b. How'd you get it? Multiply the amount of shares you own (100 shares) by the current price of the stock ($21 3/8 or $21.375), and your answer is $2,137.50.

As you learned in Chapter 5, many newspapers have daily stock listings in which you can check pricing and other facts about a particular stock. An example of a stock listing can be seen in the following figure.

A typical stock listing found in the newspaper.

	52 Weeks Hi	Lo	Stock	Sym	Div	Yld %	PE	Vol 100s	Hi	Lo	Close	Net Chg
	26⅜	19¼	ShawmutNtl	SNC	.80	3.7	8	2143	21½	21⅜	21½	– ⅛
	29¼	25⅝	ShawmutNtl pf		2.33	9.0	...	44	26⅜	26	26	– ¼
n	7	3½	ShawmutNtl wt			...	...	27	5	5	5	– ⅛
	14⅞	9¾	ShelbyWill	SY	.28	2.6	22	13	10⅞	10⅝	10⅞	+ ⅜
	68⅞	56⅞	ShellTrans	SC	2.72e	4.0	23	1688	68¼	67⅞	68⅛	+ ⅞
	37½	29½	SherwinWill	SHW	.56	1.7	17	1177	33⅜	33	33¼	– ⅛
	25⅝	13½	Shoneys	SHN		...	10	4366	14¾	14⅜	14⅜	– ⅛
	12⅛	9⅝	ShopkoStr	SKO	.44	4.5	10	106	10	9¾	9⅞	...
	23⅜	14⅝	Showboat	SBO	.10	.6	14	598	15½	15⅜	15½	+ ⅛
	30¾	15⅛	SierraHlth	SIE		...	17	391	26½	26	26½	...
	21⅞	17¼	SierraPac	SRP	1.12	5.7	11	219	20⅛	19¾	19¾	– ¼
	43⅞	30½	SignetBk	SBK	1.00	2.6	11	1288	39⅛	38⅝	39	– ⅜
s	26⅞	16	SiliconGrph	SGI		...	26	2180	23⅞	23¼	23½	– ½
n	28	22¼	SimonPrpty	SPG	.95e	3.6	...	335	26½	26⅛	26⅜	...
	25½	14⅝	SingaporeFd	SGF	1.03e	5.6	...	150	18½	18⅛	18¼	– ⅛
	39¼	31	Singer	SEW	.20	.6	19	172	32⅜	31⅞	32⅜	+ ¼
	14⅝	10⅜	SitheEngys	SYT		...	cc	11	10⅞	10¾	10¾	...
	14⅞	11¼	SizelerProp	SIZ	1.12f	8.6	22	191	13⅛	13	13	– ⅛
▼	10⅞	5⅛	SizzlerInt	SZ	.16	3.1	dd	4784	5¼	5	5⅛	– ⅛
	24⅛	16½	Skyline	SKY	.48	2.5	14	145	19½	19⅜	19⅜	– ¼
	16⅞	11⅜	SmartFinal	SMF	.20	1.3	20	138	15	14¾	15	+ ⅛
n	12⅞	10⅜	SBHighInc	HIO	1.15	10.2	...	1115	11⅜	11⅛	11¼	...
n	26½	24⅜	SmithResdntl	SRW		...	...	204	25⅜	25⅛	25¼	...
	6½	4⅛	SmithCorona	SCO	.20	4.6	26	174	4½	4⅜	4⅜	– ⅛
	17⅝	7¾	SmithInt	SII		...	73	4241	16¼	15¾	16	+ ⅛
	26¼	18⅛	SmithFood	SFD	.52	2.5	16	150	21⅜	21	21	– ⅜
	35¼	26⅜	SmithklBeech	SBH	1.06e	3.2	...	370	32⅞	32⅝	32¾	+ ¼
	31¼	23⅞	SmithklBeech eq	SBE	1.06e	3.6	...	2562	29⅛	29	29⅛	+ ⅛
	26	20¼	Smucker A	SJMA	.50	2.1	22	80	23⅞	23½	23½	– ½
	23⅜	19⅜	Smucker B	SJMB	.50	2.3	20	1414	21½	21⅜	21⅜	...
	44⅜	34¾	SnapOn	SNA	1.08	2.9	17	1232	36¾	36¼	36⅝	+ ⅛
	23	14¾	SnyderOil	SNY	.24	1.3	29	130	19	18¾	18⅞	– ⅛
	31¾	24	SnyderOil pfA		1.50	5.9	...	26	25½	25½	25½	...
n	38	23¼	SocQuimica	SQM	.51e	1.9	...	139	28½	27½	27½	–1¼
	38¾	10⅜	SofmorDk	SDG		...	16	473	16⅝	16⅛	16½	+ ¼
s	34	17¾	Solectron	SLR		...	24	4966	28⅜	27⅞	28⅛	– ¼
s	36½	26	Sonat	SNT	1.08	3.3	18	1621	32½	32⅛	32⅜	– ⅜
	23⅜	15¼	SonatOffshr	RIG	.24	1.3	33	67	19	19	19	...
	63¼	41½	Sony Cp	SNE	.47e	.8	...	134	59⅛	58¾	59	– ⅝
	19¾	10¾	Sothebys	BID	.24	1.9	35	594	12⅜	12⅛	12⅜	...
	48¾	40	SourceCap	SOR	3.60	8.6	...	2	42	42	42	– ⅛
	32½	27⅛	SourceCap pf		2.40	8.6	...	20	27⅞	27¾	27¾	...

What Should I Do?

Investors should always plan on investing in stocks for the long-term. Gurus who predict that the stock market is going to plunge or soar don't really know. In fact, no one really knows how high or low stocks will go in a relatively short time frame. Whether you're investing in stocks for growth and appreciation or just to receive the dividend income, thinking and planning for the long-term is a strategy that wins hands down.

What if you only have $1,000 to invest? Is choosing growth and appreciation over dividend income better? Which approach works best for you? It all depends on your financial goals. If you have time on your side, such as 10–15 years before junior starts college, you need your money to grow rather than concern yourself with earning income along the way. Stick with the price appreciation focus. It could be considered the buy low and sell high approach, although remember you're doing this over a long period of time. If you are looking to realize large capital gains, this strategy should be your main focus.

If you're looking to maximize growth potential from a stock over the long term, you can start off with $1,000, depending on which stock you buy. You might not be able to purchase 100 shares (a round lot) at first, but you can purchase an odd lot (less than 100 shares) and just keep purchasing additional shares over the long-term.

Secret
It isn't that difficult to read a stock quote. Just keep in mind that you need to know the company name or ticker symbol to first locate your quote. Some basics? The HIGH, LOW, and CLOSE represent the highest and lowest prices the stock hit during one trading day, and the price at which it closed.

Careful
Don't get caught up in the wave of investor euphoria or gloom and doom and base your decision to buy and sell on what the crowd is doing. When stock prices are going up, your gut instinct is to buy more, just as when stock prices are dropping, your heart tells you to sell. Don't let that happen. Think long-term.

Those investors who seek income from these stocks typically just buy and hold the stock. They don't necessarily focus on the potential for price appreciation; rather, these investors want to earn income from their stock investment. You can invest your $1,000 here, too, but in order to increase your income (larger dividend payments) you are going to have to increase the number of shares you own.

What Else Do I Get?

You may be wondering what other perks you get for owning part of a company in the form of stock. Unlike a bond, which has a maturity date, the life of a stock is infinite. Common stock never has a maturity date and can continue paying dividends and growing in value forever and ever. Plus, stock investors can't lose more than 100 percent of their investment. No matter how much money my company loses, as a shareholder you are not liable for anything.

Guess what? You also get voting privileges on important corporate matters, such as who to elect for a board of directors. Most companies are run as a "one-share/one-vote rule." If you have 100 shares then you get 100 votes. Easy enough. As you'll see in Appendix A of this book, there are also some shareholder freebies that you might be entitled to, depending on which company you invest in.

But I Prefer Preferred Stock

There is another type of stock that exists—*preferred stock*. Preferred stock is similar to common stock in that it reflects ownership in a company. Preferred stock owners do not get voting rights as common stockholders do, but they are entitled to receive their dividends before common stock shareholders. Plus, if the company is liquidated—that is, it goes belly up—claims from preferred stockholders are satisfied before those claims from common stockholders.

The other difference between common and preferred stock is the value of the dividend. When you purchase a preferred stock, the dividend has already been set at the time the shares were issued. Paid on a quarterly basis, the dividend payment does not fluctuate in price and does not depend on how well the company is performing.

Trading in the Pits

Most investors think of the New York Stock Exchange (NYSE) located at 11 Wall Street when they think about trading securities. And it's true—many of both the common and preferred stocks and some bonds issued by America's largest companies trade at the NYSE. Wall Street is one of the most recognized and most powerful streets in history because of the New York Stock Exchange.

Secret
If you are faced with buying an *odd lot*, broker commissions will be higher than usual because you are purchasing less than 100 shares. You may see if the broker can give you a discount, go through a discount or deep discount broker, or see if the company has a *dividend reinvestment program* where you can purchase fractional shares of stock directly from the company with very small transaction fees.

But what exactly is the NYSE? If you've ever been in the visitor's gallery that overlooks a major financial exchange's trading floor, it might seem like the building's been overrun by a bunch of Neanderthal men and women screaming at each other. The correct definition of a stock exchange is a place where buyers and sellers (traders) come together to transact business. These financial wizards trade securities by agreeing on a fair price based on the supply and demand for these securities.

An order to buy or sell stock goes through a process as follows:

1. You, the client, place an order to buy 100 shares of stock by calling your broker.

2. The broker will typically send your order electronically to the order department in the brokerage firm.

3. The order is electronically "sent" via the broker-age firm's order department to the floor clerk at the exchange.

4. The floor clerk then passes the order onto the brokerage firm's floor trader.

5. The floor trader looks for another floor trader who is selling those 100 shares (remember, for every buyer there has to be a seller and vice-versa).

6. These two traders agree upon a price.

7. The order is executed.

8. The floor clerk reports the execution price back to the order department.

9. The order department gives a copy of the executed price on the order ticket back to the broker.

10. The broker calls you with your executed price. Within the next two days, you should receive a trade confirmation in your mailbox stating all of the transaction information.

> **Secret**
> Because preferred stocks have an already-determined dividend price, investors choose to buy this stock when they are looking for a steady flow of income rather than price appreciation.

The total number of the major financial exchanges in the United States is 14. For a list of some of the most popular financial exchanges, check Appendix D in the back of the book.

> **Bet You Didn't Know**
> The American Stock Exchange is known as the "curb exchange" because until the 1920s, all trading that took place before the building was constructed occured on the street curb until they moved inside.

Additionally, you should understand another exchange called the *NASDAQ*, which stands for National Association of Securities Dealers Automated Quotations. Until recently, it was known as the *over-the-counter* market (OTC). The NASDAQ is not a physical trading exchange like the New York Stock Exchange or the Chicago Stock Exchange but rather a computerized system that provides brokers and dealers with price quotations for stocks traded over the counter. You can tell if a stock is traded on the NASDAQ by the number

>
> **What?**
> *Preferred stocks* are securities or shares representing an ownership interest in a company and have "prefer-ence" over the common stock shares. Most buyers of pre-ferred stock are large corpora-tions and institutional buyers.

187

of letters in the ticker symbol. Typically all other exchange-listed stocks have one, two or three letters in their ticker symbols; NASDAQ listed stocks have four.

May I Take Your Order, Please?

When you order your favorite sandwich in your local greasy spoon, you have certain particulars that need to be met. Ketchup, mustard, hold the mayo, no onions, and lettuce and tomato on the side, please. These days not only do you have to worry about the order coming out right, but also about the price. Have you seen how much a turkey club sandwich can go for these days?

Secret
The trading hours for most financial exchanges are 9:30 a.m. EST to 4:00 p.m. EST.

If you ordered that turkey club sandwich, would you let your server decide what should go on it? What if you bought a house? Would you let the realtor make all of the decisions as to how much she thinks you should pay for the house? I don't think so. The same common-sense applies when you "order" your stock. As a smart investor, you can determine how you want to order your stock.

When you buy or sell stock, you shouldn't just say to your broker, "Okay, I'll buy 100 shares of that company stock and I want to buy it at whatever price you think is best." (What's the old saying? There's a sucker born every minute.) This section explains how to be a smart stock trader.

Knowing how to trade stock won't make you an elitist, but it will put you ahead of the game. You see, when you buy or sell a stock, you are making a trade. When you buy shares of stock through an initial stock offering, your money is going to the company. When you buy or sell the shares in the secondary market through the brokerage firm, your money doesn't go to the company but to the seller. In a trade, there always needs to be a buyer and a seller.

The seller could be anyone. You don't see that person. It could be me. It could be your Aunt Gert. The seller is someone who has also called up his or her broker and put in an order to sell a certain number of shares.

Where do the buyer and seller meet to make the trade and close the transaction? On the floor of a stock exchange. It doesn't mean you can jet to the nearest stock exchange and take your stock certificates to the floor and sell them. You need to execute your orders through a brokerage firm. Remember, for every share you decide to buy, there's another investor on the other end who has decided to sell.

Here's a list of the most common types of orders you execute through your broker to either buy or sell shares of stock. These orders are placed over-the-phone with your broker—you don't need to be there for him or her to write the ticket or electronically send in the order. Once the order is executed, you'll receive a confirmation in the mail detailing all of the information.

GTC

GTC stands for *"good-till-canceled."* You tell your broker that you want to buy shares of stock at a particular price, and the broker won't trade until that price is met. However, your order remains "good-till-canceled"—it doesn't expire until you cancel it. For example, if you wanted to buy 500 shares of QRS Company stock that is trading at $30 a share but you think the stock is worth $28, you would put in a GTC order for 200 shares at $28. Until you cancel that order, it remains in effect. Therefore, you don't pay for the GTC order until it is executed.

Careful

If you ever use a GTC order, follow the stock price closely so you can cancel the order if you think the stock price will fall below your order price. If you place the order and never follow the stock price, your order could get filled and you wouldn't know it until the trade confirmation arrived in the mailbox.

What if the price never comes down to $28? Don't ever say never when it comes to trading stocks. The price could drop, but it also could be a long time before it does. Meanwhile, you lose the opportunity to have your investment appreciating in a stock.

Another drawback to a GTC order is when the stock falls below your order price immediately after your broker executes the order. If the stock trades at $30, then $29 1/8, and then continues to slide to $27, you'll still buy 100 shares of stock at $28, even though the stock has already slipped to $27. Your portfolio is now down $100.

Market Maven

Imagine telling your broker that you want to sell all 300 shares of your THE Computer Company stock at whatever price it is trading. That's known as a *market order*. This type of order is the most common order used by investors. You buy or sell a specified number of shares immediately at the best available price. Here's how it works.

If the last trade was at $29 1/2 and you enter a market order to sell, you'll probably get the price *close* to $29 1/2 a share. However, the actual price could be higher or lower if the price of the stock changes before the order reaches the trading floor or trading post. Most of the time, brokerage firms handle market orders rather quickly. If the price of stock changes dramatically by the time the order is received at the trading post, you're stuck with it, whether it's favorable or not.

When you place a market order, be sure to ask your broker for the *bid price, ask price*, and *last trade price* of

What?

The *bid* is the highest quoted price that any prospective buyer will pay for a security at a specific moment in time. The *ask* value is the lowest quoted price that any prospective seller will sell a security at a specific moment in time.

the stock you want to buy. A broker gets this data from his or her computer terminal or ticker machine, and it looks similar to this:

29 1/2	29 1/4 B	29 3/4 A	30,700 V
(last trade)	(bid)	(ask)	(volume)

The last trade is the price at which the last trade was transacted. The bid is the price you would get if you sold the stock right now and the ask price is what you buy the stock at if you bought it immediately. The volume represents the number of shares that have currently exchanged hands or traded so far that day. Using the preceding example, if you were to put in a market order to sell your shares, you would get a price of $29 1/4 (the bid) or close to it.

Limit Up or Down

This one's a little more tricky. A *limit order* is an order to buy or sell shares of stock, but only if you can get it at the price you want or better. This order can be a *day order* (it expires at the end of the trading day if not executed) or a GTC order. An example? If you want to sell 500 shares of a certain stock but only at a price of $18 or better, you would enter a limit order stated as "sell limit at $18." If a buyer is willing to pay $18 1/8, your broker would sell your stock at $18 1/8—remember, it is at the price you want *or better*. If the best price available is $18, then your order is executed. However, if the highest bid is only $17 7/8, then your order is not executed and your shares are not sold.

This type of order *does not* give the broker any discretion whatsoever. Even if the stock price has been rising all morning and your broker has a hunch it'll continue to rise, the broker CANNOT wait a while before submitting your order to try and maximize your profit. He or she must place the order immediately.

Stop Right There!

Using a *stop order* is tricky as well. With this type of order you buy a stock above or sell a stock below its current market price. Wait—this sounds like the opposite of buying low and selling high, right? In order to understand its definition, let's compare it first to a limit order. A limit order is an order to buy or sell shares of a stock at the price you want or better, right? A stop order is similar—it's an order to buy or sell shares of a stock when its price hits the price you specify. However, once the specified price is reached, your order then becomes a market order.

A stop order has a few useful purposes. If you bought stock at $20 a share and over a period of two years the stock price appreciated to $50 a share, you have a very nice profit. Still you feel that the stock can go even higher, but you don't want to lose the enormous profit you built up. You end up torn between selling the stock that you have and hanging onto it for a little longer aiming for a higher price.

Here's how a stop order can help alleviate your problem. If you enter a "stop loss order at $48," then *if and only if* the market value of the stock drops to $48, does your stop loss order become a market order to sell. Your shares would then be automatically sold at about $48 a share. Mazel tov! You have protected your profits. If the stock price doesn't rise, the order is not executed.

There's another type of stop order you should know about, the stop limit order. You would use a *stop limit order* as a way of overcoming the uncertainty of not knowing what the execution price will be after the order becomes a market order.

Break it down into two parts using a hypothetical example. A stop order is an order that is treated as a market order once the specified price has been traded (reached). For example, if you put in a "buy stop order at $23," that indicates that you want to buy the stock once its price hits $23 a share. Once that $23 price has been reached, your order becomes a market order and you get the best prevailing price. (It isn't necessarily $23 but as close to it as possible, unless the stock price is volatile.)

What?
If you have placed a *sell stop* order or a *buy stop* order and the current trading price gets further and further away from the stop order price, you may want to change your stop order price to one that is closer. For example, if the stock is at $50 a share and you bought it at $40 a share, but are afraid the price is going to drop, you could put in a "stop order at $48" to ensure a profit in case the stock price does drop.

Here's the second part. The limit order is an order that you place when you want to buy or sell a stock at the *exact price indicated*. If the price isn't reached then it isn't executed. Combining the two together forms a stop limit order. It allows you to specify the limit price, either trying to get the maximum price you'll pay if you were to place a stop limit to buy or the minimum price you'll accept if you place a stop limit to sell.

Stay with me, folks. A stop limit order to buy is executed as soon as the stop price (or higher) is reached, and then an attempt is made to buy at the limit price. Therefore the order does *not* become a market order. If the attempt is uneventful and you don't get the limit price, the order isn't executed. A stop limit order to sell is executed as soon as the stop price (or lower) is reached, and then an attempt is made to sell at the limit price. Therefore this order also does *not* become a market order. Again, the order is not executed if you don't get the limit price.

The Least You Need to Know

➤ Buying stock represents ownership in a company. For example, if you bought 100 shares of a company's stock and there are 100,000 total shares outstanding, you own 1/100 of the company.

➤ When a company announces that it is making company stock—either common or preferred—available to the public, it makes an *initial public offering*. Any time after this that the company announces the availability of additional stock is known as a *secondary offering.*

➤ When you invest in stock, you are making a trade through a broker. In the world of stock trading, there is always a buyer and a seller.

➤ Know the different types of orders you can place when you make stock trades. They include a market order, a limit order, good-till-canceled, day order, a stop order, and stop limit order. The most commonly used order is a market order.

➤ When you want to make a profit on a stock trade, you must buy the stock at a lower price than what you sell it for. *Buy low and sell high*—the fundamental rule in investing!

Basic Stock Investing Strategies

There's more to investing in the stock market than just buying low and selling high—although that is the number one strategy to earning a profit.

But what is considered low? And high? How do you know exactly what is the *right* price for you? And, how do you know if it's even the right stock investment for you and your portfolio?

In this chapter you'll learn a few easy strategies that you can implement to learn how to compare stock prices and what types of stock are available for you to invest in.

The Most Commonly Asked Question in the U.S.

"So, what did the market do today?"

When you ask someone how the market did today, what does the question really mean? Technically, you are referring to the Dow Jones Industrial Average (DJIA) that everyone—market watchers, the media, and consumers—follows. The DJIA is used as an indicator of how well or how poorly the entire stock market did that day.

It is surprising to learn that the DJIA is calculated from only 30 stocks, known as *blue-chip stocks*. These stocks represent between 15 and 20 percent of the total market value of all stocks traded on the NYSE. Most of these blue-chips are manufacturing companies, but a few service companies are included, too. For example, IBM is commonly referred to as "Big Blue," because it is one of the largest components of the DJIA. Other easily recognizable blue-chip stocks are Eastman Kodak (EK), McDonald's (MCD), and Sears (S).

In Chapter 18, you learned how to read a daily stock quote to find out current data about a particular stock. If you were to take a bundle of stocks of all different types and lump them together, essentially with a few financial formulas you could have an "average" or an index. All these averages or indices give you an idea of where a stock is going. Today, there are more than 20 major indices you can follow. These indices are always listed in *The Wall Street Journal* and many times in the local newspapers. For a complete listing of the most frequently-used indices, see Appendix D in the back of this book. The DJIA is the most common index. Another is the Standard & Poors 500, which is calculated from 500 stocks (including the DJIA's 30 blue-chip stocks).

Secret
The reason an index is a useful tool for investors is because it gives a good indication of the performance of that particular market sector, such as utility stocks or small company stocks. Therefore, use an index as a means to gauge how your stock is doing by comparing one to the other. You shouldn't necessarily base your sell decision on whether an index is performing 5 percent, 10 percent, or even 20 percent better as a whole compared to your stock; rather, use it as a guideline.

An investor typically uses one of these averages or indices as a benchmark to gauge how his or her portfolio is doing by comparing returns from these benchmarks to his or her personal investment portfolio. For example, if your portfolio were to be heavily weighted in airplane, trucking, and railroad stocks, you would follow the Dow Jones 20 Transportation Stock Index to get a good "read" on the market performance of this sector. The Dow Jones 20 Transportation Stock Index consists of 20 of the largest companies in the transportation business. These companies include Burlington Northern Railroad, Federal Express Company, and TWA Corporation.

And if you were to buy and sell only utility companies, such as your electric company, gas company, or telephone company, you would monitor the Dow Jones 15 Utilities Stock Average. Companies listed in this index include Commonwealth Edison Company, Pacific Gas & Electric Company, and Southern California Edison Company.

Another reason these benchmarks are used is because of the historical data that they can provide. If you want to find out how utility stocks performed during a recession or how blue-chip stocks fared during inflation, these indices and market averages can tell you. Important: Using these benchmarks enables you to determine which stocks would be wise to buy or sell given a specific economic environment.

Other popular indices and averages include the AMEX Market Value Index, which tracks the average of stocks traded on the American Stock Exchange; the NASDAQ Composite Index, which tracks all of the stocks traded on the National Association of Security Dealers exchange (these stocks tend to be more volatile than those on the DJIA); and the Wilshire 5000 Index, which is the broadest measure of all of the indices—5,000 stocks are tracked.

No matter which index you choose to follow, you should do the following:

1. **Understand the components in each index.** The stocks that make up the Dow Jones Industrial Average are totally different from those in the Standard & Poors 500 (which is also known as the S&P 500). Once you know which stocks are in each index, you'll be able to choose which index to follow.

2. **Check to see if the index is made up of smaller indices.** This is just for informational purposes. Many times, a large index, such as the Wilshire 5000, which consists of 5,000 different types of stocks, will represent a broader measure of stocks. Because a larger, broader index covers a greater percentage of the market activity of all stock issues traded, larger indices are good benchmarks for gauging how your investments are doing. If the indices continue to increase by a large margin and your investment portfolio as a whole is going nowhere, consider reallocating some of your stock positions.

3. **Research how the major market indices performed during inflationary periods and recessions.** Investigating the performance of each index during those past economic periods will let you know which stocks to choose during certain economic time frames. For example, let's say you're interested in the airline industry, and you look into the historical performance of a transportation stock index to see how airline stocks perform during periods of recession. If the index's performance was down during the last recession and all previous recessions, and economists are currently forecasting another recession, don't consider purchasing transportation stocks for your investment portfolio.

Following an index sometimes turns into "beating the index" (or at least trying to). Many professional money managers use the big indices, such as the S&P 500, as a benchmark that they have to "beat." It's a difficult feat to accomplish, and most professional money managers just try to equal the market.

A Quick Word About the S&P 500

Aside from the Dow Jones Industrial Average (DJIA), the S&P 500 is an often-looked-at (and mirrored) index. The S&P 500 index consists of 500 stocks chosen for market size, liquidity, and industry group representation. It is a market-value weighted index, which means stock price times the number of shares outstanding, with each stock's weight in the Index proportionate to its market value. The largest industry group represented in the S&P 500 are industrial companies, with almost an 80 percent representation, and the majority of these stocks are traded on the New York Stock Exchange.

Bet You Didn't Know

What does it take for a stock to be delisted from the S&P 500? If a merger, acquisition, bankruptcy, or restructuring occurs, an in-depth analysis is done, but in the case of a merger, a company is removed from the Index as close as possible to the actual transaction date.

Picking a Few Winners

Knowing when the right time is to be in the stock market shouldn't be difficult.

Really?

Seriously. It's *always* the right time if you do your research, buy (and eventually sell) good-performing stocks, and learn to be patient. An overnight success really takes a lot of time. Investing and patience go hand in hand.

Before any secrets are revealed, know the different types of stocks that exist; when buying a stock, choose one that has objectives consistent with your investment goals, as described in the following few sections.

Growth Stocks

Secret
The idea of investing in growth stocks is to buy and hold the security. It is the easiest way to make money in growth stocks over the long term.

Investing in growth stocks is one of the easiest ways to make money over the long-term. Why? Because the companies that issue them are built for growth. The long-term buy and hold approach typically works best here. Growth stock companies are those that exhibit faster-than-average gains in earnings and profits over the last few years and are expected to continue doing so. You can expect average annual returns between 12% and 15% or even more *over the long run* with a growth stock, *but you must remember to think long-term.*

Today's investors lap up these company stocks like a dehydrated sheepdog on a steamy August afternoon. This, meaning the demand, pushes the stock prices even higher. Then something happens, like a change in management or less-than-anticipated company earnings, for example, and the stock value sinks.

Growth stocks typically do not offer dividend payments to shareholders. Some examples of company growth stocks are in the sectors of computers, biotechnology, health maintenance organizations and retailing stocks. Companies include WalMart, Xerox, Eastman Kodak, and Abbott Laboratories.

Investors in search of high returns from growth companies get too excited about the potential growth and forget the price. The best way to determine if you are paying too high of a price for a growth stock is by looking at the company's *P/E ratio*. This stands for the price/earnings ratio. Technically, the figure is derived from taking the price of the stock divided by company earnings. It indicates how the price of the stock is valued.

You also need to look for the company's earnings growth rate, which tells you the rate at which company profits increase on a year-to-year basis. If there is a high earnings growth rate, typically there is a high P/E ratio. It would be an ideal investment if you found a growth stock with a high earnings growth rate with a lower P/E ratio. For example, if XYZ Company's profits are growing at 20 percent a year and its price/earnings ratio wasn't growing as much, the stock would be a bargain because it hasn't realized its true value yet.

Income Stocks

You can get capital appreciation and steady income from income stocks. A stock with solid dividend increases can actually pay more over time than if you were to invest in bonds. Examples of income-producing stocks include electric, gas, and telephone companies, and some banks, too. Commonwealth Edison and Pacific Gas & Electric are income-producing stocks.

What? WHAT?
Traditional book value is simply the shareholder's equity divided by the number of shares of stock outstanding. However, you should look at the company as a whole, and use the aggregate market capitalization of the company divided by the current shareholder's equity when determining a potential investment in a stock.

Secret
Income stock prices are greatly affected by the general direction of interest rates because when interest rates fall, the stock prices on income stocks tend to rise. This makes the dividend income you can earn just as competitive as other income-producing investments, such as bonds.

Secret
Try and find companies that are consistently raising their dividends and don't carry a lot of bad debt when searching for a good income-producing stock.

Income stocks tend to be less volatile, and they are an appropriate choice for those investors who can't afford to take on a lot of risk. In the past, the typical stereotype of income stock shareholders were widows and orphans because they both need the income without a lot of risk. Today, income stocks offer high yields for those investors who are seeking more income out of their investments rather than price appreciation.

Cyclical Stocks

Cyclical stocks ride the economic highway. Companies that are closely tied to the ups and downs of our economy are considered cyclical. Careful, though, because to profit handsomely, you have to time your buys and sells.

Examples of cyclical company stocks include automobile manufacturing, steel, and paper companies. The reason these types of companies are cyclical in nature is because they incur a lot of costs to run their manufacturing plants. When the economy is growing, production is up, and consumers are utilizing the products these companies produce (increased demand), cyclical companies can meet these high costs and even pocket a profit. But, if the economy isn't doing well and consumer demand is down for these goods and services, company earnings can drop. See why learning about the economy is so important?

Because cyclical stock prices are so volatile, it's a little difficult to time your investing. You should buy cyclical stocks when their well has just about run dry but their situation can't get any worse. Then, you should sell cyclical stocks when they are enjoying record profits and everything seems hunky-dory.

Initial Public Offerings (IPOs)

One of the most risky opportunities in the stock market is an IPO. You learned in Chapter 18 that when a privately held company goes public, an initial public offering is held for investors to buy stock (ownership) in the company. True, an IPO stock can soar to two or three times its value in just one day, but over the long run, IPOs are extremely sensitive to the general direction of the stock market. Be careful.

Careful

Because initial public offerings indicate the very first time a company went public, there is no track record or performance information about the stock. Therefore, you do not have a lot of data to research and compare. Be careful!

These are also called *new issues*. Stock prices on new issues soar right after the offering because of all the hoopla that had been put into the offering. Soon after the new issue is out, the stock price typically drops.

Investing in the stock market can work for or against you depending on how much research you do. Research your investment choices carefully. Don't act on a hot stock tip from your neighbor. Find out what type of business the company does, if it has a lot of debt, and what the competition is doing. Once you invest, then you'll want to continue monitoring company business. Has the business changed? Is it providing a level of service above and beyond the competition? Is debt increasing?

One of the best ways to learn how to pick winning stocks comes from observation. Look around you. Many times a good stock choice will come from paying attention to your surroundings. If, for example, everyone is drinking Coca-Cola, and it looks like it's not just a fad but a habit that's here to stay, see what type of information you can find out about the company.

Secret
Remember when considering inves-ting in the stock market that one of the best sources of information about a company is its annual report. (A pro-spectus is issued only when there's an initial public offering.) This information gives the com-pany's current financial status and changes in the business operations.

Also worth mentioning is that you shouldn't necessar-ily focus on the *price* of a stock. Why? If you expect to double your money over the long haul, price should be a concern but not the driving force behind your decision to pick a winner. Plan to invest for the long term. Even if you hear a story of a stock purchase that made your brother-in-law Billy a financial windfall overnight, don't put your life savings in it with the hopes of becoming a quick millionaire.

Instead, remember all of the work that you did at the beginning of this book. You know your financial goals by now and are working on getting there. But you could destroy all of your goals just like that (snap your fingers) if you give in to temptation.

Which Comes First? The Market or the Stock Price?

When making a stock purchase decision, it's more important to know if the market is temporarily overvalued than it is to know if one company stock is trading higher than usual. A market is overvalued when a number of stocks are trading at a price that's higher than what they're truly worth. They're "rich," like a huge slice of double-double choco-late fudge marble-glazed cocoa cake.

Figuring out if the market is overvalued requires complex financial formulas and ratios (and what seems to be the equivalent of an accounting degree), but the way to get around that is to discuss your questions with your financial adviser.

Once you know this, you'll get a better idea of whether you should buy the stock you're interested in. If the stock is trading for much less than it's worth, that's like buying a $20 stock for only $10. That's a bargain and known as *value investing*. However, if the stock is overvalued, give it a second thought before you buy it. Would you want to pay $40 for a $30 stock?

Also, you can compare your financial adviser's information to the Dow Jones Industrial Average or S&P 500. This is another reason why studying an index is so important. It tells you when the *entire* market is undervalued or overvalued.

When the DJIA earnings are higher than your stock's earnings (P/E ratio), consider the stock to be a good value and a good buy. However, if the situation was reversed and the stock's earnings were higher than the market's earnings, your stock is trading for more than what it's worth.

Sometimes investors pick winning stocks by checking out companies that have just made a new low for the past 12 months, or unsuccessful takeover and merger candidates. If one buyer thinks a company is a good value, maybe others will come along and think the same thing.

And, don't forget, have a selling target price in mind even before you purchase the stock. Don't just buy a stock and then plan on it going through the roof. Pick your target point and stay with it. You'll learn more about when to sell a stock in the next chapter.

Learning About Shorting Stocks and Margin Accounts

Shorting a stock is not for the faint of heart. Here's why:

As an investor, you can pay part of the purchase price for a stock trade and borrow the remaining balance from your brokerage firm. This service isn't free, though. The brokerage firm charges you interest. Before you can do this, you need to set up a margin account and sign a margin agreement. Once this account has been established, the money you pay for the trade is the *margin* and the money that you borrowed is your *debit balance*. That's what you owe the firm (eventually). The stocks that you buy serve as collateral for the loan. Because the firm loaned you the money, the stocks are registered in *street name*, which means they are registered in the name of the brokerage firm. They get their money back when you sell your securities.

Bet You Didn't Know

Securities are usually registered in the street name, unless any of the following occur:

➤ The certificates (stock or bond) are sent to your house and then registered in your name.

➤ The certificates are registered in your name but held by the brokerage firm in its safe (in *safekeeping*). Most brokerage firms charge up to $50 a year for this service *per security*.

➤ If the certificates are held in street name (not your name, but held by your brokerage firm), you do not incur a fee.

You may be asking yourself why anyone would want to borrow money to buy stocks. Because you expect the price of the securities to rise at a faster rate than the amount of interest you'll pay to borrow the funds. It gives you *leverage*.

Here's a hypothetical example of how leverage works in a stock trade. Assume that you have been watching Goodyear Tire Company trade at $20 a share and expect the price of the stock to double within the next year or so. You can afford to invest $2,000 for 100 shares. You could, of course, buy 100 shares for $20 a share, pay $2,000 (plus commissions), let them appreciate to $40 next year, and sell them for $4,000, making a $2,000 profit. You've doubled your money—100 percent profit.

What happens if you margin the securities? You would put up 50 percent of the purchase price, according to Regulation T, which is a securities law created by the Federal Reserve board in response to the chaos that occurred during the stock market crash of 1929. It requires investors to post 50 percent margin on all stock securities. The remaining 50 percent you would borrow from the brokerage firm. In this case, you would still invest $2,000 of your money, but you would also borrow $2,000 of the firm's money and buy 200 shares. Now you've invested a total of $4,000. Assuming that the stock did double in value, you would be able to sell your shares for $8,000. Of course, you have to pay back the $2,000 plus interest that you borrowed. This interest is known as the *broker loan rate*.

Bet You Didn't Know

Prior to the 1930s, there was no minimum restriction on the amount of margin investors had to post. That's why so many people lost money during the stock market crash of '29 because many investors had margined their securities and they couldn't come up with the money required to pay back the margin loan.

Let's assume the rate was 5%. For a $2,000 loan, 5% would equal $100 for a year. After you repay the loan and interest, here's how your profit would sum up:

$8,000 (sale of stock) – ($2,000 (paying back the loan) + $100 (interest on the loan)) = $5,900.

$5,900 – $2,000 (your money) = $3,900 (your net profit).

Therefore the return on your investment is close to 200 percent, much, much greater than 100 percent! You've almost doubled your profit.

If you have margined some of your securities and the price falls, the brokerage firm will require you to deposit additional money into the margin account to bring it up to the required minimum level. This additional deposit is required because the stocks are the collateral for the loan. As collateral, if they drop in value, you need to make up the difference. Therefore, the present value of the stocks you bought on margin must equal the loan amount (Reg T = 50 percent). Make sure your broker tells you how much your account has to drop (it's usually 25 percent, but check with your broker or financial adviser *first*) before more money needs to be deposited.

Bet You Didn't Know

While using margin to buy securities sounds great, there are times to avoid it. First of all, just as stocks go up, they can also fall. Therefore, trading on margin could increase your losses if the price of the stock drops. Second, not all securities are marginable, and depending on the rules, some securities allow much less than 50 percent to be margined. Third, even if the price of the security doesn't move at all, you still lose because of the amount of interest you pay for borrowing the money.

Another type of trade that must be done in a margin account is a *short sale*. A short sale is when you sell a stock that you don't own, but instead borrowed from the brokerage firm. When the price of the stock *falls*, then you would buy the stock back at the lower price and keep the difference as profit.

Remember all that "buy low and sell high" stuff? Well, here you're "selling high and then buying low" to make a profit. Imagine that, an exception to the rule. Here's an example of why you'd do this.

XYZ Company is trading at $10 a share. Bad news is leaking out and you think the stock is going to go into the toilet. In your margin account, you would profit from the stock's decline by borrowing 100 shares from your broker (known as *shorting the stock*), selling it short at $10 a share, waiting for the price to drop to $2 a share (or whatever your target price is), buying 100 shares back at $2 a share, and then returning the shares to your broker. This gives you a gross profit for yourself of $800. Not bad.

Let's see how this looks mathematically.

XYZ Company stock current market price:	$10 per share
You borrow 100 shares:	100s (s = short)
Total value or your investment:	$1,000s (s = short)
Price drops to $2. Current value of your investment:	$200
You buy back the shares at $2 a share:	$200
$1,000 (short sale of stock) – $200 (bought stock back) =	$800 profit (less commissions, of course)

However, there is an inherent risk. The market value of the security could rise. Then you would be selling short and buying the stock back at a higher price (because you have to return the stock you borrowed from your broker). This situation is extremely risky because your maximum loss is unlimited.

The Least You Need to Know

➤ When you invest in the stock market, plan to invest over the long term. The average long-term time period is about five years. Don't expect to make a killing overnight in the stock market. You'll only lose your shirt—and then some.

➤ Market indices and averages like the Dow Jones Industrial Average give investors an idea of the general direction of the stock market. Use them as a benchmark to see how your investment portfolio is doing.

➤ When you choose to invest in a stock, keep in mind your investment objectives. Decide whether you want to invest for growth potential (price appreciation) or income (dividends).

➤ You can borrow money to purchase securities (buying on margin) or borrow stocks to sell (selling short) from your broker by opening up a margin account. However, trading stocks on margin is quite risky if the market value of your stocks drops dramatically. Selling short can also be risky if the value of the stock rises.

Chapter 20

Selling Your Stocks

In This Chapter

➤ Finding how fear and greed can cloud your decision to sell

➤ Knowing when to take your profits

➤ Determining the best time to cut your losses

Want to make a million dollars in the stock market? All it takes is a little knowledge…and a lot of time. But even more important, even before you purchase your stock, you must think of the best price to buy—and sell—it at.

Buying and selling securities requires you to know when to hold 'em and when to fold 'em, as this chapter explains. Think of the best price to buy a security at, but determine a target price to sell at, too. Don't buy a stock, a bond, or even a mutual fund just because it's a "good buy." That's only half the battle.

One of the best ways to determine a target price is to reflect on your financial goals again. What are you saving and investing your money for? Is there a specific amount? If you need $20,000 for your daughter Lisa to go to college in ten years, at some point you are going to have to sell your investment to get the cash to pay for tuition, room, and board. Deciding what you need the money for aids in targeting a selling price.

Rule #1: Getting Rid of Fear and Eliminating Greed

Never, ever believe your stock price will always rise, just as you should believe that it won't always fall. There are always two sides of the coin in trading stocks. Just make sure you're not flipping the coin of greed and fear.

Take this hypothetical example—but by all means, don't try this at home!

Mr. and Mrs. Jones just had a baby girl. Because the Joneses have already started their financial planning (they were smart and read Chapter 3 of this book), one of their biggest financial goals and priorities is to pay for their daughter's college education. Because they have 18 years until she starts college, the Joneses decided to allocate a large portion of their investment portfolio to long-term growth stocks to help pay for their daughter's future education.

How'd they do it? Each year, Mr. and Mrs. Jones invested $2,000 in several long-term growth stocks that had good earnings over the past ten years. The Joneses want this criteria and know how to get this information because they learned how to research the company through *Value Line* research reports and the annual report the company sent to them. (Guess where they learned how to do that. That's right, Chapter 5.)

Now the daughter is six years old and wants a Shetland pony (I said this was hypothetical). Mr. Jones, of course, cannot deny his daughter a pony. He needs cash fast—she's whining and her birthday is right around the corner. So he takes out $3,000 (or whatever the going rate is for a four-legged mammal) and expects to double his money from a stock tip he overheard in the barber shop.

The $3,000 is then invested in a sexy new IPO tech company trading at $15 a share. Mr. Jones has read a number of recent articles on the IPO market, and how many investors make a bundle in the first few days of trading after the offering, so he is confident of an immediate windfall. (Meanwhile, the college investment account has been reduced because he took this money out.) Guess what happens? The stock price goes to $8 after eight days of trading. Mr. Jones isn't satisfied—he wants to double his money. The stock price goes to $5.50. Mr. Jones, however, decides to cut his losses, and eliminates his position, selling his stake at a loss. (It helped reduce his tax liability on his personal income tax return; however, his daughter was displeased—no pony.)

This is a good example of how greed can get the best of you. In some way, Mr. and Mrs. Jones will now have to allocate a few more dollars each year if they are to stay on track with their financial objective of meeting their daughter's future education costs.

The bottom line is that you need to stick with your investment objectives or you'll never reach your financial goals. If you must have some "greed" money, allocate $20 to $30 a

Secret

Recognize how easy it can be to become greedy when trading stocks. You can protect your profits and give greed a swift kick by placing a stop loss order (see Chapter 18). Your broker will sell the stock if the price drops to a specific point, but remember to raise the stop loss order if the stock price continues to rise.

month for you just to do whatever you want with it. I don't recommend this, however. Your first priority should be to meet your financial goals.

Now let's take a look at how fear can cloud your investment decision. The Smiths, who live next door to the Joneses, are very conservative and frugal people. They don't live beyond their means. In fact, they buy the basic necessities and save all the rest of their money.

Eeeek! They save their money! Where? In a low-interest bearing savings account earning a 2.27% annual yield, which is comparable to the national average mid-Summer 1997, according to *Bank Rate Monitor*, an industry newsletter.

The Smiths think they're smart, because they've identified all of their investment objectives and their financial goals. However, they are too afraid to risk any of their principal, so they opted for the safety of an insured bank savings account.

Very respectable, but not very smart. If the Smiths are die-hard conservatives, a portion of their money can be kept in a money market deposit account. However, they won't reach their financial goals in the time required. The fear of losing their money is too overwhelming for them. This is how fear clouds your investment decision to buy.

You can also have fear about selling a stock. Some investors, for example, might be losing sleep over their first stock purchase. They are so fearful of having the stock drop from $20 a share, let's say, to $5 a share overnight that they decide to sell all of their shares the next trading day at the current price of $21 a share. Sure, they can sleep better at night, but the stock is now trading at $29 a share. Fear can cloud your decision as to when to sell if you are not keeping up with the current events and information about the company, its earnings, its financial reports, and the general direction of the financial market and industry.

Fear Not—It's a Stop Loss to the Rescue

Stop loss orders can help you be a little bit greedy and protect you from losing your profits. Remember, a stop loss order is when you tell your broker to sell your stock when it drops to a certain share price. Here's how to be smart when using stop loss orders:

➤ Don't put the stop loss price too close to the current stock price. If the current trading price dips just a hair before it rises again, your stop loss order would be executed and you might miss out on further profit potential.

➤ Investment analysts and a few technicians use the following rule when entering stop loss orders: Set the stop order price at ten percent below the current stock market price.

➤ Remember not to confuse a *stop loss order* with a *stop limit order*. A stop loss order protects your profits by selling your shares of stock should it fall in price to the stop loss price that you set. A stop limit order gives the investor the advantage of specifying the limit price, meaning the maximum price you'll accept in the case of a stop limit to sell.

Take the Money and Run

Every investor wants to make a lot of money. The promise of a stock price rising is invigorating. Growth potential is the single most important consideration in buying stocks, bonds, mutual funds, futures, options—you name it! Ultimately, you want to choose a stock that reaps great profit potential. Of course, the only way to reap a great profit is to buy *and sell* the stock. Otherwise, the only profit you will see is a paper profit. Typically, this type of approach is a bit more aggressive than if you were to invest in a dividend-paying stock, where you usually buy and hold it.

I won't lie to you. It is very difficult to know when to sell a stock. Sure, you have access to research reports. Comments from your broker might tell you to watch the stock one more day or maybe wait until the next market rally comes around.

Realize that you can't control the ups and downs of the stock market or whether or not your stock appreciates in value. However, you can control when you want to sell the stock and learn to identify situations when you should sell or when your stock price hits the target price you initially set, you'll be able to evaluate your decision on whether to hold or sell.

It's Better to Sell Out Than to Fade Away

As you become an educated investor, there is one thing (among many) to look for when evaluating the best time to sell your stock. It's an easy thing to spot and requires only a little more observation than usual. It's a fad gone bad.

If you bought stock in ABC Toy Company right before their hottest toy product was literally swept off the shelves by eager consumers, you probably would have witnessed a substantial rise in the stock price. Lately, though, your observations tell you that this once hot-selling toy is out. Kids are now going crazy for a new toy manufactured by a competing company. You may notice your ABC Toy Company stock trying to rally to a new high, but the price starts dropping. You're trying to decide whether to sell your shares and realize your profits.

At this point, you could use a stop loss order and tell your broker to sell the stock automatically when it drops below the stop price. This way you protect your profit—even if the stock price rises. In fact, every time the stock price advances, cancel the old stop loss order and enter a new one with a higher selling price.

Merger Mania

Another time to realize your profits is when a company merger is anticipated. Waiting with bated breath, investors pounce on rumors of company mergers. Typically, the stock price will jump sky high with the high hopes of the pending merger, only to drop when the merger actually takes place. What happens is that the interest created by rumors flying brings in new investors, pushing up the stock price. When the merger mania subsides, the interest in the company drops, and so does the stock price. It brings to mind an old adage that some investors follow: Buy on rumor, sell on fact. Regard it as just that—an old adage.

Splitsville

If you hear that the company you have stock in is planning a *reverse stock split*, you should probably sell your stock. Often when a company announces a reverse stock split, the stock price tends to end up trading lower in value. This is the opposite of a regular *stock split*. Here's what happens.

Let's say ABC Toy Company is trading around $2 a share. The company wants investors to purchase the *outstanding shares* (all the shares that exist) of stock, but no one is willing to buy. Even the big boys in the company can't convince anybody on Wall Street to buy. The low price may be the factor that's scaring off the investors, which makes it seem like ABC Toy Company isn't performing all that well.

Instead of trying to increase sales even further, which would ultimately increase earnings and push the stock price higher, ABC Toy Company might announce a reverse stock split. As an investor, you would receive fewer shares at a higher price. Don't be alarmed. Your market value remains the same. Let's say you owned 1,000 shares of ABC Toy Company, which is currently trading at $2 a share. If ABC Toy Company decided to execute a one-for-ten reverse split, the number of shares you owned would be reduced (for every ten shares you had, you would now have one share) but the current stock price would increase. Here's the math.

What?

The board of directors will announce a *reverse stock split* when they decide their stock is trading too low and no one is buying. If you have two shares, they'll be combined together as one. The remaining securities are still yours, but at a higher market price. Conversely, a *stock split* occurs when the current company stock price is too high. So the company splits the stock to make it more affordable to buy. For example, a two-for-one stock split means that for every share you own you'd get an additional share. The stock price would be cut in half, but the total dollar value remains the same.

> **Before:** 1,000 shares @ $2/share = $2,000
>
> **After:** 100 shares @ $20/share = $2,000

Why would a company do this? By raising the price of the stock (without issuing any additional shares), the company makes the stock price more attractive to Wall Street buyers and brokerage firms. Usually big brokerage houses won't even deal with stocks that trade below $5 a share.

Why would there eventually be a drop in value in the new stock price? Studies show that if a stock is trading at $2 a share one day and $20 a share the next without any substantial gains in company profits, investors become wary of the stock because the increase isn't based on anything tangible. Investors might oppose this higher price, and then the stock price would fall. Also, big-time traders know that reverse stock splits may cause the price of the stock to drop, so they short sell the stock (see Chapter 19). This puts further downward pressure on the stock price.

Patience, Patience

After choosing the stocks you want to buy, it's equally important to choose when you want to sell. Remember you are the only person who can make that decision. Unless something really good or terribly drastic happens to a company, a stock price tends to move up to its yearly high and then trade back down.

Another rule is patience. This is how brokers benefit from the average investor by following an "active trading" model. Remember: Patience and discipline pay off when you are trying to realize your profits. Many times, I have followed a stock for a year or more before it hits the right mark—a good quality stock with a low price. Discipline helps you buy the right price, and patience enables you to sell at the right price, too. If a broker calls you and tells you that you can make a great profit from a good stock that he's promoting, ask him to send you information so you can analyze the company. This strategy can save you a lot of trouble and money.

Cutting Your Losses

No one—not even wise old Uncle Merle—knows the highest price your stock will hit before it tanks. Understand, though, that if you don't realize your profits, you may have to cut your losses.

It *is* difficult to pinpoint exactly when you should cut your losses, but if your stock is trading well below the price you bought it at, consider cutting your losses. For example, if you bought 100 shares of a stock at $40 a share, and now it's trading at $20 a share, your market value dropped 50 percent. Your stock would have to double in price—*gain 100 percent*—just for you to be back where you started.

What?

Cutting your losses is a favorite phrase among brokers. It means you haven't realized your profits, usually because the stock price has dipped and hung below your purchase price. "Sell your stock if it falls 20 percent below what you bought it for to cut your losses!" they exclaim.

As a rule, keep the following guidelines in mind:

➤ **Take the time to review company news**. Has there been any negative publicity that caused the price of the stock to drop? But might it blow over in time? Make sure you keep abreast of all company information. Contact the shareholder services department if you have questions. Call your broker or financial adviser for some additional research material or helpful answers. Finally, make sure you continue to follow the financial reports that are sent to you.

➤ **Is the drop in price a big drop that occurred in just one day or has it been steadily declining?** If it is a big price drop that has occurred in just one day, take a step back and review the situation. Why the drop? Is it bad news that'll just have a temporary effect or is it the shape of things to come? If it's a temporary situation, you don't have to sell your stock. However, if the price has been steadily declining for a while, review all of your research information and consider cutting your losses.

➤ **Perhaps an investor who holds a large block of stock sold all of it.** Many times when this happens it can send the stock price tumbling even though all of the company's ducks are in order. Call the company and find out.

Cutting your losses does have an advantage (if you can look at it this way). Depending on the tax rules, you are allowed to apply these losses to your tax return to reduce your adjusted gross income (AGI). For more information on taxes, read Chapter 32.

Another Reason for the Fall

Selling your stock when everyone else wants to buy it has been one of the tricks of the trade, according to a few fundamentalists. You may be able to buy low and sell high using this strategy.

The concept rests on the theory of supply and demand. The more demand for a given level of supply, the higher the price. The less demand for a given level of supply, the lower the price. The idea behind it is that if more investors want to buy the stock than there are shares available, then the price will rise. On the other hand, if more people want to sell the stock than there are buyers for it, well, then the stock price will drop. Ultimately, when other investors want the stock and the price increases, tally ho! You'll sell your shares for a profit. This just shows you that a stock's price is determined by the laws of supply and demand.

The Least You Need to Know

➤ Making a profit requires you to buy the stock low and sell it higher. If you buy the stock at a low price and it is trading up from where you bought it, there's no profit until you sell it—although the price appreciation does look good on paper!

➤ Realizing your profits is the ultimate motive for investing. However, if you let the two negative emotions—fear and greed—get in your way, your profit potential might be reduced. Watch out for that trap! Make your decision based on your original investment goal.

➤ Only you can make the decision about when to sell your stock. Several key indicators—such as a decline in a fad product, an anticipated merger, or a rumor of a reverse stock split—can mean that it's a good time to sell.

➤ As your stock approaches—and then hits—your initial target price, reevaluate the company, its performance, and so on, as if you were making the purchase for the *very first time* to determine whether or not you think it's worth it to continue holding. However, while you are doing this, remember to keep your original investment objectives and goals in mind.

➤ Don't sell in a haphazard fashion to cut your losses. Take the time to review company news and see if there has been any bad publicity. Check to see if a number of investors dumped several large blocks of stock. Also investigate the possibility that the stock has been declining for some period of time.

MAXWELL, DRIPS—
YOU'RE IN.

Chapter 21

Getting into the Game with DRIPs

In This Chapter

➤ Beginning with as little as $10

➤ Understanding why dollar cost averaging is important

➤ Using resources available to help meet your goals

When you think of the word "drip," the irritating trickle of water that keeps you awake at night comes to mind, or perhaps the class geek. A drip is really steady droplets of falling water. As they fall, the droplets begin to collect and the water begins to rise.

Now apply this drip theory to investing. If you drop a little bit of money on a steady, consistent basis into an investment program—with little or no commissions—what do you get? A dividend reinvestment plan (DRIP). This chapter tells you how investing in DRIPs can add up to an ocean of net worth.

Got Ten Bucks?

The concept of a DRIP really started back in the 1950s through a program called the "Monthly Investment Plan." This program was sponsored by the member firms (brokerage firms, usually) of the New York Stock Exchange. On a monthly or even quarterly basis, customers in these member firms were allowed to invest a minimum of $40 in the investment plan. Unfortunately, this concept did not catch on—either the brokerage firms were fed up dealing with the paperwork or didn't have enough time to allocate to this program. This plan was the precursor to the first DRIP that was offered by AT&T in the 1960s.

In the past, the strongest emphasis of dividend reinvestment plans was placed on purchasing a few shares of stock at a time instead of receiving a cash dividend. For example, as you learned in Chapter 18, a company can offer a dividend to its shareholders in the form of cash or stock. So instead of receiving a dividend check in the mail for a measly $1.50, you invest that dollar and a half back into the company. A DRIP enables its shareholders to accumulate a growing number of shares of a company's stock without paying high commissions.

Today, DRIPs are offered by more than 1,000 companies and closed-end mutual funds (which you learned about in Chapter 13). DRIPs build wealth slowly through accumulating small shares of the stock or fund and enabling you to bypass a stockbroker and high commissions, because you purchase the shares directly from the company. If the company does charge a fee, it's typically quite nominal. In fact, more than 100 of these companies offer investors the advantage of purchasing company stock at discounts of 3%–10% below the current market price of the stock.

Most DRIPs permit investors to send in an optional cash payment (OCP), which could be as low as $10. This enables you to purchase additional shares. For example, if a company stock was trading around $50 and you send in only $25, you receive a fraction of a share—in this case, half a share. These fractional shares continue to build and you receive that fractional part of the dividend.

Bet You Didn't Know

Here's one way to boost the Christmas season: If you invest in the Wrigley Company's DRIP program, you'll receive a surprise—a container with 20 packs of chewing gum!

Secret
Begin early with a DRIP program. It doesn't require a lot of money to invest and is a great way to meet your long-term investment goals.

Keep in mind that when you send in additional payments, your account isn't usually credited immediately. Many companies invest these payments once a month or every quarter. That's why it's important to time your purchases. If a company makes its investment date on the 25th of each month and you send in your payment on the 1st of each month, your cash sits there for 24 days earning no interest. The company is just holding onto it until the investment date.

Let's look at an example of how a DRIP works. Suppose you are interested in investing in XYZ Company. However, based on your personal finances, you've determined you can only allocate a few dollars per month to purchasing their stock. Based on your research, you find out that the company has a pretty solid background and the stock currently trades at around $42 a share. You can purchase 100 shares at $42 a share or whatever the current market price is and pay $4,200 plus commissions. If you don't have enough money for 100 shares but want to invest because XYZ Company produces a good product, you can participate in their dividend reinvestment program since you found out through your research, by calling the shareholder services department, they offer a DRIP program. If, for example, you wanted to buy one share through a dividend reinvestment plan, you would send in your check for $42 (plus whatever minimal fees there are) to enroll in the DRIP program. Again, the shareholder services department will send you an application complete with instructions.

Going on the Record

Here's where a slight drawback arises. Not all companies that are publicly traded offer DRIPs. With those that do offer them, in most cases, you have to become a shareholder of record to enroll. The next section shows you how to get started.

Step-by-Step Process to Investing in DRIPs

You can accomplish just about anything these days with a step-by-step guide, even in investing. When you're ready to invest in a dividend reinvestment plan, simply follow these guidelines:

> **Secret**
> Some companies now offer DRIP programs especially for children. These companies include Mattel Toy Company, McDonald's, and Wrigley. Starting your children on an investment program in DRIPs is a great way to introduce them to the stock market—and make money!

1. Buy at least one share of stock that is registered in your name. This share of stock *can't* be registered in a brokerage or "street" name. Purchase the share of stock from a deep-discount brokerage firm (see Chapter 5 to find the names of a few of these) to keep your costs to a bare minimum. Don't purchase this single share from a full-service brokerage firm because it'll cost you a bundle.

2. Once you purchase the share, make sure that you tell the broker you want the stock certificate sent directly to you via certified mail. Make sure the spelling of your name is correct and your current address appears on the front of the stock certificate. If your goal is to invest in a DRIP, do not have the stock registered in your name and then held in safekeeping at the firm—that service can run as high as $50 a year. When you receive the certificate, put it in your safe deposit box if you own one. If you don't have a safe deposit box, it's not necessary to go out and rent one. It is more cost-effective to send your certificate to the company who issued the stock for safekeeping. It's typically only five bucks if the company offers this type of service.

Secret

After you set up your DRIP, avoid the hassle of paperwork by setting up the automatic withdrawal feature, if the company provides it. You need the bank account number from which the funds will be transferred and your bank's ABA number, which is the routing number. Next, pick a day when you want to have the funds transferred, which should be no later than five days before the company makes its investment purchase.

3. Notify the company that you are a shareholder of record and that you want a DRIP application and prospectus. Make sure you read the prospectus to determine whether there are any fees or charges, what the minimum and maximum optional cash payments are, and when they make their purchases. Fill out the application and send it in. After you sign up for a DRIP through the company, you don't need a stockbroker to reinvest the dividends.

Some companies don't require you to buy one share through a broker at all. This type of approach is known as a direct-purchase plan. Minimums on these direct-purchase plans start as low as $20. Keep in mind that some companies require you to reside in the state where the company is headquartered.

Whether you have to buy that first share through a broker or not, DRIPs give you a chance to invest in some well-performing stocks with little seed money. The biggest plus is that you are able to buy shares without paying hefty brokerage fees. It's a "do-it-yourself" investment strategy. That's why brokers don't like DRIPs, of course.

Other DRIP Features

Tired of buying your grandchildren toys for Christmas that they quickly toss aside, having become mesmerized by the box the toy came in? Through DRIP programs, some companies make it easy for you to give a stock as a gift. Plus, the stock can appreciate, whereas the toy usually winds up on the "Under $2" table at your next garage sale. All you do is contact investor services at the company and open an account in the recipient's name. The company sends a gift certificate representing the shares to the recipient.

Also check to see if the DRIP you're considering offers electronic funds transfer service. This feature enables you to have automatic withdrawals made from your bank account to your DRIP account on a steady basis. This saves time and paperwork for you.

Bet You Didn't Know

If you invest in McDonald's DRIP program for your child (or even you!), you'll receive a "mock" stock certificate.

Dollar Cost Averaging

Making regular investments of a fixed amount of money on a periodic basis helps you
~~take~~ advantage of dollar cost averaging, one of Wall Street's biggest secrets to long-term
~~success.~~

~~...~~is investment strategy, you avoid making initial pur-
~~...~~y on Wall Street begins with our favorite rule, folks—buy
~~...~~ost averaging, you'll never buy all your investments at the
~~...~~t not all. That's the beauty of this strategy. With the same
~~...~~(or however often you choose to invest), you buy more
~~...~~ the market is low than when prices are high.

~~...~~ you want to invest $200 a month for the next 12 months
~~...~~Currently, the fund is trading at $10 a share, so your initial
~~...~~20 shares. Table 21.1 shows what happens when the market

Cost Averaging Works for You!

	Dollars Invested	Share Price	Shares Purchased	Total Shares to Date
	$200	$10.00	20.00	20.00
	$200	$12.50	16.00	36.00
March	$200	$14.00	14.29	50.29
April	$200	$13.00	15.38	65.67
May	$200	$13.00	15.38	81.05
June	$200	$9.00	22.22	103.27
July	$200	$10.00	20.00	123.27
August	$200	$11.25	17.78	141.05
September	$200	$13.50	14.81	155.86
October	$200	$15.00	13.33	169.19
November	$200	$14.50	13.79	182.98
December	$200	$14.00	14.29	197.27

Total Number of Shares:	$197.27
Total Investment:	$2,400.00
Total Value of Portfolio:	$2,761.78
Net Profit:	**$361.78**

When you invest in a dividend reinvestment program or a direct purchase plan, you are
practicing dollar cost averaging. It can't guarantee you a profit, nor can it protect you

against loss, but it does enable you to buy more shares in a mutual fund or stock as prices are declining and buy fewer shares as prices rise. However, if the financial markets keep dropping, at the end of the 12-month period you'll have a loss. That's why you need to use this strategy over a period of several years. (Mutual funds are the biggest source of dollar cost averaging investing. You saw how it works in Chapter 13.)

Where Can You Sign Up?

We know that investing in stock is not for rich folks only. Even small investors can participate in the stock market through DRIPs. You can start with investing as little as $10 in some of America's best companies and accumulate shares over a period of time using dollar cost averaging.

Secret
Even though it only takes a few bucks to start investing in a DRIP, you still need to do your homework on the company. This isn't a "buy and hold forever" investment. You can do that, but you also need to keep on top of the quality of the company's financial position and its strength in its respective industry. See Chapter 5 to learn how to get information about a company's performance.

The best source that I can recommend to keep up with the latest DRIP information is the monthly publication *DRIP Investor*, (219) 931-6480, which is considered as "Your Guide to Buying Stocks Without a Broker." This newsletter updates you each month on which DRIPs are worth looking into. The publisher, Chuck Carlson, also provides free to new subscribers *The Directory of Dividend Reinvestment Plans*—truly the bible of the DRIP industry. This more than 140-page directory sums up everything you need to know about all DRIPs, including tidbits such as minimum and maximum OCPs, fees and charges (if any), and a special performance rating.

You can also join the Low Cost Investment Plan of the National Association of Investors Corporation, also known as the NAIC (**http://www.better-investing.org**). The NAIC can be reached by mail at NAIC, National Association of Investors Corporation, P.O. Box 220, Royal Oak, MI 48068, Attention: (Dept. Name), or by phone at (248) 583-NAIC.

You join the NAIC and they will provide you with a wide variety of information on how you can invest in DRIPs and what companies provide the feature where you can buy directly through them. The NAIC typically charges you about $5 for each investment.

The Least You Need to Know

➤ Investing in the stock market isn't just a rich man's game. Small investors can buy stock with as little as $10 in a dividend reinvestment program.

➤ By using dollar cost averaging, you'll never make all your purchases at the top of the market, which catches many investors. Instead, you buy more shares when the price rises and when the market price drops.

➤ Contact the *DRIP Investor* newsletter at (219) 931-6480 for a year's subscription to stay on top of the latest news and developments in the DRIP industry. Another program to look into is the Low Cost Investment Plan of the National Association of Investors Corporation (NAIC).

Chapter 22

Understanding the Risks Involved with Trading Stocks

Trading stocks or bonds has its inherent risks. Volatility (rapid change) in the stock market can take even the strongest-stomached investors for a wild ride. The possibility of not being able to reinvest your money at the same rate of return is apparent in a down market. Plus, there's always the possibility that you won't have access to your money as quickly as you need it.

One example of what I consider to be risky is making your investment decisions based on what other people are saying or doing. While it's true that words of wisdom come from elders and those who are more experienced, one of the best ways you'll learn about investing is by making your own mistakes. Obviously, you want to avoid making as many mistakes as possible, and this chapter gives you some solid advice, rather than old maxims, that can help you become a successful investor.

Don't Follow John Q. Public

There really isn't a John Q. Public for those of you who want to know. The entire population of America can be considered John Q. Public. All those people with two-point-five kids, a dog, a white picket fence, a station wagon, and a house in the suburbs make up John Q. Public (as do those carrying bus passes who have a cat but no children or a fence…you see where I'm going with this).

You should only invest in a security when you have done all your homework—not when the John Q. down the street says the market is ready to rally.

Here are some tips to keep in mind:

1. You can listen to your friend's stock tips, but don't blindly invest in the stock without doing your own research. This includes getting a company's annual report, its prospectus (if it's a new offering), and research reports, such as *Value Line,* or researching on the Internet at various financial sites. You need to make sure your friend's advice is credible.

2. Many times, investors get their stock recommendations from "financial experts" who promote their most recent stock strategy on popular financial television programs. While this information may be coming from a professional, such as a portfolio manager or notable stock trader, wait before you contact your broker. You need to do your own research here, too.

3. Pay attention to any special information that's reported in the media. This information includes but is not limited to the following:

   ➤ Company layoffs, hiring freezes, or even hiring booms.

   ➤ New products or services coming out into the market.

   ➤ Any existing products or services being recalled or taken off of the shelves.

   ➤ Whether a company did not report profits this year even though it usually does have a profit.

   ➤ Whether a company reported its first-time profit.

What?
Investors who buy stocks that are out of favor and nobody else wants are called *contrarians.* There are several mutual funds that invest using contrarian methods, too, such as Crabbe Huson (**http://www.contrarian.com**), Kemper-Dreman High Return Fund, and Robertson Stephens Contrarian Fund.

Listening to the recommendations of the media—whose members consider themselves the experts about what John Q. Public is doing or should be doing—doesn't always work when it comes to investing. In fact, you can achieve investment success by not following the crowd. Instead, you should do your homework and challenge the masses!

What happens when you invest in a way that's contrary to what everybody else is doing? You may come out ahead. Suppose you're investigating a stock as a potential investment. You've been following the stock price for awhile, hoping to pick up on a potential profit opportunity. Only a few people are investing in the stock, and you haven't heard any solicitations from any brokers about the company. After you do your homework to make sure this is a good quality stock, you may discuss this with your financial adviser or just buy it on your own. Not many investors are demanding shares for this stock, so the price is low.

As luck might (hypothetically) have it, the company announces pretty favorable news and the stock price takes off. Investors are now clamoring to buy the stock on their brokers' recommendations. This increase in demand may push the price up. Other investors are buying this stock at much higher prices than what you paid for it. You can now sell it and make a tidy little profit.

While the above sounds like an impossible dream, it isn't. True, there'll be times during your investing lifetime when all of your investments won't act favorably. But, as you become an educated investor, you can save money on commissions by doing it yourself, interact with your financial adviser, and still make intelligent investment decisions on your own without following the crowd.

Ignore the Fads

Investing in fad stocks is another way you can be misled by John Q. Public. A fad stock is nothing more than a relatively short-term, popular stock. Think of a fad stock this way: How long did bell-bottoms last? (I don't care what the fashion world says.)

Investors jump on the bandwagon and buy up whatever stock is hot right now. It could be a technology stock, a manufacturing stock, or some type of automobile stock. The price moves up so fast, word gets out on the street, and the price moves up more. Investors pour money into this stock even as the price rises, but in this case, the overinflated stock price is not a true measure of the company's worth.

Secret
Make sure you understand the difference between a fad stock and a company that produces fad products. A company that makes fad products, such as popular diet drinks and clothing, could be a potential investment worth researching.

Don't buy a fad stock just because it is in the public limelight. Remember, the secret to making money on Wall Street is buying low and selling high. Investing in a fad stock will only be profitable if you catch it before it became a fad.

Get Rich Quick—And Pay for It!

Individuals in the financial services industry exist to perform several functions: assist customers with their trades, provide investment advice, and charge their customers large fees for doing the previous two functions. What they shouldn't be doing is making *all* your financial decisions for you, or pressuring you to do something you wouldn't otherwise do. Financial advisers are available to you to help you create your financial goals, work with you along the way to modify those goals (as needed) and meet those goals.

The majority of brokers and financial consultants are honest, but I want you to be aware that investment scam artists do exist—and, boy, are they unethical. Many times when consumers talk with their brokers, the consumer gets so wrapped up in dreams of making money that he or she will forget to ask specific questions about the investment. The greed factor usually comes into play as thoughts of a financial windfall sandblast your brain.

One of the biggest investment scam artists in the Twentieth Century—possibly of all time—was Charles Ponzi, an infamous investment swindler who in the early 1900s formulated the "get rich quick" scheme. He preyed upon everyday people just like you and me, promising to pay 50% interest if the victim would lend him money for a month and a half.

Well, Ponzi took in millions—almost $10 million, to be exact. He paid back his original investors with new investors' money. Time (and the arm of the law) caught up with him, though. He couldn't pay back all of the money, and millions of dollars were lost by the gullible public. Arrivederci, Ponzi.

Bet You Didn't Know

Unfortunately, various types of Ponzi schemes continue to prosper even today. There is always a sad story to tell of an elderly couple who was hoodwinked into believing that sharply dressed, Ponzi-copycat swindlers were telling the truth about making a fortune. Sadly, the couple invested their life savings and poof! It was gone.

One way to learn how to buy the right stocks is to determine which investments you should avoid. Beware if any of the following occurs:

➤ **Don't believe that you'll make a fortune overnight from someone claiming that you can...especially if it's over the telephone.** Making a good fortune takes time and patience. To protect yourself and your money, ask the solicitor for written information. If you receive some type of information and it appears to be fishy, either contact the National Association of Securities Dealers (NASD), 9513 Key West Avenue, Rockville, MD 20850, toll-free (800) 289-9999; relay the information to the Securities and Exchange Commission (SEC) at (202) 272-7460; or line your bird cage with it.

➤ **Be wary of brokers you don't know who promise sky-high investment returns.** If you are consistently receiving high-pressure sales calls from a broker you don't even know, you may want to check out his or her prior working history at the NASD. If the broker is from a commodity or futures brokerage firm, contact the National Futures Association, 200 West Madison Street, Suite 1600, Chicago, IL 60606, toll-free (800) 676-4632.

➤ **Don't buy any type of investment from someone who says it's inside information.** Even if this person is promising his hot stock tip will double your money, trading stocks based on inside information is illegal. And the regulators will do something about it. (There are a number of high profile people sitting in jail because greed got the best of them.)

➤ **Ask where the stock is traded.** Familiarize yourself with the different types of financial exchanges (see Chapter 18). If the broker says it trades on the NYSE or AMEX, ask him to send you some information to support the claim. If he says he doesn't know or it's getting ready to trade on a specific exchange, BEWARE! Better yet, hang up the phone!

On a final note, I would like to share with you one phrase that stuck in my head from my consumer economics class in high school: If it sounds too good to be true, it probably is.

The Least You Need to Know

➤ If you follow what everyone else is doing in the investing arena, you may pay a higher price for an investment than if you were to buy based on your own research.

➤ One of the most famous investment scams—the Ponzi get-rich-quick scheme—is still thriving today. Be wary of any broker who uses high-pressure sales tactics to get you to invest your money. If the broker continues to bug you, contact the NASD or the SEC.

➤ If it sounds too good to be true, it probably is.

Chapter 23

Researching Your Way to Your Investment Goals

In This Chapter

➤ Subscribing to the many investment newsletters

➤ Helping you with your investment planning

➤ Getting access to these newsletters

Ask anybody for advice about investing in stocks, bonds, mutual funds, or any type of investment. Many individuals know of someone who has a story to tell of how his stockbroker made him a fortune. Brag, brag, brag. For every story like this, you can count on a hundred stories of how bad investment advice wiped somebody out.

Asking for advice is okay, but you can't believe everything you hear. Reading about investment advice is even better, but don't believe everything you read, either. This chapter will explain how to find additional resources for reliable stock investment information, but is not the panacea to replace an investment professional.

Read All About It!

There are a little more than 100 newsletters that give stock advice. And that's just about stocks! Most of these investment newsletters reflect the personality of the writer. If the writer is having a good day, well then she might be bullish on specific investments. But if

Secret

Don't buy an investment newsletter until you see a sample copy, especially if the subscription price is several hundred dollars. Instead, ask for a trial subscription to check out the style, writing, and advice found in the newsletter. The Select Information Exchange, (212) 247-7123, gives you a list of more than 50 different financial newsletters. They offer a package of 20 trial subscriptions for only $11.95. Happy reading.

the writer got up on the wrong side of the bed, well, gloom and doom might be the day's motto. That might sound a little farfetched, but most investment newsletters cover the interests of the author.

Subscribing to a financial newsletter is one way to get investment advice. A multitude of different types of newsletters exist, and each covers just about every different type of investment strategy available. Some letters use technical analysis and are chock full of charts and graphs—it's up to you to decipher them! Other letters use fundamental analysis and discuss the value of a company and the potential for earnings growth. Still others provide information about initial public offerings, hostile takeovers, inside company scoops, foreign information, and our current economic situation and how it impacts investments. You name it, it's probably being published in a newsletter somewhere.

Is any of this advice rewarding? Some newsletters give solid advice and justify their positions. These newsletters can be a real plus in picking out the right investments. Many others do not give good advice and often mislead subscribers.

It's a shame because many of these financial newsletters are costly and could range in price from $29.95 up to $450 a year. To make matters worse, sometimes the subscription department refuses to send out sample copies unless you have a paid subscription. But it doesn't cost anything to ask!

Secret

For those of you who like to stay connected, consider several of the online or Internet research tools that can help you with your stock and other investment selection. Some top-notch sites include The Motley Fool (**http://www.fool.com**), Standard & Poors, Morningstar (**http://www.morningstar. net**), and Hoovers (**http://www. hoovers.com**), for example.

A word of caution. These financial newsletters don't have to be registered with the Securities and Exchange Commission (SEC), which is the legal arm of the securities industry.

How to Tell the Good from the Bad and the Ugly

I found the best and most respected service that tracks nearly all newsletter recommendations and rates their performance is *The Hulbert Financial Digest*. This is the newsletter of newsletters. They offer a five-issue trial subscription where you can have access to the ratings of the top 130 newsletters over a period of several years. The manner in which *The Hulbert Financial Digest* rates the newsletters it covers is based on three time periods: eleven years, five years, and from January 1987 to the most recent quarter (first, second, third, or fourth).

To receive a monthly five-issue trial subscription or even their annual subscription, which is $135 per year, call (703) 683-5905 or write to 316 Commerce Street, Alexandria, VA 22314. If you're still a little unsure about subscribing, you can get just a list of the newsletters that *Hulbert* reviews. The cost is only $20.

Bet You Didn't Know

There are more financial newsletters that cover the stock market and investing in stocks than any other investment product.

And Now for Some News About Other Investments

What about bonds, mutual funds, futures, and options? There are plenty of newsletters about all of these! Many of these newsletters just give factual information and data; others report opinions about the current events in the market. The following lists are suggested newsletters, however this list does not comprise the entire financial newsletter universe. Use the following information as guidelines.

Tracking Bonds

The newsletters that track the bond market tend to be even more expensive than those newsletters that cover stocks. Plus, they're quite complex. After reading the section about investing in bonds in this book, your best bet would be to contact several trade associations for additional information about the bond market.

The only non-profit trade association, the Bond Investors Association, offers subscriptions to three different newsletters: *High-Yield Securities Journal*, which covers the junk bond market and preferred stocks; *Bond Investors Newsletter*, the association's general newsletter covering the entire bond market; and *Defaulted Bonds Newsletter*, which uncovers any corporate or municipal bonds that have defaulted. This last publication is mainly geared toward institutional clients and really isn't for the individual investor.

The first two newsletters published by the Bond Investors Association are some of the most cost-effective newsletters for individual investors. They offer sample copies before you subscribe. Contact the editor at (800) 472-2680 or write to P.O. Box 4427, 6175 N.W. 153rd Street, Suite 229, Miami Lakes, FL 33014. A one-year subscription to the *High-Yield Securities Journal* is $125 and gives you 12 issues (a three-month trial subscription is only $45). If you would like to receive the *Bond Investors Newsletter*, it costs $85 a year for 12 issues. No trial subscription is available.

If you want a newsletter that thoroughly covers municipal bonds, the *Public Investor* newsletter tracks the developments in this market and is aimed solely at public investors. This publication is distributed to both members and non-members through the Government Finance Offers Association in Chicago. Call (312) 977-9700 for a one-year subscription (12 issues at $85 for non-members, $70 for members) or write to 180 N. Michigan Avenue, Suite 800, Chicago, IL 60601.

Mutual Attraction

Mutual funds also deserve a big nod, because there are so many different ways to choose a mutual fund. There are more than 3,200 mutual funds that exist today, making up about a $6 trillion market. How can you sift through all of them and tell the best from the rest?

One way to pick a mutual fund is through a mutual fund rating service. For those of you who want to subscribe to a mutual fund investment newsletter, you have several to choose from. Most are published on a monthly basis, analyze funds based on their objective (growth, income, or both), and then give a thumbs up or thumbs down on the fund. Two of my favorite mutual fund investment newsletters are *Sheldon Jacobs' No-Load Fund Investor* and Don Phillips' *Morningstar 5-Star Investor*.

Jacobs' mutual fund newsletter covers 793 no-load and low-load funds—more than any other newsletter. It provides fund news and tables listing mutual funds' performance on a one-month, four-month, five-month, one-year, two-year, three-year and five-year annualized basis. A few articles always catch a subscriber's eye, but the gist of the publication is the performance tables. The No-Load Fund Investor is published monthly. Subscription price? $109 for 12 monthly issues, and for $20 more you also receive *The Handbook of No-Load Funds*, which is published annually. It's about as big as the Chicago Yellow Pages telephone book. Call (914) 693-7420 or write to P.O Box 318, Irvington-on-Hudson, NY 10533.

Careful

Please, please, please, keep in mind that I'm not telling you to go and sink all of your money into a subscription service. None of these letters are registered—nor do they have to be—with the SEC. Rather, consider these newsletters recommended reading to further enhance your knowledge about the financial markets.

You can also subscribe to Don Phillips' newsletter *Morningstar 5-Star Investor* for its informative list of 500 chosen funds in various categories. This newsletter is a must for all mutual fund investors. Even if you aren't a mutual fund investor, the information found in this newsletter is invaluable and extremely user-friendly. The five-star rating is the highest rating Morningstar gives to those mutual funds that meet certain criteria based on different categories.

Phillips' investment newsletter is also the most economical: $65 for a one-year subscription, with free samples upon request. Call toll-free (800) 876-5005 anywhere in the U.S.; write to Morningstar, 225 W. Wacker Drive, Chicago, IL 60606; or log onto their website at **http://www.morningstar.net** for further information.

Predicting the Options and Futures

Let's not forget the speculative crowd out there who wants to read up on those risky investments—options and futures. Because these financial markets change so rapidly, publishing a newsletter about them would be silly. Timeliness is of the essence. By the time you received an options newsletter or a futures newsletter, the markets could have changed so drastically that any investment advice would be out of date.

If you'd still like to read up on these investments, a few publications exist to whet your appetite. The Futures Industry Association publishes a complimentary magazine called *The Futures Industry*. All you have to do is send in your request to FIA, 2001 Pennsylvania Avenue, NW, Suite 600, Washington, D.C. 20006. If you have any questions about the magazine, contact the editorial department at (202) 466-5460 for further details.

One of the better reports I have found is *Managed Account Reports*, which tracks the performance of commodity pools and funds. This publication follows commodities that are "pooled" together in one big basket and managed by a professional. This report is available for $265 a year. Call (212) 213-6202 or write to 220 5th Avenue, 19th Floor, New York, NY 10001 for a sample copy.

No Newsprint, Only You and Your Keyboard

As you know, investment newsletters can assist you in market analysis as well as point you toward specific securities and emerging industry groups. Websites such as the Wall Street Journal (**http://www.wsj.com**) charge a fee to subscribers. On the other hand, sites such as Money magazine (**http://www.pathfinder.com**) and Business Week (**http://www.businessweek.com**) are free to visitors.

Hundreds of financial advisors publish their own investment newsletter online, but usually the available material is substantially edited, often little more than extended headlines or mere teaser ads with no content. In fact, based on my research, a lot of newsletters are outdated (several haven't been updated for three months or more), obviously not something you want to spend too much time on in today's rapidly changing market. But, many do offer free trial subscriptions to the real thing so you won't waste too much time or money.

Tip: Keep your expectations to a minimum for now and hopefully in the near future you'll find more quality newsletter information on the Internet.

The Least You Need to Know

➤ Investment newsletters are to be used as a guide to learn more about the financial markets. Don't treat them as the cure-all to your investment plan.

➤ None of the investment newsletters are registered with the Securities and Exchange Commission. They don't have to be. Keep this in mind before you place a trade from a recommendation in a newsletter. Do other research to confirm that the investment's a good idea.

➤ Contact one of the following two newsletters that track the performance of most of the financial newsletters that exist. These are considered the "newsletters of newsletters": *The Hulbert Financial Digest* at (703) 683-5905 or *Timer Digest* at (800) 356-2527.

Part 5
Looking for Income?
Consider Bond Investing

A bond, no matter what type, is an IOU. A junk bond? An IOU. Municipal bonds? Still IOUs. Corporate bonds? Again, bonds are IOUs from the issuer, promising two things—to pay a set rate of interest and repay your original investment at a later date.

Making money on bonds used to be the most simple, safe investment around—invest your money in a bond at a fixed rate of return, wait a spell, and boom, there's your income.

But the bond world has changed over the past several decades. The rise and fall of interest rates has caused both glory days and mayhem for bond investors. New and different types of bonds flourished in the markets during the early 1980s. It's trickier now, but you can still make a tidy sum in the bond market, as this part of the book explains. So gear up and let's go!

Chapter 24

Getting a Grip on the Bond Market

In This Chapter

➤ Understanding what a bond is

➤ Knowing the risks involved in investing in bonds

➤ Applying a financial strategy for conservative investors

A *bond* is basically an IOU. Taking this one step further, a bond is a debt instrument that is issued by corporations, the U.S. Government, foreign governments, and cities and states. Think of it this way. An issuer of a bond, like the U.S. Government, is a borrower of monies. You, the investor, are a purchaser and a lender of monies.

These debt instruments pay you interest in exchange for your "loan." In this chapter, you will learn about the ins and outs of bond investing, how following the direction of interest rates plays a role in your bond portfolio, and what type of fixed-income strategy works best for you.

How Much Do We Owe?

The United States bond market is the largest bond market in the world. In fact, if you were to break it down just by corporate bonds and municipal bonds alone, the new issue volume size of all corporate bonds in 1996 was almost $400 billion.

In the bond market, buyers and sellers figuratively meet to agree upon a price to buy or sell bond securities. Bonds are not typically traded on a financial exchange with the exception of a few corporate bonds. Those are traded at the American Stock Exchange. But they're not stocks, so what's the difference?

In Chapter 18, you learned stock represents *ownership* in a company. If you bought 100 shares of XYZ Toy Company and there were 100,000 shares outstanding, you own 1/100 of the company. Bonds do not work this way. As a bond investor, you are *lending* your money to the corporation or government. This "loan" requires the bond issuer (the corporation or government borrowing your money) to pay you the amount borrowed plus interest over a period of time. Therefore, you are a lender, not an owner.

Traditionally, a bond issued in the United States specifies the following things:

➤ A fixed date when the amount borrowed must be paid back. This date is the *maturity date*. Although there is a stated maturity date, this doesn't mean that you have to hold the bond until it has matured. You can sell it at any time prior to its maturity date.

➤ A coupon rate. Most bonds also pay you interest. The amount of interest that is paid reflects the coupon rate that is stated on the bond. The coupon rate can be either a fixed rate that pays you the same amount of interest every year, or a floating rate where the amount of interest is adjusted periodically based on some pre-determined index.

➤ The *face value*, also known as the *par value*, is the amount of the original investment, or principal. This amount is equal to the amount that you agreed to lend to the borrower.

Here's what a typical bond trade would look and "sound" like: "I bought $1,000 worth of an 8% bond due on September 18, 1997." This means that you invested in a bond with a $1,000 face value, an 8% coupon rate, and a maturity date of September 18, 1997.

The Continuing Saga of Bond Prices and Interest Rates

The following principle is the cardinal rule to know if you want to understand bond investing:

As interest rates go up, bond prices go down.

And when interest rates go down, bond prices go up. This is why it is said that interest rates have an inverse relationship with the bond prices. Just remember that they move in opposite directions of each other. Repeat to yourself: If interest rates rise, bond prices go down.

Suppose you own thousands of dollars' worth of government bonds that were issued in the early 1980s with coupon rates between 12% and 15%. These bonds are still earning that interest even today, and you can't earn that kind of interest on government securities now.

So what do you think investors are willing to pay you for your 12%—15% coupon bonds? Because today people are only able to buy government bonds at an average 7.12%, for example, some investors are more than willing to pay you a higher price for your high coupon bond. This is where the inverse relationship between interest rates and bond prices begins. The investor is willing to sacrifice dollars now to buy the bond because he will get it all back when he cashes in on the higher annual coupon payments generated from your securities. Therefore, because interest rates are constantly changing, the value of outstanding fixed-income securities (bonds) fluctuates as well.

Interest rates are represented in *basis points*. For every basis point that the interest rate goes up or down, the discount rate goes up or down 1/100 of a percent. So if you hear someone shout "Oh, the Fed raised the discount rate by 150 basis points!", you will know the Federal Reserve raised the discount rate by 1.5%.

What?
The *principal/face value* is the amount of money the bond issuer agrees to repay to you on the date of maturity. This will vary depending on the type of bond that you are buying. The *maturity date* is when the issuer of the bond must repay the principal back to the bondholder plus the final interest payment. Sometimes, the phrases "the bond is due" or "is coming due" are used interchangeably with the date of maturity.

What?
Basis point. This is the smallest measure used in quoting yields on all bonds and notes. 100 basis points = 1%. 10 basis points = .1%. 1 basis point = .01%.

Crash Course in Current Yields

Do not confuse the *coupon rate* with the *current yield*. Remember, the coupon rate is the stated rate on the bond and does not change. The current yield is the coupon rate divided by the market price of the bond. Because the market price of the bond fluctuates throughout the day, the current yield is constantly changing.

For example, let's say you bought a bond with a 10% coupon rate at a price of 90. The price of 90 means that you have paid 90 percent of the face value of the bond. Because the bond has a face value of $1,000, the total market value is equal to $900 ($1,000 × .90 = $900). The annual interest paid on this bond is equal to the coupon rate multiplied by the face value. In this case, it would equal $100.

The current yield at the time you bought this bond was 11%. You can determine the current yield of the bond by dividing the annual interest payment by the dollar price you paid for the bond (or the current market value if the price has changed), and then multiplying the result by 100 to get a percentage, as the following figure illustrates.

How to determine the current yield of a bond.

$$\left(\frac{\text{Annual Interest Payment of the Bond}}{\text{Total Market Value of the Bond}} \right) \times 100 = \text{Current Yield}$$

$$\left(\frac{\$100}{\$900} \right) \times 100 = 11.11\%$$

Earlier you learned that every bond has a maturity date, and you may wonder what it has to do with how much interest you will earn over the life of a bond. This is easy. You receive an interest payment at least annually, if not semi-annually, every year until the bond matures. Therefore, if you have a bond that matures in ten years, you will receive interest payments for the next ten years. These interest payments are only a portion of the total return on a bond.

The *yield to maturity* is a measure of the total return that you can expect to earn if you hold the bond till maturity. Sometimes known as YTM, this amount takes into account the coupon rate, the bond's current market price, and the years left until the bond matures. It is a pretty difficult calculation, but your broker should be able to tell you what it is. Just know that the result represents the estimated return you can expect to receive if you hold the bond until maturity.

Buy Bonds at Your Own Risk

If you follow the direction of interest rates, you can determine the price movements in the overall bond market. Before you invest, you need to understand that price swings can mean significant profits or terrible losses to bond buyers.

Typically, the longer the length of maturity of the bond, the higher the rate you will earn. If you are lending your money to the U.S. Government or a corporation for a longer period of time, you'll want a higher rate for doing so, right?

In exchange for lending your money out for a longer period of time, you should expect to receive a higher rate—but you also incur more risk, which includes price risk. Keep the following risks in mind when you are investing in any bond, and make sure your broker supplies you with enough information about a bond to comfortably evaluate these risk factors:

➤ Ask yourself if the borrower—such as a city government, state government, corporation, or even the U.S. Government—will be able to pay back the amount borrowed from you plus the interest promised at regular, semi-annual intervals. This is known as credit risk. Answering this question will require you to understand the concept of how bonds are rated. Just as you used to get grades on tests in school, they get a grade from such rating agencies as Standard & Poor's, Moody's, and Fitch Investor Service. (More about this later in the chapter.)

➤ Inflation will creep up and the money you get back in the long run will be intrinsically worth less. The risk involved here is known as *purchasing power risk*, which we discussed in Chapter 4. As you follow the economy and the business cycle, pay attention to any inflationary trends that might push interest rates above the coupon rate of the bonds you own. You may want to sell your bond before interest rates exceed the coupon rate, because you don't want your money locked up in an investment that cannot even keep up with the pace of inflation. However, you have to make the decision to sell quickly. Why? Because as inflation rises, the purchasing power of the interest payments you receive gets smaller and smaller. In addition, rising inflation leads to higher interest rates, which will cause bond prices to fall.

> **Secret**
> Among bonds that have the same coupon rate, those with a longer maturity have greater price sensitivity. This means that their prices will fluctuate more for a given change in interest rates. Among bonds with the same maturity date, those with the lower coupon rate have a greater price sensitivity. Knowing this should help you better anticipate how much the value of the bonds you own will change in response to fluctuations in interest rates.

➤ As with any type of investing, there is always reinvestment risk. When your bond matures or if you decide to sell it before maturity (hopefully for a profit), you don't know what the investment climate will be at that time. You can't count on it being the same as when you bought the bond, especially if you bought a longer term bond. If you sell the bond before maturity and interest rates are lower than when you bought it, you are forced to accept a lower yield on a new investment. This scenario is known as *reinvestment risk*.

➤ If interest rates drop after you buy your bond, and you decide to sell it before maturity, you will get a higher price than what you paid. However, you can't always count on the interest rates dropping. If you need to sell your bond and interest rates are higher than when you purchased it, you're going to have to accept a lower price than what you paid. This is known as *interest-rate risk*.

Rate That Risk

Bond securities do receive grades, just as schoolchildren do after taking a math test. In fact, before buying any bond, you should find out its investment grade, or *rating*. Companies like Moody's, Standard & Poor's, and Fitch's Investor Service grade most bond securities. Each of these services uses a different rating scale, taking into account different risk factors.

Here's an example of what a rating scale might look like.

Moody's	Standard & Poor's	What Does It Mean?
Aaa	AAA	Highest quality
Aa	AA	High grade
A–1	A+	High medium grade
A	A	High medium grade
Baa–1	BBB+	Medium grade
Baa	BBB	Medium grade
Ba	BB	Speculative grade
B	B	Not desirable
Caa	CCC	Very low standing

Secret

If you buy a bond that is rated "not desirable," you will receive a higher yield; however, there is a lot more credit risk involved than if you were to invest in a high-grade bond. This is part of the risk-reward scenario in investing.

Bonds with lower investment grade ratings will usually offer higher coupon rates than bonds with higher ratings. If the coupon rate were the same no matter what the rating, who would buy the lower rated (riskier) bond? In exchange for loaning your money when there's a higher investment grade risk, you receive a higher interest rate. This is where trading risk for reward comes into play.

It's also important to note that even when the ratings for bonds are equal, interest rates for short-term bonds (that is, bonds with closer maturity rates) are typically lower than interest rates on long-term bonds (bonds that mature further in the future). For example, if you invest in short-term Treasury bills (which have maturities of one year or less), you will receive a lower rate of interest than if you parked your money into a long-term government bond with the same credit rating.

Secret

For the most part, the only thing you need to understand about the yield curve is that it is typically positive, which is upward sloping. It is typically positive because investors who are willing to tie up their money for longer periods of time are usually compensated for the extra risk with higher yields.

Never buy an unrated bond. If the issuer does not apply for and receive ratings on its bonds, the bonds will be harder to resell to any investor—institutional or regular Joe. Don't take a chance on a bond that hasn't been rated.

The Basics of the Yield Curve

The following figure represents a normal yield curve. This graph represents the fluctuations in interest rates that occur over time and affect bonds of the same quality with varying lengths of maturity.

The result looks like a curve, which is exactly what it is, a yield curve. The vertical axis shows the yield, and the horizontal axis shows the term. The curve tells you if short-term interest rates are higher or lower than long-term rates.

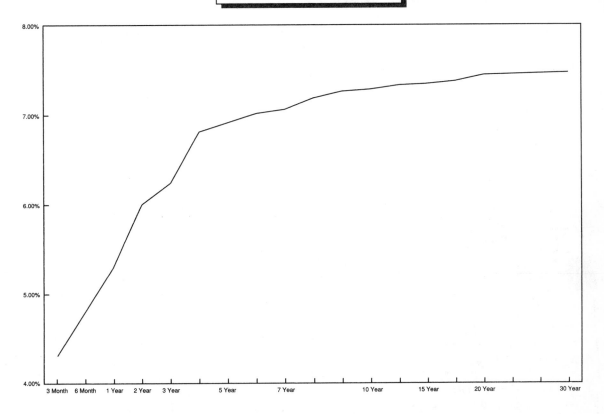

➤ If short-term rates are lower than long-term rates, the yield curve is a *positive yield curve* or normal yield curve.

➤ If short-term rates are higher than long-term rates, the yield curve is a *negative yield curve* or an inverted yield curve.

➤ If there is little difference between the two, the yield curve is *flat*.

Think of it this way. If I borrow money from you for ten years instead of one, you are going to charge me more interest for borrowing it for a longer period of time because you don't have any use of your money at all during those ten years.

So why study the yield curve? It isn't that difficult. You can even plot the points on the graph and make your own curve. If you understand how easily the yield curve works, you can make your own judgments about the direction of both long-term and short-term interest rates based on the shape of the yield curve. This can assist you in making a decision about when to buy and sell bonds.

An upward-sloping yield curve implies that interest rates are expected to rise in the future. Because of the inverse relationship between bond prices and interest rates, you would expect bond prices to fall. On the other hand, a downward-sloping yield curve indicates that interest rates are expected to fall. Therefore, bond prices will rise.

What If Interest Rates Flip-Flop?

If, after a bond is issued, interest rates should rise or fall, the market value of the bond drops or rises. Here's what happens next.

➤ **If interest rates rise and I'm a saver.** You don't have to worry about keeping a portion of your money in savings, a money market deposit account, or even a certificate of deposit because rates are going up. That means you'll earn more money on your money.

➤ **If interest rates rise and I'm a borrower.** Don't panic. Shop for the best rates around, whether you are borrowing the money for a new car, new house, or new whatever! But don't take too much time doing so if rates keep going up.

➤ **If interest rates rise and I'm an investor.** You may want to look into short-term investments with maturities of two years or fewer (a short term Treasury-bill, for example). Not only do you not have to tie up your money for a long period of time, but the interest income you receive is free from state and local taxes. (Hopefully you'll invest the proceeds again and not buy a new set of golf clubs.) Longer term investments, such as a 30-year bond, might not be a wise move if rates are going to keep rising. Why? Because you could lose out on earning a higher interest rate, thus foregoing a larger amount of semi-annual interest payments.

Secret
If you are looking into buying a house, you may want to check out a fixed-rate mortgage instead of an adjustable-rate-mortgage. The rate you receive on your mortgage is fixed and cannot change. However, the adjustable-rate mortgage, although a few percentage points lower than a fixed rate, will rise as long as rates keep going up! up! up! It all really depends on how long you plan on living in the house. To best determine your personal finance needs in homebuying, consider both books *The Complete Idiot's Guide to Buying and Selling a Home* and *The Complete Idiot's Guide to Managing Your Money* to help you with your home-buying and mortgage process.

As an example, let's say I issue a 20-year, 9% corporate bond, and you want to buy one (interest payments would be $90 a year on a $1,000 bond). That means that you are buying a bond, issued by a corporation that will mature 20 years from now. Over the next 20 years, the bond will pay you 9% in interest every year.

Let's say the bond in our example is for $1,000, and five years down the road you can't wait till maturity and want to sell—but there are still 15 years to go. The bonds that have a maturity of 15 years (you have to compare apples to apples) offer a better yield: 11%

because interest rates have gone up. If you try to sell your 9% corporate bond for its full face value, you will have a hard time doing so. After all, who would want to buy a 15-year bond yielding 9% a year (that's $90 a year in interest income) when you could buy a 15-year bond yielding 11% (that's $110 a year in interest income). You might have to sell your bond for less than its face value.

➤ **If interest rates fall and I'm a saver.** You'll want to find the best-paying money market deposit accounts around to keep a portion of your cash liquid (not really liquid, like Kool-Aid, but "available").

➤ **If interest rates fall and I'm a borrower.** When mortgage rates fall, you'll play the "should I/shouldn't I" game of wondering if rates have hit their lowest point before you borrow money to build a new house, to refinance a house, or to buy a new car.

➤ **If interest rates fall and I'm an investor.** If you invest in the stock market—through stocks, DRIPs, or stock mutual funds—you'll probably be in for a good upwardly mobile ride. Typically when interest rates fall, the stock market reacts favorably. Bond prices rise, too. Before you figure out your strategy with your bond investing, you need to consider a few important factors.

If you are a current bondholder, you need to determine why you are holding the bond. For example, are you holding it for reasons of *capital appreciation* (meaning you are buying the bond at a low price and a high yield and selling it at a high price and low yield to make a profit)? Are you holding it for *income* (meaning that, as a bond investor, you are more interested in getting as much of an interest payment—yield—as you can with a specific level of risk? As long as you identify which type of bond investor you are, you will know what to do in a changing economic environment.

Using our previous example, if after five years you want to sell your bond and interest rates are falling, prices on bonds would be going up. Therefore, you can sell your bond that yields $90 a year in interest income at a higher price because the current market rates are much lower.

The Ladder to Succesful Bond Investing

Chutes 'N' Ladders is an all-time favorite for American children. You roll the dice and move the corresponding number of spaces. If you plan your strategy (and with a little luck), you'll move up the ladder. The faster you move up the ladder, the closer you come to winning the game. But there's a little more risk involved at the top of the board. The possibility of landing on a chute increases, and if you land on a chute, you sail back down and have to start all over again.

Structuring a ladder (no chutes, though) to accommodate your bond portfolio is a worthwhile strategy for some folks. Unlike the game, a bond ladder involves more time and patience, but the rewards are much greater!

A bond ladder is not an actual physical device, but a strategy of investing your money in bonds. When you create a ladder, you invest in bonds with maturity dates scheduled consecutively over a number of years. A laddered portfolio includes a range of securities with varying maturities.

Here's how it works. If you want to invest $100,000 of your investment portfolio in bonds, you could choose to divide the money into a number of parts rather than sink all $100,000 into just one bond. Let's say it's January 3, 1998, and you are strategically planning out your bond portfolio. You decide the best strategy is to ladder your bond portfolio with Treasury securities.

You may want to divide up your money into ten parts of $10,000 each. You would buy U.S. Treasury securities (usually Treasury notes) that mature year after year starting in 1999. Therefore, the longest maturity date would be the year 2008. After you construct your laddered portfolio, the idea is to hold on to the bond securities until maturity. As the bonds mature, you would reinvest the proceeds at the end of your ladder. For example, in 1999, when your first bond matures, you would reinvest the proceeds in a bond that has a maturity date of 2009.

Your laddered portfolio would look like the following.

Bond	Amount	Investment	At Maturity
Bond 1	$10,000	Invest in 1-yr. Treasury bill @ 5.67 yield	Matures next year
Bond 2	$10,000	Invest in 2-yr. Treasury note @ 6.22 yield	Matures in 1999
Bond 3	$10,000	Invest in 3-yr. Treasury note @ 6.57 yield	Matures in 2000
Bond 4	$10,000	Invest in 4-yr. Treasury note @ 6.76 yield	Matures in 2001
Bond 5	$10,000	Invest in 5-yr. Treasury note @ 6.94 yield	Matures in 2002
Bond 6	$10,000	Invest in 6-yr. Treasury note @ 7.02 yield	Matures in 2003
Bond 7	$10,000	Invest in 7-yr. Treasury note @ 7.08 yield	Matures in 2003
Bond 8	$10,000	Invest in 8-yr. Treasury note @ 7.20 yield	Matures in 2005
Bond 9	$10,000	Invest in 9-yr. Treasury note @ 7.26 yield	Matures in 2006
Bond 10	$10,000	Invest in 10-yr. Treasury bond @ 7.29 yield	Matures in 2007

A bond ladder is a financial-planning tool that defines a simple way to increase yields without taking on much more risk. You increase your yields because, by extending maturities, you take advantage of the higher rates paid on longer-term bonds. There's your answer to the $64,000 question.

Plus, if rates move even higher, you will always have a bond security coming due (maturing) that year to take advantage of any other higher-yielding investment. Remember, though, this investment strategy only works if you hold these bonds until maturity. If you follow through with this system, you will always be able to take advantage of the most recent interest rates with the monies that are maturing. Even if rates are going lower, keep in mind that you don't have to worry about having all of your money locked into a lower rate since you alternated your maturity periods. What a way to ride the rates!

Secret

You can protect some of your liquidity by scheduling your shorter-term securities on your bond ladder to mature at times when you know you need the funds. For example, if you are planning to buy a house next year or if your granddaughter is starting private school, you can stagger the maturities on the securities to come due when you need the money. You are in control!

The Least You Need to Know

➤ A bond is nothing more than an IOU from its issuer. The issuer could be a corporation, the U.S. government, a foreign government, a city, or a state. Regardless of who it is, the issuer is the borrower, and you are the lender. Because you lent them your money for a certain amount of time, the issuer promises to pay you back in full on a certain date, plus pay a set amount of interest (the coupon rate).

➤ There is an inverse relationship between interest rates and bond prices. When interest rates go up, bond prices go down. When interest rates go down, bond prices go up.

➤ Even though bonds were once thought to be the investment for safety, they do not escape all risks. Look at the investment pyramid in Chapter 4 to see where they fit into the scheme of things.

➤ Creating a laddered portfolio by investing in bonds with staggered maturities can reduce some risk and increase yields.

➤ If you follow the yield curve, you can pretty much figure out the direction of both short-term and long-term interest rates. If you figure out the direction of interest rates, you can pattern your investment decisions about buying and selling bonds accordingly.

➤ Unfortunately, no one can accurately predict future interest rates. So no one can predict future bond prices, either.

Investing in Uncle Sam

When you think of the U.S. Government, what images come to mind? Uncle Sam and the red, white, and blue? Hefty tax bills? The Pentagon? What about investments?

The U.S. Government is one of the most common and safest places you can invest your money. Why? Because the U.S. Government puts its full faith and credit on all of its Treasury securities. As you read this chapter, you'll learn what types of Treasury securities exist and how you can make money from them.

We Want You!

A rather reputable trader named Bernard Baruch used to say, "I'm not as concerned about the return on my money as I am about the return *of* my money!" Investors in Treasury securities followed this old maxim to the letter.

Why would the Treasury, which is the financial arm of the U.S. Government, need to borrow money? The Treasury issues debt instruments (securities) in the form of *Treasury bills, Treasury notes*, and *Treasury bonds* to finance its deficit spending.

Bet You Didn't Know

In 1945, Treasury bills didn't even exist, but today they make up the second largest component of debt—about $832 billion.

What?

Credit risk shows the financial soundness of the company that is borrowing money through issuing fixed-income securities. Companies with a strong financial position, good income prospects, and a low level of outstanding debt probably will receive a high credit rating. There are two major rating agencies, Standard & Poor's and Moody's, which provide credit ratings on issuing companies that can assist you in determining credit risk.

The U.S. Government debt is the money that the government has borrowed over the years, and it keeps growing. Therefore, when you invest in any of these Treasury securities, you are loaning the government your money to help finance its deficit spending.

One of the biggest reasons people invest in Treasury securities is because anyone who invests in them will receive their money back when promised. There really isn't any credit risk when you invest in Treasury Securities.

Traditionally, Treasury securities have the reputation of being safe investments. They are backed by the full faith and credit of the U.S. Government. No other bond investment (with the exception of the Ginnie-Mae securities described in Chapter 26) can make this claim. Due to the safety factor, however, the interest rates paid on Treasuries are lower than that on comparable bonds of different issuers.

An onset of new fixed-income products in the early 1980s and the wide swings in interest rates in the past few decades have caused Treasury securities to rise and fall more frequently than in the past. Some of these new fixed-income products have wild names, too: LYONs, TIGRs, CMOs—there's always a goofy acronym in the investment world!

Secret

If the economy is experiencing a slowdown or a recession, consider looking into better fixed-income investments, such as Treasuries.

Fixed-income securities do experience a lot of price volatility. When interest rates rise, bond prices fall. That means that the value of your bonds fluctuates either higher or lower than the original purchase price, depending upon the general direction of interest rates.

The value of Treasury securities also rises and falls along with that of other fixed-income securities, but Uncle Sam's claim to fame of being a creditworthy borrower keeps

Treasury investors sleeping soundly at night knowing that when they wake up, their principal will be safe.

Investing in securities with high credit quality is usually most apparent during economic downturns. During an economic slowdown or even a recession, investors usually make a shift to quality. Why? During these hard times, companies with a lower credit rating may have difficulties in meeting the interest payments and/or principal obligations of their outstanding debt. You are more likely to see companies file for bankruptcy during hard times versus prosperous times. As a result, investors will move toward those investments that hold a high credit rating during poor economic conditions.

Three Ways to Security

The three main classes of Treasury securities are defined as the following: Treasury bills (T-bills), Treasury notes (T-notes), and Treasury bonds (you guessed it, T-bonds). Each is backed by the full faith and credit of the U.S. Government. The differences lie in the minimum investment amount and the length of available maturities.

Interestingly, market watchers view Treasury securities as benchmarks to the interest rate world. The U.S. Treasury bill is so widely quoted and compared to other investments, it is quite astounding. In fact, big-time investors and financial gurus will speak of how well or how poorly an investment did compared to a similar Treasury security.

Treasury bills are considered a discount security and Treasury notes and bonds are coupon securities. The difference is that discount securities, such as T-bills, don't pay any interest. You purchase the securitiy at a "discount" from its face value, and at maturity you receive the full face value. The difference between the discount price and the face value received at maturity is the "interest" earned on the investment. Coupon securities (T-notes and T-bonds), on the other hand, pay interest semi-annually and the face value at maturity. The interest payments that you receive are federally taxable but exempt from state and local taxes.

Treasury Bills

Commonly referred to as T-bills, these securities are issued with varying maturity dates: three-month, six-month, and one-year maturities. They are sold in minimum increments of $10,000. Treasury bills represent the second largest component of debt.

A T-bill is different from the other Treasury securities because of the way the interest payments are calculated. There is no specified interest rate at all. Investing in a T-bill would work as follows. Typically, you would buy a T-bill at less than its $10,000 face value. For example, if you bought one six-month T-bill, you would not pay $10,000 for it but rather an amount that is less, perhaps $9,500. Because you are buying the T-bill for less than its true value, you are buying it at a discount from its face value.

It's math time. If you bought a $10,000 six-month T-bill for $9,500 and held it until maturity (when you would receive the face amount of $10,000 back), you would receive $10,000 on the maturity date. The return on this investment is $500.

$10,000 – $9,500 = $500

The difference between the price you bought it at and the price you sell it at is your interest. In this scenario, you earned 5.26% over six months on your investment ($500/ $9,500). (Annually, your return would be 10.52%.)

Pricing of Treasury bills is also quoted differently than the other Treasury securities. T-bills are quoted in terms of discount yield, not dollar price. Here's how a quote on a T-bill might look:

Bid   **Ask** (sometimes referred to as "offer")

8.00   7.75

The first thing to realize is that these quotes are discount yields and not dollar prices. The quote given above reads as follows: Bid equals 8.00%, and Ask equals 7.75% (not $8.00 and $7.75). The Bid is the maximum price that a buyer is willing to pay and the Ask/Offer is the minimum price that the seller is willing to receive.

The difference between these two prices is referred to as the Bid-Ask spread. Because T-bills are discount securities and the quote is in terms of discount yields, reading the quotes can be confusing, but hopefully I can make it easy for you.

The bid price will always be lower than the asking price. You may ask, "Then why in our example is the Bid (8.00%) higher than the Ask/Offer (7.75%)?" Well, T-bills are quoted in terms of the discount from the face value and not dollar prices. If you were to try and convert the discount yield to a dollar price you would do the following:

1. **Calculate the Dollar Discount.** Multiply the face value by the discount yield, and then that number by the fraction of the year. (Here, there are 360 days in a year, not 365.)

   Face Value × Discount Yield × t/360, where t is the actual number of days to maturity. For our example, lets assume t = 360, therefore, the dollar discount would be:

   $10,000 × .08 × 360/360 = $800

2. **Calculate the Dollar Investment.** Subtract the Dollar Discount from the face value.

   $10,000 – $800 = $9,200

3. **Calculate the Dollar Price.** Divide the Dollar Investment by the Face Value, and then multiply that number by 100 (Dollar Investment / Face Value × 100.)

   $9,200 / $10,000 × 100 = $92.00

If you followed these steps in calculating the Ask/Offer price, you would obtain a dollar price of 92.25, therefore, in terms of dollar prices our quote would read as follows:

Bid = 92.00 Ask/Offer = 92.25

As you can see the Bid is less than the Ask/Offer.

Treasury bills are sold by the Treasury department at weekly auctions to all types of purchasers, both institutional and retail. The auctions of the three- and six-month T-bills occur every Monday at the Federal Reserve Bank in New York City. You don't have to travel to New York City to buy a T-bill; you'll learn where to go later in this chapter. The trades settle on the Thursday following the auction.

Longer-Term Maturities: T-Notes and T-Bonds

The length of maturity for Treasury notes is longer than T-bills—between one and ten years. Treasury notes represent the largest segment of Treasury debt financing.

Unlike T-bills, Treasury notes, also known as T-notes, carry a definite interest rate on the face value of the security and pay interest every six months. Plus, you do not need as much money up front to buy a T-note. The minimum investment for a two- and three-year note is $5,000, and additional increments can be added. Usually, during the third week of every month, there is an auction of two-year Treasury notes.

Treasury bonds are the longest-term Treasury obligations and mature over ten years or more. In February, May, August, and November, the Treasury department auctions off T-bonds to investors. The minimum amount required for investment is $1,000. By the way, Treasury bonds make up $501 billion of the U.S. Government's total debt.

The pricing on Treasury notes and bonds is quoted in 1/32 of one point and in terms of yield to maturity. Each 1/32 is equal to $.3125, assuming a $1,000 face amount. For example, if you saw a quote on a ten-year Treasury note in the financial section of your paper that read 94-14, it would cost $944.375 to buy it.

Here's a simple way to remember the pricing on Treasury notes and bonds. Split the quote into two parts. If the quote read 94-14, take it apart, so 94 is the first part and 14 is the second part.

Let's start with the second part first. This part of the quote represents the number of 32nds. In the example, the second part is 14/32nds, which equals .4375. Add this to the first part (94), and you get 94.4375 as the price. Because bond prices are quoted as a percentage of face value, when trying to calculate the dollar cost of the bond you take the quoted price divided by 100 and multiply it by the face value:

94.4375 / 100 × 1,000 = $944.375

Careful

There are a few assumptions made when calculating the yield-to-maturity. First, all interest payments can be reinvested at the yield-to-maturity. Second, you must reinvest all of your interest payments. This means that if you purchase a note or a bond that is quoted as having a 7.00% YTM, you take all of your semi-annual interest payments and reinvest those proceeds at a rate equal to 7.00%. The reality is that it is highly unlikely that you'll be able to reinvest all proceeds at that rate.

As mentioned earlier, when you read a bond quote in a newspaper you will see a dollar price and a yield-to-maturity (YTM). This yield-to-maturity represents the approximate return on your investment if you were to purchase the security at the quoted ask/offer price and hold the security to maturity.

One more thing. When you purchase a T-note or a T-bond, you will receive a full six months' worth of interest on the next scheduled coupon payment date *no matter if you held the security for the full six months or three days*. To compensate for this, the seller is going to charge you for the interest that has accrued for the time that he or she owned the security. So the total cost to you will be the dollar price plus any accrued interest. The prices that you see in the newspapers are only the dollar price and do not include any accrued interest.

For example, if you bought a $10,000 face value 8% T-note on February 15, and interest payments are made on January 1 and July 1 of every year, it has been 46 days since the last payment. Take 46 and divide it by the actual number of days between January 1 and July 1. Get out your calendars! Assuming February has 28 days, the total actual number of days should be 181. (Add up the first six months of the year.)

So now the whole calculation looks like this:

Accrued interest = principal × rate × time

= $10,000 × 0.040 (that's 4%) × 46/181

= $101.65

Secret

When you buy Treasuries at auction, they are purchased directly from the U.S. Government. When you purchase them through a brokerage firm, a bank, or thrift (savings and loan), you are buying them on the secondary market, which is usually from another investor.

Now what about those semi-annual interest payments you receive? If you really want to be a math whiz, figure it out with this formula: accrued interest = principal × rate × time. The principal "ingredient" never changes. But the rate and time factors are different.

For example, to figure out how much interest you're going to receive on your Treasury notes (and even your Treasury bonds), know that you are paid semi-annually, meaning every six months. So for a $10,000 face value 8% T-bond, you will use half the annual rate to make your calculations. Cut the 8% in half to 4%, and plug it into the rate section of the formula. Therefore, every six months you'll receive $400.00. That's your fixed return.

Fortunately, you don't have to whip out the calculators or consult the math nerd in your son's trigonometry class. Whenever you buy a T-note or T-bond, the interest payments are already calculated for you. I just wanted to see if you were paying attention. Those of you who didn't follow, back up and try again. After all, it's your money!

Buy, Sell, or Hold?

Here are some buying scenarios that can help you make decisions about buying, holding, and selling treasury notes and bonds.

➤ If you buy a ten-year Treasury bond and hold it until maturity, you'll receive the face value of the bond.

➤ However, if you were to sell the bond before it matures, then you are exposed to any swings in interest rates and the ups and downs in prices that are currently happening in the bond market. As a result, the proceeds you receive can be different than the face value.

➤ If you bought a ten-year T-bond with a face value of $1,000 at 95 ($950) with a 10% coupon rate and held it until maturity, you would get $1,000 when it matured. Plus, over the ten years, you could collect $50 every six months in interest payments.

➤ But what if it's only four years into the life of the bond and interest rates are falling? Your ten-year T-bond is now worth more than what you paid for it. You know this because you understand that when *interest rates fall, bond prices rise*. You may sell the bond before it matures, thus following the cardinal rule of buying low and selling high. However, once you sell the bond you give up any future interest payments and just keep your profit. Keep in mind that your profit can only be invested at the new, lower rates.

Secret
Because bond prices move in the opposite direction of interest rates, there is more price volatility (ups and downs) in longer-term Treasury bonds. The longer the maturity, the bigger the swings (up and down) in prices as these bonds are bought and sold.

Secret
Buying Treasury securities directly from the Federal Reserve saves you money because there are no fees involved. The catch is your account is debited a service fee (like a commission) that the institution includes as a "transactional cost" for purchasing the Treasuries for you. You could pay an additional $40 to $70. If these fees seem sky-high, keep in mind that the Federal Reserve doesn't charge a penny for any securities transactions.

Where to Buy 'Em

In the last section, I mentioned that you can purchase Treasury securities at auction. Images of a fast-talkin', gavel-swingin' guy in a three piece polyester suit are probably running through your mind, but a Treasury auction is different. Polyester suits, perhaps, but no gavel.

Secret
For those of you who have a son or daughter—or even yourself!—who'll be attending college someday, use the money you receive when you redeem your savings bonds to pay for college tuition. You do *not pay partial or any federal tax on the interest you earn on the bonds*, but you must meet specific tax qualifications. Check with your financial or tax adviser to determine which bracket you fall under.

Treasury securities are auctioned off (sold) from the Federal Reserve bank or a branch (you'll see where the 12 branches are located across the country in Appendix C) and not the Treasury department in Washington, D.C.

Buying Treasury securities directly from the Fed (or any of its branches) is the easiest—and most cost-effective—way to purchase them. You do not pay any fees when you buy Treasuries directly from the Fed. You don't have to live near a Federal Reserve branch to purchase Treasuries, either. You can either visit one to buy Treasuries or call them to get more information about buying Treasury securities directly—sometimes it is done through the mail.

To purchase a Treasury security, you would put in a *non-competitive bid* at one of the Treasury auctions, which means you accept whatever average rate you get for the securities you want to buy. After you buy a Treasury, your purchase will be noted as being in *book-entry* form, which means that you don't receive the certificate, but rather are "on the books" with the Treasury department and your interest payments are sent directly to your home.

It is extremely easy to buy or sell Treasuries because there is such a huge market for them. Why? Because of the high degree of safety and the principle of receiving interest income.

➤ **Treasury Bills.** Three- and six-month bills are auctioned every Monday; the one-year T-bill is auctioned in the third week of every month.

➤ **Treasury Notes.** The Treasury regularly issues coupon securities (both T-notes and T-bonds) with maturities of two, three, five, seven, and ten years. These are the only maturities available. However, if you want to buy a four-year Treasury note, for example, you would buy a five-year Treasury note that is one year old. Every month, two-year and five-year notes are auctioned. The three- and seven-year notes are auctioned at the beginning of the second month of each calendar quarter, which is February, May, August, and November.

➤ **Treasury Bonds.** Treasury bonds with maturities of ten years and 30 years are also auctioned on the second month of each calendar quarter. If you wanted to buy a 25-year T-bond, again, you would buy a 30 T-bond that is five years old.

In addition to gaining knowledge about Treasury securities, you should also be aware of a distant "cousin" that Treasuries have—savings bonds.

Basics About Savings Bonds

Savings bonds, like other Treasury securities, are safe—they are backed by the full faith and credit of the United States Government. Plus, the interest you receive on them is free from state and local taxes. However, you'll have to report any interest on your federal tax return from any savings bond investment.

> **Careful**
> Make sure the savings bonds are registered in your name so you can get the tax benefit where applicable.

The reason savings bonds have been so popular among Americans is because they are available in smaller denominations. You can buy them for as little as $25 each, with other denominations of $50, $75, $100, $200, $500, $1,000, $5,000, and $10,000.

How do savings bonds trade? Well, you don't buy them at a brokerage firm or at auction, nor are they bought and sold on the floor of a financial exchange.

> **What?**
> *Noncallable*, shown as "NC" on a bond certificate or trade confirmation, means the issuer cannot "call back" and redeem your bond before the date of maturity.

Instead, you can purchase them at your local bank or thrift, at a Federal Reserve branch, or even through company-sponsored payroll deductions.

Here's how they work. If you were to buy a $100 savings bond, you would pay $50 for it. There is no set maturity date and you don't receive any interest. But you redeem them when they mature for the full face value, in this case, $100. When you redeem them you will owe federal tax on the interest.

So why should you invest in Uncle Sam? Because the Treasury securities issued are considered one of the safest investment vehicles around. Treasury bonds, for example, are *noncallable*, which means the Treasury cannot call your bonds in before maturity. Other types of bonds—corporates, municipals, and government agencies—they can.

The Least You Need to Know

➤ Investors purchase Treasury securities because of their high degree of safety. They are conservative investments and provide a steady stream of income every six months if held to maturity—with the exception of Treasury bills, which you buy at a discount and receive your interest income on the day of maturity.

➤ Treasury notes and bonds trade in 1/32 of a point, which is equal to $.3125 per $1,000 face amount. When a Treasury security is trading below $1,000, which is known as par, it is said to be trading at a discount. This is why Treasury bills are considered to be priced at a discount to yield. If it is trading at $1,000, it is trading at par. It the Treasury is trading above $1,000, it is priced over par at a premium.

➤ Another Treasury security is the savings bond, which can be purchased in smaller denominations with as little as $25. However, because they are bought at a discount, you only pay half of the face value of the savings bond when you invest.

Chapter 26

Investing in Other Types of Fixed-Income Products

In This Chapter

➤ Knowing who Freddie, Ginnie, and Fannie are

➤ Understanding why you should invest in them

➤ Learning about a few other friends of theirs

As you know by now, the largest debtor of the United States is...the United States.

The U.S. Government borrows primarily to finance its annual budget deficits, which still exceeds $100 billion as of 1996. Yet, despite the incredible size of its accumulated deficit, U.S. Government securities and agency bonds are still considered to have less "credit risk" (that is, risk of default) than any other bonds in the world.

To further develop your knowledge about bond investing, this chapter explains how some nicknames and a few acronyms describe the different types of bonds that exist and what makes them different from Treasury, corporate, municipal, and junk bonds.

Three Playschool Buddies

In the last chapter, you learned about the IOUs of the U.S. Government, Treasury securities. Additionally, the U.S. Government has established various entities (branches of the government) that implement federal policy and political "stuff." These entities are known as *agencies* and are divided into four different classes: agriculture, transportation, housing, and education. Even though these agencies receive the support of the U.S. Government, many are not owned by the government at all.

Secret
While federal agencies do have the sponsorship of the government, their bonds are *not* backed by the full faith and credit of the U.S. Government, like Treasuries. However, the government does own some of these agencies and bonds issued from them are almost as safe as Treasuries.

These agencies, like the U.S. Treasury, borrow money directly from investors for their own purposes. Recalling that bonds are IOUs (where a borrower receives money from a lender and promises to pay back the amount plus interest), these agencies issue bonds to investors. Depending on the agency, most minimum denominations are as high as $25,000 per bond.

The names of the three best known agencies bring to mind three little schoolchildren all gleefully playing together: Freddie Mac, Fannie Mae, and Ginnie Mae. These agencies are the General National Mortgage Association (GNMA), Federal Home Loan Mortgage Corporation (FHLMC), and Federal National Mortgage Association (FNMA). To understand how they trade and how you can profit from investing in them, it's important to comprehend what they are.

These agencies provide investors with an alternative to other fixed-income investments. If you were to compare these agency bonds to Treasury bonds, it's like comparing apples and oranges. Sure, they're both fruit, but they have different characteristics. The biggest difference in these agency securities is the feature that makes investing in them so interesting—mortgages.

So My House Is Involved?

A mortgage is a legally binding agreement made between a borrower (mortgagor) and a lender (mortgagee) where the borrower pledges his property in order to secure the funds from the lender. There's a whole slew of mortgages, which include a *fixed-rate level payment* (known as a traditional mortgage), an *adjustable rate mortgage* (ARM), and a *graduated payment mortgage* (GPM). All you need to know about here is the traditional mortgage.

What?
A *fixed-rate level payment* (also referred to as a traditional mortgage) is typically a 15- or 30-year mortgage with a fixed interest rate.

A traditional mortgage has a level monthly payment made up of principal and interest that is paid over the life of the loan. The principal part of the payment is used to pay off your loan balance. As time passes, the amount of your principal loan balance will decline until the final payment when your loan balance is zero. This is referred to as *amortization*. During the early stages of the loan, your monthly payment is interest. At the end of the mortgage, your monthly payment is mostly made up of principal.

Here's the key. As a mortgagor, you have the right to prepay your mortgage at any time without penalty. Since these agency bonds are made up of mortgages, the prepayment right is critical to how these agency securities (now referred to as "mortgage-backed securities") are priced.

What?
Mortgage-backed securities consist of a pool of residential mortgage loans.

Ginnie Mae, Fannie Mae, and Freddie Mac Step In

So how do these three playschool buddies relate to all of this mortgage business? That's easy. These agencies have been created to pool together—purchase individual mortgages (like yours!) from banks and savings and loans—a large quantity of mortgages and produce mortgage-backed securities. These mortgage-backed securities offer higher yields (and thus more credit risk) than Treasuries.

Since these mortgages have been pooled together, the issuer reduces the credit risk associated with owning a particular mortgage. For example, if you were looking for higher yields and wanted to invest in the mortgage market, you could purchase the mortgage of Joe Smith of Portland, Oregon. Therefore, you assume all of the risk of Joe Smith. If he defaults on his mortgage, you get his piece of property, but that's not what you wanted. With a mortgage-backed security, you own a piece of many mortgages, thereby spreading your risk.

Ginnie Mae, Fannie Mae, and Freddie Mac issue these securities. They pay monthly rates of interest and principal (remember, they're mortgages), although these amounts fluctuate from month to month. You purchase these from a full-service or discount broker—no need to go to our nation's capital to knock on agency doors.

Ginnie Mae

Ginnie Mae is owned by the department of Housing and Urban development. Its purpose is to maintain a healthy housing industry by creating and contributing to even more available funding in the housing market.

Ginnie Mae was introduced in 1970. Since its inception, investing in Ginnie Maes, and the entire mortgage-backed security market, has skyrocketed due to the higher yields that are offered to investors. In exchange for a lot more risk, most investors want to earn a better yield on their investment. Plus, you get monthly interest payments rather than semi-annual interest payments offered from Treasuries.

Bet You Didn't Know

Ginnie Mae was the first mortgage-backed security ever introduced.

What this agency does is put its guarantee on *packages* of VA and FHA mortgages. So a pool of mortgages are lumped together and sold as one package. These pools (put together by banks and savings and loans) are sold to investors as *participation certificates*. They provide payments of interest and principal to investors (the participants). These packages are also known as *pass-thru certificates* because these interest payments are passed through to investors. It's not a physical thing that occurs, just a concept.

Ginnie Mae investors receive interest and principal payments monthly, corresponding with the homeowners' monthly mortgage payments. You will see more how these securities work when you read up on CMOs (collateralized mortgage obligations) later in the chapter.

Let's illustrate this further. If you bought a house and took out a 30-year mortgage, your bank might lump it together with a few other 30-year mortgages and sell it as a package deal to the Ginnie Mae agency. You and the other new homeowners in the package are making your monthly mortgage payments (which are made up of principal plus interest). Ginnie Mae then sells the package as participation certificates. The interest plus principal payments that you are making are passed through to investors. All interest and principal payments are taxable on all levels.

Freddie Mac

Part of the government housing sector of the government is an agency called the Federal Home Loan Mortgage Corporation, known as Freddie Mac. This agency used to be wholly owned by the government, but since 1989, it has been partially owned by a different organization.

Here's the best way to describe what Freddie Mac does. When you take out a mortgage from your bank, your bank may decide to sell the mortage to another party and pass the risk on to someone else. These traded mortgages are known as *mortgage-backed securities*. Each type of mortgage-backed security differs in name, purpose, pricing, risk factors, and coupon rates.

Because Freddie Mac isn't a wholly owned government agency, these bonds are a little more risky than Treasury securities. But, because Freddie Macs are a federal government agency bond, not a true Treasury bond, you receive a slightly higher yield on a Freddie

Mac than on a Treasury. Why? Because the more risk attached to a bond investment, the higher the yield you receive. That's the relationship between risk and reward. For example, a Treasury bond may pay you 7.5% in interest, but a Freddie Mac bond with the same maturity date may get you a better rate (8%–8.5%).

These bonds can trade at a discount, at par, and at a premium. Although, because of the higher yield involved, Freddie Mac bonds often trade below par (at a discount). You can also buy stock in Freddie Mac, because the agency is listed on the New York Stock Exchange as a publicly traded stock. Its ticker symbol is FRE.

Fannie Mae

Fannie Mae stands for the Federal National Mortgage Association (FNMA) and falls under the housing sector in the government. Keeping in mind that this is a mortgage-backed security will make it easier to understand how this agency works.

Bet You Didn't Know

The minimum pool size for Freddie Mac is $100 million. Ginnie Mae and Fannie Mae require a minimum pool size of only $1 million.

Fannie Mae sells bonds to raise money to buy and sell two different types of mortgages—FHA and VA mortgages—from banks across the country. FHA mortgages are for those folks who are looking to buy a house and have income below a certain limit. VA mortgages are available to people who are veterans of the armed forces.

Let's use an example to illustrate how Fannie Mae works. If you bought a house and secured a VA mortgage (you are a veteran, of course), your bank sells that mortgage to an agency, in this case, Fannie Mae. Fannie Mae then repackages the mortgage in the form of mortgage-backed securities (Fannie Mae bonds) and sells them to investors. Fannie Mae then promises its investors that it will pay back the principal plus interest as the mortgage on which the bond is based comes due, whether or not you pay the mortgage back.

How They Trade?

Bonds are one of the best ways for you to achieve your financial goals, because they allow you to lock in a set rate of income for a certain period of time. Because you have locked in the rate you know how much interest income you will receive in your interest payments. This type of certainty provides a firm, solid foundation for your financial plans.

You know that if you were to buy a Treasury security from the U.S. Government, you would be lending the government your money in exchange for their promise to pay you back in full at a later date plus interest. The same thing goes for bonds issued by agencies such as Freddie Mac, Fannie Mae, and Ginnie Mae. They borrow money from investors like you with the promise of paying you back in full at a later date with interest. But, the interest income you receive can fluctuate.

Bonds issued from these agencies trade in 1/32 of a point and the prices of these bonds move in the opposite direction of interest rates. Just to recap, let's say you buy an agency bond for $25,000 and it is yielding 10%. If interest rates fall to 5% over the next several years, what happens to the current market price of your bond? It goes up—maybe even to $25,500. Why would it go up? Because other investors would kill to get their hands on a bond that pays 10% when all they can currently get their hands on are bonds that are only paying 5%. So, they wouldn't mind paying the $25,500 to get a higher interest rate.

When one of these agencies wants to sell bonds to investors, the agency will hire an investment banking firm to sell them for the agency. Many of these investment banking firms only work with bond investments; therefore, they are known as *bond dealers*. In exchange for distributing and selling these agency bonds to the investing public (that's you and me), these bond dealers and investment banking firms receive a commission for every bond it sells. Keep in mind that you can buy an agency bond from a brokerage firm, too.

What's in It for the Broker?

How do these bond dealers, investment banking firms, and brokerage firms make money on the deal? By "marking up" the price of the bond. If you buy a ten-year Ginnie Mae bond with a face value of $25,000, that means in ten years it will mature for $25,000. When you bought it, you paid $24,950, which means it was trading at a discount because the current price was cheaper than the face value.

Secret
When you buy or sell a fixed-income security, such as a mortgage-backed security, versus equities (like stocks), the broker has hidden the price of the commission in the trade on the fixed-income security. You can ask what the commission is, but it's not guaranteed you'll get an answer.

This is where the financial firms will make their money. What they do is take the current price and mark it up. The current price plus the mark up is what you'll pay for the bond, which should be shown on the trade confirmation you receive in the mail.

With agency bonds, you'll pay a commission because you *have* to buy them at a brokerage firm, investment banking firm, or bond dealer. There isn't an auction for these bonds as there are with Treasuries. When you buy them, you hold them in your account in "street name."

CMOs

Known as a collateralized mortgage obligation, a CMO is a type of mortgage-backed security. Think of it this way. The outside is the mortgage-backed security, and the inside is made up of all of these mortgage loans. If you are a homeowner, you know that mortgage loans are made up of monthly payments of principal and interest. Think of this as the guts of the mortgage-backed security.

If you invest in a mortgage-backed security, consider the following:

➤ You are investing in a bond. Therefore, you buy it either at a discount, at par, or at a premium. It has a face value and a maturity date, just like all other bonds do.

➤ You receive two separate payments made up of interest and principal. Both types of payments vary, depending on several factors (more on this in a minute).

➤ The risks involved are geared toward the movement in interest rates, but specifically, mortgage rates.

As homeowners pay down their mortgages, and as more principal and less interest are paid on their mortgages, that principal and interest are passed through to you, the mortgage-backed security investor. The statement that you get from your brokerage firm will tell you and separate how much you received in interest payment and how much you received in principal payment.

> **Secret**
> Studies have shown that the average 30-year mortage loan is paid off in 12–15 years. What does this mean to a mortgage-backed security investor who doesn't invest in a CMO? You're not quite sure of the exact maturity date of your investment.

When you receive these payments, though, is quite uncertain. If mortgage rates fall in general, those homeowners with high monthly mortgage payments might refinance their mortgages. Investors in mortgage-backed securities would then receive less in interest payments.

Imagine the situation like this: If interest rates on 30-year fixed rate mortgages fell to 7% nationwide average, many homeowners would consider refinancing their mortgage. However, many mortgage-backed security investors received less in interest payments because of the big wave in refinancing. However, as an investor, you would receive more of a payment in principal, but you won't be able to reinvest that money at a higher rate because interest rates have come down.

What if interest rates rise? Well, no one would refinance, for one. Thus, as a mortgage-backed security investor, you would receive little in principal payments. Therefore, you won't have as much to reinvest in other investments that could currently give you higher interest income than you would be earning on your mortgage-backed security.

Where does a CMO fit into this? It was invented to relieve the prepayment worry, which is what you get when all of those homeowners refinance their mortgages. A CMO is a mortgage-backed security sliced into different pieces of pie. These slices are known as *tranches* (which is the French word for "slices," mais oui!).

Some of the prepayments that homeowners gave that were funneled into the mortgage-backed security are put in the first slice until the mortgages are completely paid off. The next batch of prepayments are put into the second slice until they are completely paid off. And so on and so on, until all of the tranches are retired or matured.

The benefit of a CMO is that you can pick the tranche you want. Each tranche has a different maturity date and coupon. So if you think you'll need the money you invest five years from now, you would pick a CMO with a tranche life of five years, for example.

A Word of Caution

Mortgage-backed securities and CMOs are a great way to get a better yield than if you were just to invest in plain-vanilla Treasury bonds. However, they do carry more risk because of the greater exposure to interest rates swings and the uncertainty of final maturity.

The small investor also has a difficult time meeting the minimum denomination to invest in a mortgage-backed security: $25,000. Because of this high initial investment, several mutual fund companies have set up mortgage-backed security mutual funds so that even the smallest investor can sink money into a tranche, with initial deposits as low as $1,000.

If there is one thing—okay, two things—that I could stress about investing in any bonds that are issued by different agencies, they are:

1. With the exception of Treasury STRIPS and Ginnie Mae bonds, the rest of these agencies are not backed by the full faith and credit of the U.S. Government.

2. As with Treasury securities, prices on all of the bonds mentioned in this chapter move inversely with interest rates.

Secret
Understand that zero-coupon bonds, as they get closer to maturity, must rise in price to equal the face value. There's no ifs, ands, or buts.

ZEROs, or Zero Coupon Bonds

Zeros are also known as *zero-coupon bonds*, and they get their name from the fact that they are issued with no coupon rate at all. The interest rate given on the bond is zero. Zero-coupon bonds are issued by the Treasury department, corporations, municipalities, and government agencies.

So why would you buy a bond with no interest rate? First, you need to understand how it works to see how you can potentially make money from zero-coupon bonds.

Bet You Didn't Know

On April 22, 1981, JC Penney became the first corporation to ever issue a zero-coupon bond. It was priced at $33.427. Following its debut, General Motors and IBM began issuing zero-coupon bonds.

Instead of receiving regular semi-annual interest payments as you would on a Treasury bond, a zero-coupon bond is bought at a deep discount from its face value, kind of like a savings bond.(Buy a $50 savings bond for only $25, and when it matures you get the 50 bucks.) Zero-coupon bonds are similar. You make money off the increase in the bond price as the bond approaches maturity. Thus, you try to buy the bond at the lowest price possible (its deep discount price) to get the face value when the bond matures.

Bet You Didn't Know

Zero-coupon bonds are a popular investment because you know how much money you'll be getting when the bond reaches maturity, and what that date is. Also, because you don't receive any semi-annual interest payments, you don't have to worry about reinvesting that portion of money. However, you are taxed on these interest payments on all levels.

Who buys zero-coupon bonds? Most investors in zeros buy them because they know when they're going to get their money and they know how much they'll receive. Based on that principle, investors use zero-coupon bonds as a way to match their future liabilities. For example, a parent who knows that ten years down the road he'll have to pay for his son's college tuition would invest in a zero-coupon bond. So if you and your spouse just had a baby, you know that approximately 18 years from now your child will probably attend college. So you can buy a zero coupon bond that matures 18 years from now.

Or, let's say you want to retire in 30 years. You can buy a zero-coupon bond today and match its maturity date (or close enough) to the day you plan on retiring. Today, you know how much money you'll be receiving on your date of retirement.

Who Sells Zeros?

Buying zero-coupon bonds is easy. You can buy them at any full-service or discount brokerage firm. When you call up, your broker will give you a bond's current price along with its face value and the number of years it has until maturity. Plus, you will learn the yield that you will be locking in at that particular price. Even though you won't receive regular interest payments, you still need to know what the yield is because it is factored into the calculation of how the bond will grow from its discount price to its face value at maturity date.

Plus, the quote you get from the broker will include the mark up (which is hidden from you), which is the amount of commission the broker makes for selling the bond.

When getting a quote on zero-coupon bonds, ask your broker the following:

➤ What's the current price?

➤ How much is the mark up? (You can ask, but an answer is not guaranteed.)

➤ What's the maturity date?

➤ How much money do I receive at maturity (what's the face value)?

➤ What is the yield to maturity that I will be locking into? (Make sure you ask this one!)

Want to know how to make money on these zero coupon bonds? Here are some hints:

➤ If you expect interest rates to fall, purchase zero-coupon bonds with the longest maturity. Zeros have the greatest price sensitivity for a given maturity.

➤ If you expect interest rates to rise, you don't want to be holding zeros. Why? Because you could be receiving higher income from another investment with the higher rates.

Secret

The longer you tie up the money, the cheaper the bond will be. For example, if you bought a ten-year zero coupon bond worth $10,000, you might only pay around $5,000, but if you can wait 20 years for the payoff, you might only pay $2,500 for the bond.

It Sounds Too Good to Be True

Here's the catch. The price on a zero-coupon bond reacts more to the changes in interest rates than any other type of bond. Why? Because the only cash flow (income) you receive is on the date of maturity.

If you are trading zero-coupon bonds as a way to buy low and sell high, there is much more risk involved because these bonds react so intensely to interest rates. If you bought a ten-year zero coupon bond at a discount and plan on selling it within the next six years instead of waiting to maturity, you have no idea what interest rates and bond prices will be like six years from now. You might get lucky and the value of the bond would rise; therefore you could sell it and have a profit. If bond prices fall, you are faced with the decision of selling the bond and having a loss, or holding onto it for the full ten years so you can get the face value.

Zero-coupon bonds can be purchased for maturities from six months to 30 years, so you can pick a maturity date that fits your needs and your financial goals. Plus, you can buy a zero for as little as $1,000. You can really make this $1,000 go a long way if you hold the bond until its maturity date.

STRIPs, CATs, and TIGRs

You can invest in a zero-coupon bond that is made from a Treasury bond. These types of zero coupon bonds are known as STRIPs, which stand for Separate Trading of Registered Interest and Principal of securities. What a mouthful!

STRIPs were first issued in 1985. They are made up of Treasury notes and bonds, where the interest coupons have been separated from the principal security. In a sense, the interest coupons were "stripped" from the principal and now have their own identity as a separately traded investment security. Because they are derived from a Treasury bond, these zero-coupon bonds are backed by the full faith and credit of the U.S. Government. Way to go, Uncle Sam!

Now, a few brokerage firms have launched their own names for this type of zero-coupon bond. For example, Merrill Lynch created Treasury Investment Growth Receipts, or TIGRs. Others? Salomon Brothers, one of the largest bond houses in the world, came up with CATs (Certificates of Accrual on Treasury Securities) as a way to label a zero-coupon bond.

The benefits of these zero-coupon bonds are three-fold. If they're issued by the Treasury, you get the backing of the U.S. Government, and you get a slightly better yield if you buy and hold them to maturity than if you were to buy a Treasury bond and hold it to maturity. Lastly, you can buy them at a discount.

There are mutual funds that deal specifically with investing in these types of zero-coupon bonds, known as zero-coupon bond funds, which you can buy directly from a mutual fund company instead of going through a broker and paying a higher commission.

The Least You Need to Know

➤ One way to earn higher interest rates on your bond investments is to invest in bonds that are issued by federal agencies. The most popular are Federal Home Loan Mortgage Corporation (Freddie Mac), Federal National Mortgage Association (Fannie Mae), and Government National Mortgage Association (Ginnie Mae).

➤ Unlike Treasuries, these bonds that are issued by federal agencies are not auctioned. If you want to invest in them, you must purchase them from a brokerage firm.

➤ Zero-coupon bonds allow you to match up future liabilities. For example, if you know that your child will be starting college in 15 years, you can invest in a

15-year zero-coupon bond, pay a discount price for it, and realize the full face value 15 years later to pay for tuition. Remember, though, you do not receive any interest payments but you *are* taxed on them (known as a phantom tax). Therefore, you must report this to the IRS on your income tax returns.

➤ Mortgage-backed securities offer investors rates sometimes from 1.5% up to 3% higher than Treasury securities with similar maturities. Proceed with caution, though, as the prices on mortgage-backed securities react more to interest rate movements than Treasuries do.

Corporate Raiders and Muni-Takers

Throughout this section on bond investing, you will find one rule that keeps popping up: Bond prices move in the opposite direction of interest rates. I'm sure this rule seems repetitive, but knowing it and timing your bond investing around it will enable you to make money on Wall Street.

In this chapter, you will uncover a lot of information about two *very* different types of bond investments—corporate bonds and municipal bonds. Even though they carry many differences in terms of how investors are taxed, the yields that you can earn, and the risks associated with each, both offer investors the opportunity to make some pretty decent money.

Float Me a Note

Several chapters ago, in a galaxy far, far away, you learned how corporations raise money, known as capital: through a stock offering. Another way these corporations can raise money is by selling bonds. When a corporation sells bonds, they are known as *corporate bonds*. Easy enough?

These bonds represent a loan from the investor to the borrower, which is the corporation. So if I owned a company and needed to raise more money, but I didn't want to offer more stock to public investors, I could have a *bond offering*. You, the investor, would loan me the money to raise my capital by investing in my corporate bonds. In exchange for this loan, I promise to pay you back in full—with interest—at a later date. The interest that you receive is taxable on federal, state, and local levels. As a bondholder, you are a creditor to my company, not an owner; you would be a stock owner (or shareholder, as it is commonly known) if you were to buy stock.

Why would a company want to sell bonds? Well, a corporation could borrow money from a bank, but the interest rates on bank loans are too high. By eliminating the bank, the company gets the money at a lower rate of interest. In addition, they probably have a longer period of time to repay the money than if they had borrowed it from the bank. Typically, banks loan money to corporations for no longer than five years.

Secret

Most brokers do not like to sell bonds in increments of less than $5,000—although it does happen. You can buy less than $5,000 worth of corporate bonds, but the mark up (commission you pay) on them will be much higher.

Here's what I would do in a bond offering. Overall, my company needs to raise $20,000,000. Therefore, I hire an investment banking firm, known as the *underwriter*, to "manage" the bond offering in order to make it available to all investors—including you. I plan on paying back all of my lenders over a period of ten years, and I am willing to pay you an 8% interest rate for letting me borrow the money. Whether you want to buy one bond or one thousand bonds, the details remain the same.

If I can't borrow all of the money through the bond offering from investors, I have to either cancel the bond offering or make my terms more attractive to other investors. The bond offering is very similar to a stock offering since there are underwriters—the investment banking or brokerage firm. Many times, these firms deal primarily with bond offerings.

Corporate bonds are issued in denominations of $1,000 and are quoted in the same way Treasuries are. They trade in 1/32nds of a point, just like all other bonds.

What?

The *floating rate* is the rate on a corporate bond that is constantly changing, which is why it is considered an adjustable rate. The rate will rise and fall along with the general direction of interest rates.

Now, before you can analyze and invest in corporate bonds, you have to learn the jargon that goes along with them. If you want to buy a few bonds that my company is offering, you need the following information:

➤ The name of the corporation, in this case my company name, which is also known as the *issuer*.

➤ The interest rate on the bond, also known as the bond's *coupon rate*, and when it is paid (expressed in terms of months and dates).

➤ The date of maturity.

➤ Whether or not the bonds are callable. In other words, can the corporation "call them back" and redeem the bonds before the date of maturity?

➤ Fixed rate or *floating rate*. Do the bonds have a fixed rate, a constant rate paid to the bondholder until maturity. Or do they have a floating rate, an adjustable rate that is constantly changing. The floating rate will move along with the general direction of interest rates.

Secret
If you invest in a corporate bond that carries a floating rate, know that your interest payments will also be adjusted accordingly. If interest rates fall, the interest payment that you receive will decline, also. However, if interest rates rise, your interest payment will increase. Remember, though, the price of the bond moves in the opposite direction of interest rates.

Here's an example of how my corporation might describe a corporate bond that you could invest in. Check out the lingo.

CLH—FA-15—8 1/2% of '09

So what does all this mean? "CLH" stands for my corporation name: Christy L. Heady, Inc. "FA-15" represents the months and dates you will receive an interest payment. In this case, F means February, and A means August. The 15 represents the date in those two months you will receive the payment. Therefore, FA-15 means you will get interest payments on the 15th of February and August. (There are your semi-annual interest payments, just like you would receive on most other bonds.) The 8 1/2% is pretty easy to decipher. It's the coupon rate, the fixed rate, you will receive on the corporate bond if you hold it until maturity. Speaking of maturity, the '09 stands for the year 2009, when the bond matures.

The difference with the interest payments on corporate bonds is that they pay their interest on either the 1st or the 15th of the two months, which are six months apart. Look at Table 27.1.

Table 27.1 How'd Ya Figure Out That Date?

You receive interest	1st of the month	15th of the month
January and July	JJ	JJ-15
February and August	FA	FA-15
March and September	MS	MS-15
April and October	AO	AO-15
May and November	MN	MN-15
June and December	JD	JD-15

Once you can translate the bond abbreviation, you can get a corporate bond quote. Table 27.2 gives an example of how my corporate bonds would be priced in the newspaper.

Table 27.2   Corporate Bond Prices as They Would Look in the Paper

Bonds	Cur Yld	Vol	High	Low	Close	Net Chg.
CLH 8 1/2' 04	8.58	15	100 3/4	98 5/8	99	–1/2
(a)	(b)	(c)	(d)	(e)	(f)	(g)

Here's what each of the numbers in Table 27.2 means:

(a) This is similar to the bond description you translated before. CLH stands for my company name, the 8 1/2% represents the fixed rate you would receive as an investor, and the '04 represents the year in which the bond would mature.

(b) 8.58 represents the current yield. This figure is obtained by dividing the coupon rate by the current price. It tells you what your income return is.

(c) This tells you the number of my corporate bonds traded that day. In this case, only 15 bonds traded.

(d-f) These give you the high, low, and closing prices of this corporate bond (the price fluctuations) for the previous trading day. The highest price recorded for my corporate bond was 100 3/4, meaning the highest price of the bond was $1,075.00. The lowest price was 98 5/8, which is $986.25. However, the closing price was neither its high nor low for the day (although that does happen). It was 99, which equals $990.00.

(g) Net change represents the difference in price from the previous day's trading activity to yesterday's trading activity. This is expressed in points. Therefore if today is Wednesday and you're looking at the paper, you would be reading all about Tuesday's trading activity. The net change on Tuesday compares the closing price of the bond on Monday with the closing price of the bond on Tuesday. The bond was down 1/2 a point, which is $5.

Playing the Game of Risk

Why are corporate bonds more risky than Treasuries and federal agency bonds? Because they are *unsecured.* This means that they are only backed by the issuer, which is the corporation.

For example, if you invested in a corporate bond issued by my company, you would receive your interest payments and your principal back on the maturity date based on my corporation's ability to repay you. I pay you these interest payments and your principal back in full on the maturity date out of my company cash flow (the money that I take in from the services/goods I sell) and my profits. Because these bonds are unsecured, they are known as *debentures.* In the event my company goes under, there is nothing that backs the default except for my corporation's word.

Unsecured Corporate Bonds

Corporations experience many highs and lows in the business world. Company sales might be booming one year and hit the skids the following year. Competition is fierce among many business corporations and industries. All companies are vying for basically the same bottom line—a profit.

No matter where we are in the business cycle (as you recall from learning about economics in Chapter 2), every corporation is affected in some way, shape, or form. Therefore, because of the ups and downs in the business marketplace, corporate bonds that are not secured are considered riskier than government issues. However, you would receive a higher yield on them in exchange for the higher degree of risk.

What happens if you own a corporate bond and the company goes into default? That is actually a rare case scenario, because less than 1% of all corporate bonds are ever affected by default. However, if you did have to state your claims during a bankruptcy proceeding to receive your loan back (remember, this is a loan you've given the company), you would be paid before stock-holders would receive their settlements.

> **What?**
> A *mortgage bond* and a *mortgage-backed security* are completely different things. A mortgage bond is issued by a corporation and is secured by real estate being used as collateral in case the issuing corporation of the bond goes belly up. A mortgage-backed security is based on a pool of mortgages that are sold as a package to investors and are backed by federal government agencies.

Secured Bonds

In contrast, if I issue *secured bonds*, the bonds are backed by an asset of the company should my company go into default. Examples of assets include real estate and equipment. These corporate bonds are then given different names, depending on what is being used as collateral. For example, if you buy a secured corporate bond that is backed by real estate, it is known as a *mortgage bond*. If the bond is backed by equipment that my corporation owns, the bond is known as an *equipment trust certificate*. In any event, the bonds are still corporate bonds.

Brokers make money from corporate bonds similarly to federal agency bonds. The brokers mark them up on the buy and down on the sell. If you bought a corporate bond at a price of 95, and the dealer marked it up to 95 1/2, you would be paying $950 for the bond plus $5 in commission. That's the markup. (This is just review, okay?) If you were to sell the bond at a price of 110, the broker would have to include his commission, which would be a mark down, because he would be marking down the amount you would

> **Secret**
> If an upgrade is given on a corporate bond, the yield will fall, and the price will rise because the bond is considered to be less credit risky. Make sure you follow your corporate bond investments for any upgrades.

receive. You would receive $1,100 less the mark down—let's say it's $5. So your net proceeds would be $1,095.

Bet You Didn't Know

And you never will: When a broker marks up (or down) a bond, that commission will never be reported to you.

What else makes the price of a corporate bond rise? Good news from the company will spread to the bond rating services, and it is possible an upgrade will be given.

What?

Spread is the difference between two yields on two bonds, such as a Treasury and a corporate bond, with the same maturity expressed as basis points. When the yields move away from each other, the spread grows wider. When the yields move closer together, the spread narrows.

If you want to take on more risk, corporate bonds allow you the opportunity to earn between one and two percentage points more than Treasuries. Why? Because of the lower credit rating corporate bonds receive. So how do you make money trading them? Just like you do with most other bonds:

➤ You can buy them when interest rates are high—prices are therefore low—and sell them when interest rates come down—prices would therefore rise. Thus, you would sell them for a profit before maturity.

➤ You can look for those companies that may be upgraded. If a corporate bond is upgraded, the price rises—and the interest rate falls—because it is considered to be less credit risky.

➤ You can buy corporate bonds when the spreads are wide in anticipation of the spread tightening. The spread is represented by the difference in basis points when you compare, for example, a Treasury bond to a corporate bond, both with the same maturity. For example, if a Treasury bond has a yield of 7%, and a corporate bond has a yield of 7.5%, the spread would be 50 basis points (half of a percent because 100 basis points = 1%). If after time the Treasury yield remains at 7% but the corporate bond yield drops to 7.25%, the spread narrows—25 basis points. But what happens to the price of the corporate bond? It rises because the yield fell.

Municipal Bonds—Only for the Tax-Troubled?

The biggest advantage of municipal bonds is that the interest you receive from them is exempt from federal income tax (you don't have to pay any). These municipal bonds are commonly known as munis (pronunciation: myoo-neez) and pay interest every six months.

I can see you gleefully jumping out of your La-Z-Boy chair and yelling, "Yippee! I've finally found a way to whip the IRS." Not so fast, Andretti. First, read this section to see what a municipal bond is, and then see whether or not it's even worth it for you to invest in a municipal bond. Just because you don't have to pay federal taxes on the interest income you receive doesn't mean you should invest. I'll explain why after you learn what a municipal bond is.

Several hundred billion dollars' worth of municipal bonds exist today, with another billion or two new bond issues coming out every year. There is no auction to buy and sell these; you have to buy or sell them at a brokerage firm or a bank, as long as the bank has that type of system available—not all local banks do. Again, these brokerage firms do not assess you a commission, but rather mark up the municipal bond, usually up to 2.5% of their price for the bond.

Careful
Although major cities or states issue municipal bonds, it doesn't mean there isn't any risk involved. You must review their credit rating on an ongoing basis.

There are two different types of municipal bonds: *general obligation bonds* and *revenue bonds*.

General Obligation Munis

Commonly known as GOs, these municipal bonds are issued by a state, city, or town. Another name for these general obligation bonds are "full faith and credit" bonds, because the city, state, or town puts its good name and credit on the line. Therefore, the issuer must honor its obligation to its investors, even if it means it has to raise taxes or sell off assets, such as state land.

When you invest in a GO, you loan the state, city, or town your money in exchange for— you guessed it—their promise to pay back your loan in full, with interest, at a later date. When these cities, towns, or states borrow your money, they use it to finance ongoing municipal operations.

Revenue Bonds

This other type of municipal bond is backed only by the revenue generated from the project funded by the bond issue. This is why they are called *limited obligation* bonds, because the payment of bond interest and principal depends on the revenues generated from a particular facility.

A new toll-road is a good example. If the state needs the money to build a new toll-road, the state will have a bond offering to borrow the money to build the toll-road. The money that is required to pay bond investors back their interest payments and ultimately their principal is collected from the tolls paid by travelers going through the toll booth.

In a sense, if you buy a revenue bond and are forever paying tolls, you could think of it as paying yourself.

Here are a few ways to distinguish municipal bonds from the other kinds of bonds you've learned about so far in this part of the book, as well as some things to keep in mind if you're considering buying municipal bonds:

➤ Unlike Treasuries and corporates, municipal bonds are issued in minimum denominations of $5,000 (instead of $1,000). So, if you want to buy, you have to buy it in multiples of $5,000. That means one bond would cost you $5,000, two bonds would be $10,000, and so on.

➤ The interest income you receive from municipal bonds is exempt from federal tax.

➤ Municipal bonds trade in 1/32nds of a point, just like all other bonds.

➤ Watch out for *call features*. This means that if you buy a muni-bond that is *callable* on a certain date, the municipal issuer can cash in the loan to you—that is, pay you back, only with the interest you've earned to date. (Some corporate bonds carry this feature, too.)

➤ Municipal bonds have bond insurance, which protects against the chance of the municipality going into default or even receiving a bad rating from the rating company, which would drive the price of the muni-bond down. You don't purchase this insurance, but the municipal issuer does. The three largest muni-bond insurance companies are Municipal Bond Insurance Association (MBIA), American Municipal Bond Assurance Corporation (AMBAC), and the Financial Guarantee Insurance Corporation (FGIC). If you buy a bond that has bond insurance from one of these insurance agencies, your municipal bond will receive the highest credit rating it can get: an AAA from Standard & Poor. The cost of this insurance may lower the yield you would receive, but for that extra degree of safety, some investors find that it's worth it.

Bet You Didn't Know

Municipal bonds are callable, which means the issuer can redeem the bond before the maturity date. Check to see if the muni-bonds you invest in have a call feature.

You already know that the interest you receive on a muni-bond is exempt from federal tax. Wanna know something else? In many cases, if you live in the same state, city, or town where the bond issuer is, the interest is also free from state and local taxes— although this is not true in all cases.

Because of this tax-free feature, municipal bonds pay lower interest rates than those rates offered on U.S. Government bonds and corporate bonds. Therefore, you need to compare the yields you would get on taxable bonds, such as government or corporates, with the yields you would receive if you purchase municipals.

Let's see how the tax advantages work for higher-income individuals in higher tax brackets. Table 27.3 compares the real yields on three different bonds: a municipal bond, a Treasury bond, and a corporate bond, all with the same maturity. By calculating the *taxable equivalent yield*, you can determine which is the better deal for you and decide whether or not a municipal bond is a worthwhile investment. Your answer also tells you which investment (municipal, government, or corporate) would leave you with more money after taxes.

> **Secret**
> Investors in high tax brackets should invest in municipal bonds if the after-tax yield suggests so. When you are in the upper tax bracket, you end up paying more in taxes. As a result, any time you make a profit on an investment, you are taxed at your current income tax bracket. The higher the bracket, the more tax you have to pay on the profit of your investment.

Table 27.3 Tax-Free or Not Tax-Free, That Is the Question

Type of Bond	Return	Your tax bracket			
		39.6%	33%	28%	15%
Municipal bond	5.25%	8.69%	7.83%	7.29%	6.17%
Treasury bond	6.00%	6.00%	6.00%	6.00%	6.00%
Corporate bond	7.50%	7.00%	7.00%	7.00%	7.00%

Here's how to calculate the taxable equivalent yield. Find your marginal tax rate. For example, if you were in the 28% tax bracket, take 100 minus 28 to get your denominator, which is 72. Then take the municipal bond yield (return) and divide it by your denominator. If you were interested in buying a muni-bond with a yield of 6%, you would find your taxable equivalent yield using the following calculation:

> Municipal Bond Yield Return (6%)/ (100 – Marginal Tax Rate (72)) = Taxable Equivalent Yield (8.33%)

This means you would have to earn at least 8.33% on a taxable bond in order to end up with the same amount after taxes that you'd have if you invested in a municipal bond.

> **Secret**
> Not all municipal bonds are tax-exempt, so you may be paying state and local taxes on both your municipal and corporate bond investments; Treasuries are free from state and local taxes. This adds to the attractiveness of investing in municipal bonds, because if you added your state and local tax bracket to your federal tax bracket, some of you could wind up with tax brackets as high as 50%!

The bottom line is, the higher the tax bracket, the more your taxable bond would have to pay in interest to end up with the exact same after-tax return as a municipal bond.

The Least You Need to Know

➤ Corporate bonds are IOUs from corporations. They promise to pay investors back the initial investment plus interest on a maturity date. Interest payments are paid on the 1st and 15th of two months that are set six months apart.

➤ Corporate bonds carry more risks than government bonds, because the only thing that backs them up is the company's word, especially if you buy an unsecured corporate bond. However, if you buy a secured corporate bond, there is usually some type of asset to back it up.

➤ Municipal bonds are debt obligations of a state or local government entity, and, in the event of default, the muni-bond holder would rely on municipal bond insurance, which are policies underwritten by private insurers. Muni-bond insurance can be purchased by the issuing government entity or the investor, and it says that the bonds will be purchased from investors at par should default occur.

➤ If you can figure out the taxable equivalent yield, which is the same amount you would have to earn from a taxable bond (such as a corporate or a government bond), and compare it to the yield you would get on a municipal bond, you can figure out which one would pay you more money in the end!

Chapter 28

What's All This Junk?

In This Chapter

➤ Chasing higher yields with junk bonds—but be careful

➤ Understanding why junk bonds were such a hot investment in the 1980s

➤ Deciding if they are an investment for you

If you read the last chapter, you are already one step ahead of the game in learning about junk bonds. Why? Because they are simply corporate bonds that carry extremely high rates of interest. The only difference between a corporate bond and a junk bond is that a junk bond has a much lower credit rating, which is why they pay higher rates of interest. In fact, the interest rates on junk bonds may be two percentage points higher than rates on a regular corporate bond with the same maturity.

But there is also a dark side to investing in a junk bond. As you learn more about the different types of investment products that exist, you'll see that the more interest or reward you receive from an investment, the riskier it may be. This chapter will tell you why you can make more money investing in junk bonds...if you don't mind taking on more risk!

The Risks and the Rewards

The types of companies that reward investors with high-interest bonds do so because there is the possibility that the company might not see the sunrise tomorrow. Technically, junk bonds pay such high rates of interest that the corporation may not earn enough money—either through sales or bottom-line profits—to cover the interest payments investors should receive every six months. This is why junk bonds are also called *high-yield bonds*.

What?

High-yield bonds, also known as *junk bonds,* are IOUs issued by a corporation that is considered to be in an extremely risky position, either because of potential default or lack of experience. These bonds pay extremely high rates of interest because they are below investment grade.

As a result of the associated risks, junk bonds are rated rather unfavorably by the bond rating agencies, such as Standard & Poors and Moody's. The exact definition of a junk bond is a bond that is rated BB or lower. And get this—some even have a C-rating...or no rating at all!

Some companies held their first corporate bond offering (these bonds weren't even junk bonds, they were just corporate bonds) and were given a pretty good investment grade by the rating services—only to then find themselves downgraded to a BB or lower. Any new bond offerings would be considered junk.

If these bonds pay such high rates of interest, why did the allure fizzle out? Travel back a decade, and you'll find out.

Originally Fashion for the '80s—What About the Future?

One of the biggest financial fashion crazes during the 1980s was to be in debt. The more debt you had, the more you had to show for it (cars, boats, clothing, vacations, summer homes—you name it). Consumer debt soared in the '80s.

Secret

Make sure you review Chapter 17 about the rating services that rate all bonds, and pay special attention to the investment grade given to your junk bond investments. Remember, never buy an unrated bond.

And so did business debt. During the '80s, the typical company's *balance sheet* was filled with IOUs and what-not. Forget selling company stock as a way to raise capital. Instead, many companies began offering bonds as a way to raise money. Unlike stocks, these bonds were IOUs, and that put the companies further into debt.

The greed factor was also running rampant throughout many business communities. Company takeovers and mergers—financed by junk bond offerings—were the craze during the '80s. Companies sabotaged their fortunes with a mound of debt due to the IOUs (principal and extremely high rates of interest) that they owed their bond investors.

Bet You Didn't Know

Here's a story about one '80s junk bond king extraordinaire. Remember all of the hoopla about Michael Milken, the former exec of Drexel Burnham, one of the biggest bond houses during the 1980s? His claim to fame was based on a simple concept he created for corporations to give them more financial muscle. Milken's concept took advantage of the fact that when a pretty risky company wanted to take over and buy out another company, it would need cash to do so. If it didn't have the money, it would borrow the money from investors who wouldn't mind a higher rate of interest in exchange for a bit more risk.

For example, if my new start-up company wanted to buy your company but didn't have enough money to do so, I could use Milken's concept. My company is an extremely risky venture because I fly by the seat of my pants, juggling weak profits to cover already large debts. To raise the money, I would hold a bond offering, therefore borrowing the money from public investors with the promise to pay back these investors their money at a later date with interest. However, because my company is so risky and my investors know this, I must pay them higher rates of interest which is what makes these bonds "junk." Boom! I raise the money, and I try to buy your company.

This scenario is similar to what some highly respected companies did in the early '80s. These companies would offer junk bonds to investors, loading themselves up with huge amounts of debt, in order to take over other companies. The huge amount of debt climbed because they owed a ton of money and extremely high interest to investors, and because they took on the financial burden of other companies when the takeover deals went through.

There were other factors which caused debts to get so huge that weren't due to corporate management. The impact of where the country stood in the economic business cycle (refer to Chapter 2) caused worry among these corporations. What could economics do to companies that paid interest on junk bonds to its investors? Well, when we were in a recession, the money that companies would make from sales of goods or services would fall. And if the company wasn't making enough money, it didn't have enough money to pay interest on its bonds to its bondholders. In fact, in the late '80s, it was reported that should a major recession occur, nearly 15 percent of all junk bond issuers would go belly up.

Secret

Watch out for call features on a junk bond. If you remember, call features give the issuer the power to redeem the bond prior to maturity, which is a disadvantage to the bond holder because the yield drops, and you'll have to reinvest the proceeds at the new lower interest rate.

Just how large did the junk bond market get back then? About five years ago, we weren't even in a recession, and the issuers of almost $3 billion worth of junk bonds paying extremely high yields couldn't make their interest payments anymore. This is one of the reasons the sizzle went out of investing in junk bonds.

While getting out of debt is more in fashion than carrying it these days, many investors are taking on more market risk and investing in junk bonds. The junk bond market totals nearly $310 billion as of 1996. Who still owns junk bonds? Mostly investors who do not mind taking on a lot of risk

And the Price, Please?

Prices for high-yield bonds vary with the coupon rate and the time remaining until maturity, as they do with most bonds. This is because the longer you hold the bond, the more risk there is—and you're dealing with a risky investment to begin with. However, more risk means higher yield.

> **Secret**
> If you want to invest in junk bonds but don't know which company to invest in, let a professional portfolio manager do it for you. How? Through a mutual fund, which you learned about in Part 3. You can invest in a junk bond fund and still get higher yields. Contact a few of the major mutual fund companies listed in the Appendix to obtain information about their junk bond funds.

The face value on a high-yield bond is $1,000, but most often they do not sell at their face value. Particularly when bonds are re-sold (meaning, they have already been bought at a bond offering and are then sold out in the market, which is known as the *secondary market*), many are traded at discounts because of the higher rates of interest that are offered. Purchasing a bond on the secondary market means you buy it from another investor (there always has to be a buyer and a seller) who is selling the bond. This transaction is done through a brokerage firm, and the order is executed on an exchange or in the over-the-counter market.

What influences the yield on a junk bond? The same thing that affects yields on all other bonds: the general direction of interest rates. But there's one more thing—the credit quality of the issuer. (In English, please!) This means that if a company, known as the issuer, has outstanding junk bonds with a BBB rating, and a rating service company downgrades the company, the prices on those bonds will fall. When bond prices fall, interest rates rise. Therefore, the yield on a junk bond is affected, because the investment is even riskier.

To buy junk bonds, the brokers you buy them from often want you to meet certain requirements:

➤ A five bond minimum, for an initial investment total of $5,000 (5 × $1,000 face value = $5,000).

➤ A mark up of $5 to $25 per bond, on average. Sometimes there's just a minimum charge of $35, unless it's a brand-spankin' new issue (it's never been traded before). Then there's no charge.

➤ The company name or symbol, the coupon rate, and the maturity date. The broker asks you to provide this information so he or she can get you the right bond quote and, therefore, the right price.

Are They for You?

Investing in junk bonds is not for everyone. Junk bonds have an extremely low credit rating. In order for you to determine if you should invest, you need to know the risks that are involved and pay attention to the following guidelines:

➤ Make sure you get a lot of information about the company *before* you invest.

➤ When you invest in a junk bond, treat it as if it were a stock. In other words, you should have expectations of strong price appreciation (like a stock) and periodic payments, which you should expect, but know they're not guaranteed.

➤ If you are a conservative investor and still want a fixed-income security but without the risk (or the white-knuckle experience), junk bonds are not the type of investment for you.

Secret
If you are planning to hold a junk bond until maturity, remember its riskiness depends fully on the issuer's credit rating. This credit rating is evaluated regularly by one of the rating agencies. Keep in mind that your regularly scheduled interest payments might be interrupted depending on the continuing financial strength of the company.

Bet You Didn't Know

There are special mutual funds designed for riskier investors that invest only in junk bonds. The funds are still risky, though, so be careful. Contact the mutual fund companies listed in Appendix B to see which ones offer junk bond funds.

The Least You Need to Know

➤ Junk bonds are also known as high-yield corporate bonds. Like all other bonds, they are IOUs made by a corporation to its investors.

➤ Investing in junk bonds is one of the most risky bond investments. Why? Because of the underlying weak financial strength of the issuer. However, in exchange for the risk, you receive a much higher rate of interest on the bond.

➤ Make sure you see what types of call features are associated with the junk bond. This means the issuer can redeem or cash in the bond before maturity.

Part 6
Taking the Plunge with the Commodities Market

Why include information about commodities in The Complete Idiot's Guide to Making Money on Wall Street? *It's because commodities are an everyday part of our lives.*

The next time you are at the grocery store, look at the products on the shelves or in the freezer. You'll find some of the most common elements that make up our futures market. Orange juice, wheat (found in cereal and bread), cocoa, coffee, sugar, corn, poultry, and oats are a few examples of the types of commodities—the goods—that are bought and sold on the futures market.

Plus, the commodities market allows everyday investors the opportunity to earn more money than any other type of investment. Margin requirements are less strict than yesteryear, allowing investors to pony up less cash than in the past to secure a future or options contract.

But another reason to include a chapter or two on commodities is that more and more investors are using options as a way to "hedge" their portfolios in case of wide market swings. For that strategy, and more, you'll learn in this section how you can get in on the commodities market.

Chapter 29

Learning the Basics About Investing in Futures

In This Chapter

➤ Understanding a futures contract

➤ Making a ton of money—and losing even more!

➤ Finding out why futures are so risky

So what's all this hoopla about how easy it is to make money in futures? You set your sights on a few cattle or pork bellies, and overnight you're a millionaire? That's not exactly how it works.

Futures trading tempts wanna-be-rich investors with the allure of fast action, low minimums, and the potential of reaping gigantic profits. It is extremely important that you understand what a future is before you even consider investing in one. Even investors who are extremely knowledgeable and trade futures all the time have been burned. The high-stakes game of investing in futures has been known to wipe out many fortunes.

Some examples in this chapter will tell you exactly what a future is. As you read on, you will see just how risky they can be.

Taking a Gamble

When you *speculate* in futures, you are taking a gamble. Think of it this way. When you buy stock, you have partial ownership in a company. When you invest in a bond security, it represents an IOU from the issuer to promise to pay you back in full plus interest. And mutual funds? Depending on what type of fund you invest in, you have exposure to both stocks and bonds.

Futures are a completely different story. There is no ownership, no IOUs, and no tomorrow if you lose big. I don't want to have you freak out over futures trading, but I do want you to be aware of the risks involved. First, let's take a peek and see exactly what all the hoopla has been about.

Moving Forward

Simply put, a *forward contract* (similar to a future) is a contract in which a buyer and a seller agree to complete a transaction on a specific commodity at a predetermined time in the future that is based on the transaction agreed upon today. All the details are left up to the buyer and seller.

> ### Bet You Didn't Know
>
> With a forward contract, you must make or take delivery of the commodity and settle on the delivery date.

To illustrate how a forward contract works, let's say a wheat farmer is about to plant his summer crop and estimates that it will cost $2.00 per bushel to grow the wheat. He figures out that the crop will yield 200,000 bushels at the end of the summer. So the farmer enters into a forward contract with a buyer (like a grain or bread company who needs the wheat) to sell the anticipated 200,000 bushels of wheat. The wheat will be sold at a price that represents a profit for the farmer before the wheat is even planted.

Let's add some numbers now. The buyer agrees to buy the farmer's 200,000 bushels of wheat for $2.50 a bushel. (Farmers gotta make a profit, right?) The buyer agrees to buy it six months later on September 15, regardless of the market price of wheat at that time. If the farmer grows the wheat and produces 200,000 bushels, and it only costs him $2.00 a bushel, the farmer has a profit from the transaction. Here's the math: 200,000 bushels × ($2.50 (the sale price) – $2.00 (his cost)) = $100,000. He gets this amount no matter what the market price of wheat is on September 15.

What happens if farmers growing wheat have poor crops, either due to poor weather or insects? A lot. Because of the laws of supply and demand, the supply of wheat is low, which pushes wheat prices higher—all the way up to $3.00 a bushel by September 15. Because of the already-agreed-upon transaction between the farmer and the buyer, the farmer must sell the wheat at the $2.50 per bushel price—and the farmer misses out on the additional profit potential. If he had waited until harvest time to sell the crop out in the market (instead of selling it in a forward contract), he could have made an additional $100,000 in profit on his 200,000 bushels of wheat.

> **What?**
> A *forward contract* is a commitment by the seller to deliver, and by the buyer to take delivery of, a stated quantity of a commodity or security on a future date at a price determined today.

On the other hand, if his crops only yielded 100,000 bushels, he would have to go out and buy enough wheat to honor his contract. That means he would have to buy wheat for $.50 more per bushel than he is selling it for! (These figures in no way represent any true stories. Their purpose is to mathematically illustrate the intricacies of the commodities market.)

So what is the advantage of a forward contract? Risk is somewhat limited because both parties have limited their risk and reward. The disadvantage is that both the buyer and the seller are exclusively dependent upon each other to carry out the transaction.

I Can See the Future

Now, a futures contract is a bit different. The concept is the same: pre-selling a commodity at an agreed upon price today for delivery in the future. But the delivery dates are different because they are pre-set by a financial exchange. The months in which the contracts expire are known as the current or *spot month*.

Futures contract transactions are handled on the floor of mercantile exchanges, such as the Chicago Mercantile Exchange, the Minneapolis Grain Exchange, and the New York Futures Exchange. A list of futures exchanges is provided in Appendix D.

> **Bet You Didn't Know**
> It is much easier to get out of a futures contract than to get out of a forward contract. How do you do it? All you have to do is take the opposite position, therefore, closing out your position. This way you avoid the delivery process.

In a futures contract, the transactions take place at the financial exchange and not out in a corn field or wheat field. However, the farmer and the buyer don't necessarily go to the financial exchange. The exchange brings together a number of buyers and sellers (either farmers or company reps, or even you and me) to agree upon a fair future price for a particular commodity.

What?

Futures contract are highly standardized because the specifics (the delivery date, the quantity, and the quality) of the futures contract are determined by the financial exchange.

In this type of contract, the buyers and sellers do not know who is on the other end of the transaction. For example, in this situation, a seller (the farmer, for example) would enter into a futures contract (either directly or indirectly using a broker) to sell the corn at a price he picks today. That corn is to be delivered at a pre-set time down the road that is established by the financial exchange. (For a listing of contract months, keep reading.) To sell the corn, there has to be a buyer on the other end, such as a corn product manufacturing representative. The bottom line is that sellers sell to the *clearing corporation* (the organization that "clears" the transactions—they add up all the pluses and minuses) and buyers buy from the clearing corporation.

Bet You Didn't Know

Not all futures contracts are for commodities like corn or wheat. Other futures contracts include stock index futures, Eurodollar futures, and T-bond futures.

If you were to invest in futures, you would usually do so through a full-service brokerage firm, although some discount and deep-discount brokerage firms also allow you to trade them. Since your strategy is probably just to make money from the transaction (not to buy 200,000 bushels of soybeans), you need to make sure you constantly keep up with any changes in price of the commodity or security.

Just remember that exchange-listed futures contracts require the delivery of a specific quantity of a specific commodity (like corn or wheat) at predetermined dates.

Making or Losing Millions Overnight

When you enter into a forward contract, any profits or losses are not realized until the contract "comes due" on the predetermined date. In a futures contract, however, profits or losses are realized *every day*. For example, if the price of the underlying commodity, like corn or even cattle, moves away from its price agreed upon in the contract (known as the *exercise price*), the party losing as a result of that price move (whether it was up or down) must pay the one benefiting by it. Every day the money is taken out of the loser's account and deposited into the winner's account by the clearing house.

So, how do you make money at this? First, review what you already know about commodity futures:

➤ Futures contracts are traded on financial instruments and commodities, which include various agricultural goods, and bulk products such as grain and metal.

➤ A futures contract is a contract to either buy or sell a certain amount of a commodity at a particular price within a stated period of time.

➤ That price is established on the floor of a financial exchange.

If you are going to invest in futures, you also need to understand the three types of futures traders that exist:

➤ **Speculators.** When you speculate, many people say that you are just guessing what is going to happen. In the futures market, a speculator does not own the underlying commodity (like a farmer would); that person is trying to achieve a profit from the ups and downs in the price of the contract.

➤ **Hedgers.** These traders (like the farmer, for example) own the underlying commodity. They use futures contracts to protect themselves against any changes in the price that may result in a loss for them (because they own the underlying commodity).

➤ **Scalpers.** These are the floor traders at the exchange. They buy and sell contracts and hope to gain a profit from their trades.

When you buy a futures contract, it requires you to take delivery of the underlying commodity—no matter if it is wheat, gold, pork bellies, or soybeans. This is known as *taking a long position*. The advantage of entering into a futures contract is the profit potential. The disadvantage is the danger, especially when you do not "offset" your position.

Buying a futures contract doesn't require a lot of start up money. Usually, you're only obligated to put up five to ten percent of the contract's value. So, as a hypothetical example, if you wanted to buy ten soybean contracts (one contract = 5,000 bushels),

Secret
Why trade futures instead of forward contracts? Because you know exactly what you are trading in terms of the quantity, the quality, and the delivery date. The only piece of information you need to settle on is the price.

What?

Exercise price is the agreed-upon price on the futures contract.

Secret
A futures contract requires the buyer to take delivery of, and the seller to make delivery of, the underlying commodity unless their position is closed out. How is it closed out? When one person enters into an offsetting position, opposite of his original investment.

entering into the contract would obligate you to accept delivery of 50,000 bushels of soybeans. If you were to follow through with your obligation and the price of soybeans was $1.25 a bushel (hypothetically), you would have to buy all 50,000 bushels of soybeans for $62,500.

Now we know that you aren't investing in a futures contract to end up with 50,000 bushels of soybeans. You are probably a speculator hoping to make a profit on the change in price of soybeans. So, you put up ten percent of the contract's value, which is known as *margin* (similar to what you learned in Chapter 19 about trading on margin). You now control $62,500 worth of soybeans with only $6,250. This deposit is known as a good-faith deposit.

Secret

If you're a speculator or a scalper, and you don't close out your position before the delivery date, you must take physical delivery of the goods. (And unless you live in a mansion, it might be quite difficult to explain to your spouse how the ten thousand bushels of soybeans are going to fit in your family room.)

Here's how you can make or break your bank. As the price of soybeans rises and falls, your futures contract also rises and falls in value. If the price of soybeans went up from $1.25 to $1.50, the value of your futures contract would increase to $75,000. Your profit? $12,500. Not bad for a day's work.

But all trading days are not like that. You also can lose money. If soybean prices fell from $1.25 a bushel to $1.00 a bushel and kept dropping, you would stand to lose all of your deposit money if the price kept plunging. If you lost all of your money, the price kept going down, and you didn't close out your contract (get rid of it!), you might be sent a margin call, which is the maintenance requirement you must keep in your account. This covers additional losses over your ten percent deposit.

What if you did not close out your contract? When the delivery date arrived, you would have to buy $62,500 (the exercise price) worth of soybeans, which would then be worth either more or less, depending on the day's current price. And you could either rejoice in a profit or cry over your losses—either one could be big!

Bet You Didn't Know

Only about one to three percent of futures contracts traded are settled by delivery. As long as you follow the futures markets and make the right calls, you shouldn't have to worry about feeding the cattle come supper time.

Read All About It

How do you read a futures quote in the newspaper? Just follow me. Futures quotations in the financial section of your newspaper are listed alphabetically and by commodity. Table 29.1 gives a brief explanation of how to read a futures quotation.

Table 29.1 Reading Futures Quotes for Corn in the Paper

Month	Open	High	Low	Settle	Change	High	Low	Open Interest
May	220 1/2	221 1/2	220	221	– 1/2	235	219	35,501
July	218 1/4	219 3/4	217	218	+ 1/4	225	217 1/4	12,322
Sept	211 1/2	215 1/2	210 3/4	215 1/4	+ 1/4	216 3/4	210	4,298
Dec	205 3/4	207 1/4	206 1/2	206 1/2	– 3/4	207 1/2	205 1/4	11,482
(a)			(b)			(c)		(d)

The following list describes the columns in Table 29.1:

(a) The months represent the spot month in which the contract will expire. It is usually the third Friday of those particular months.

(b) Open, High, Low, Settle, and Change. The Open price is the price at which the futures contract opens at the beginning of the trading day. The High price is the highest price the futures contract hits that day, so the Low price is the lowest price the contract hits. The Settle price is what it "closes" out at and is the price the buyers and sellers agree to "settle" on. Change represents the change in price from the previous day's close.

(c) High, Low. This represents the all-time high and low prices this particular contract ever traded.

(d) Open interest. This is the total number of futures contracts (either the buys or the sells) that have not been offset by an opposite transaction or even fulfilled by delivery, if that were the case.

If you don't want to risk much money in this high-stakes game, there are mutual funds available, called *commodity funds*, that invest in futures. You could also lose money in these funds, of course, but you won't ever be subject to any margin calls.

Investing in commodity funds takes a big chunk out of your initial investment because of the high commissions. If you are interested in tracking commodity funds, a newsletter called *Managed Account Reports* assists you in following the performance of these funds. If you are interested in a sample copy, call (212) 213-6202.

List Some Futures for Me

Table 29.2 lists a few of the different types of futures contracts, their trading months (spot month), their minimum price fluctuation, and the exchange they are listed on.

Table 29.2 Examples of Futures Contracts

Trading Commodity	Contract Months	Size	Min. Price Change	Exchange
Live Cattle	Feb/Apr/Jun Aug/Oct/Dec	20,000 lbs.	$0.0025/lb. ($5)	Mid-American Commodity
S&P500	Mar/June Sept/Dec	500 × S&P index value	5 points $25	Chicago Merc. Index Exchange
Wheat	Mar/May/July Sept/Dec	5,000 bushels	$0.0025/ bushel ($12.50)	Kansas City Bd of Trade

Before you invest in futures contracts, test your theory out on paper by running through the numbers associated with buying and selling a contract. It is much less expensive that way. Plus, if you keep abreast of weather conditions, you might be able to take some of the guesswork out because so many commodities are dependent upon the weather.

The Least You Need to Know

➤ A futures contract is an agreement between a buyer and a seller to either buy or sell a certain amount of a commodity at a particular price on a stated date. The price of the futures contract is established at a financial exchange.

➤ The month in which the underlying commodity is to be delivered is the spot month, although only one to three percent of all underlying commodities are never delivered. The rest of the contracts (positions) are offset (closed out, or resold) before the delivery date.

➤ Know the difference between a hedger, a speculator, and a scalper. A hedger owns the underlying commodity and uses futures to protect his or her position in the event of a market rise or fall. A speculator does not own the underlying commodity and benefits by entering into a futures contract to try to reap the rewards—hopefully selling the contract and making big profits. A scalper is a floor trader at a futures exchange, like the Chicago Mercantile Exchange.

Chapter 30

Hedging Your Bets

In This Chapter

➤ Knowing what different types of options exist

➤ Using options to protect against market fluctuations

➤ Using options as leverage

There are two things you can do with an option: protect yourself against any major drops in stock prices (known as hedging your portfolio) or get more bang for your buck. When you receive more bang for your buck, you are investing using a strategy called leverage, which you learned about in Chapter 19. Investing in options allows you to obtain a greater return on an investment, especially stocks and stock indexes.

In exchange for the possibility of a greater return, there are risks involved in options trading, including losing all your money in a relatively short time frame. You'll learn about these risks and a few ways you can get more bang for your buck in this chapter.

Leveraging Your Portfolio

Imagine having the chance to purchase 100 shares of stock in a company for only $500 even though the current trading price is $50 per share? You would need $5,000 plus commissions, right? Not when you trade options. For $500, you get the right to own those 100 shares of stock at its current price for a few months. Oooh, what a bargain.

Bet You Didn't Know

The financial exchange that trades stock and index options is the Chicago Board Options Exchange, **http://www.cboe.com**, founded in 1983.

What?

Strike price The price at which you can buy or sell the underlying security (typically stock). For example, if you bought an IBM January 65 call, the strike price here is 65. Purchasing this option would give you the right to buy 100 shares of IBM stock at $65 a share. If you were to buy all 100 shares it would be known as exercising your option.

What?

Expiration date. Using the same example, if you bought an IBM January 65 call, the expiration date is the third Friday in January. Expiration dates occur on the third Friday of every month for stock options. Expiration dates will vary depending on the underlying security.

And you also get to enjoy the rewards if the current trading price goes up. There's a catch, but isn't there always? As you also learned in Chapter 19, there are risks involved when using leverage. In most cases, the more leverage you use, the more risky the investment situation. Does that make options risky? It sure does, but that's why people who invest in options realize a 100 percent or even 300 percent return on their money. On the downside, it's also how they can lose all of their money. Although you could incur unlimited loss in some situations, usually the greatest amount of money you can lose when you trade options is your total initial investment.

So what are they? *Options* give you the right—but not the obligation—to buy or sell a certain quantity of stock or bond, stock or bond index, or futures contract. These are known as the *underlying securities*. The option enables you to buy or sell these underlying securities at a certain price, which is the *strike price*, up to a specified point in time, known as the *expiration date*.

When investing in options, you have the right to either buy or sell the underlying security. Options that give you the right to buy the underlying stock (or whatever security) are known as *calls*. On the other hand, options that give you the right to sell the underlying security are known as *puts*. When you exercise your right—known as *exercising your option*—on a call, then you "call away" the stock from the seller you bought the option from. When you exercise your right on a put, then you "put" the underlying security to the seller of the put.

So what do you want these options to do? When I was taking investment classes, my instructors taught us the easiest way to remember how calls and puts work. Repeat after me:

➤ When you buy an option to get the right to buy the underlying security, you are buying a *call*. When you buy a call, you want the price of the underlying security to go up. Therefore, think of it as "call up somebody on the telephone." Call up.

➤ When you buy an option to get the right to sell the underlying security, you are buying a put. When you buy a put, you want the price of the underlying security to go down. Therefore, think of it as "put down your foot." Put down.

Easy Way to Remember: Call Somebody Up on the Telephone

To repeat, when you buy a call option, you receive the right to buy the underlying security at a set price (the strike price) for a particular period of time. Typically, this period of time is just a few months.

Options are quoted in terms of dollars, so to speak. If you bought an option that is quoted at $2, it's not really two bucks, but rather $200 because underlying securities deal in round lots, equal to 100 shares for stock options. Other options are quoted with varying round lots.

Okay, now for a little quiz. If you wanted to buy an option that was quoted at $1 1/4, what would the price be? Make it into decimal form, 1.25, and multiply it by 100. The answer is $125.00. Try another one. What if you wanted to buy ten options at $3 3/4. Use the same mathematical formula. Take 3.75 (decimal) and multiply it by 100 (100 shares of stock, for instance) to get $375.00. But hey, you wanted ten options. Multiply $375.00 by 10 to get $3,750.00 (the price you'd have to pay for ten options).

Here's an example of how calls work. Suppose you want to buy a call option and you understand that you aren't necessarily buying the underlying security—just the *right* to buy the underlying security at a certain price. You buy a call option for $3 with a strike price of 60, for a total cost of $300, whose underlying security is IBM Corporation, the big computer giant. In this hypothetical example, you bought the right to buy 100 shares of IBM stock for $60 a share until November, which is about four months from now.

Currently, IBM stock is trading at $63. Your option tells you that you can purchase the stock at $60, but the current price is $63. Does that mean you already made a profit? No. You must remember to add in the *premium*, which is the price you paid for the option. Right now you are about even.

Because you own a call option, you want IBM stock price to go up in value between now and November. If, for example, IBM stock price soars to $70, your option is *in-the-money* because the current trading price ($70) is higher than your strike price ($60). Your option price could skyrocket from $3 (where you bought it at) to $10, which is what you want it to do.

Now you can do one of two things:

➤ Keeping in mind that you have the right to buy the stock, you could exercise your option. That means you "cash in" your right to buy 100 shares of IBM stock at $60 a share (those were the particulars of the options). Then you would own 100 shares of IBM stock at $60—but wait! The current trading price is $70. What you could do is sell your 100 shares of IBM stock at $70 (the current market value) and make a hefty profit.

It's math time.

Bought 100 shares of IBM stock at $60 = $6,000.

Sold 100 shares of IBM stock at $70 = $7,000.

Profit you would realize = $1,000 (less the $300 option price and not including any commissions).

Percentage profit you would realize = 233 percent return, which is $1,000 less $300 divided by $300.

➤ If you don't exercise your option but instead sell the option—sell your right to buy the underlying stock—you would still make a profit. You could sell the option for $10 each and receive $1,000. Your profit will equal the $1,000 less the $300 that you paid for the option (which is the premium).

Secret
When a person buys an option, he or she pays money for it. This money is called the premium. When a person sells an option (a form of "shorting"), he or she receives the premium.

Which is the better move? The end result is the same but selling the option is less cumbersome. It's really up to the investor, although most of the time, investors don't usually exercise their options to buy the underlying security.

If IBM stock price did not rise above $60 at all, the option would be considered *out-of-the-money* and come November, your option would expire worthless and you'd lose all $300 of your investment.

Why would someone buy a call option? Usually, the investor doesn't want to buy thousands of dollars worth of stock and instead uses a little bit of money to control a lot of shares. It's not that he or she can't afford it—although some investors might invest in options because they can't afford to buy stock. Because of the risks involved—losing all the money you paid as a premium—I advise you not to invest in options. Look at the pyramid in Chapter 4!

Easy Way to Remember: Put Down Your Foot and Protect Your Portfolio

Call up. Put down. Remember that, and you'll know the basics of options trading.

When you buy a put option, there are usually two reasons for doing it. If you are feeling bearish and expect to profit from falling stock prices, or to protect your investment portfolio (kind of like insurance).

If you think the markets are ready to take a tumble, you could profit by buying an index put option. You can buy a put option on the S&P 500, for example, in hopes that the price of the stock index tumbles.

Buying put options also provides you with some "insurance." For example, if you owned 100 shares of XYZ stock, and you wanted to protect your position because you're worried about losing money if the price of the stock plunges, you would buy a put option that has the underlying security of XYZ stock.

Think of what a put option is. It is the right to sell the underlying stock at a given price. If the price of XYZ stock dropped, you could help cushion the blow from the loss in the 100 shares of stock you already own.

Let's say you bought 100 shares of a technology stock at $20 a share about a year ago. Today, though, you're concerned about a steep decline in the price of the stock over the next couple of months because of market news and technical indicators. You think the price drop is just short-term, so you don't want to sell your stock, but you still need to protect your shares against any decline.

Here's what you do. Let's say it's the middle of June and the current market price is $25 a share and it's starting to slip to $23. You're concerned. In order to protect your position—and keep the shares—you can buy a put option with a strike price of 20, for example, that will expire in, let's say three months. Let's say the put option costs $175.00, which is your premium. The option quote would look something like this:

> ProRata Sept 20 put 1 3/4

Buying this put option means you have the right to sell 100 shares of this tech stock for $20 a share before the expiration date in September. This right allows you to sell your stock at $20 a share no matter what the current trading price is.

If the stock price keeps falling, you have the following options:

➤ You have the right to exercise your option by selling your shares of stock for $20 a share no matter what the current stock price is.

Secret
If you buy put options to protect your portfolio from downside risk, such as when there is a steep or declining market drop, your investments won't have to make up as much ground as they would if you didn't protect your portfolio.

Secret
The terms *in-the-money* and *out-of-the-money* do not indicate whether the buyer or the seller is making or losing money. These terms refer only to the actual relationship between the strike price of an option and the stock price.

What?
For a call option, *out-of-the-money,* the stock price is less than the strike price. For a put option, the stock price is greater than the strike price. For a call option, *in-the-money,* the stock price is more than the strike price. For a put option, the stock price is less than the strike price.

Secret
When you invest in index options, you never exercise your options. It just isn't done—it's cash settlement. That would mean you would have to buy or sell all of the underlying stock, and the commissions alone could buy you a new home!

➤ You can hold onto your underlying stock and "close the position," meaning, sell your put option. If you did this, you would make a profit because your put option would be *in-the-money*. If the stock dropped to $10 a share and the put option has a strike price of $20 a share, the amount of the *intrinsic value* is $10. That's how "in-the-money" your put option is.

In this scenario, if the stock price rose, your put option would be *out-of-the money* and your option would expire worthless. The amount of money you paid for the option—the premium—would be lost.

Bet You Didn't Know

For those of you who have never traded options before or who need further information, contact the Chicago Board Options Exchange, 400 S. LaSalle Street, Chicago, IL 60605 or call (312) 786-5600, (**http://www.cboe.com**). They should send you informational brochures as requested.

And Your Time Is Up

When do listed stock options expire? Are you ready? On a Saturday! Listed stock options expire on the Saturday following the third Friday of the expiration month at 11:59 p.m. EST. Check to see when your options expire.

No, you don't have to worry about missing your favorite cartoons, because the final trading day of the week for *options* closes at 4:30 p.m. EST on the business day before the expiration day. By this cut-off time, you need to notify your broker whether or not you're going to exercise your option. This is why options are said to also have *time value*. This reflects any additional amount that purchasers of options are willing to pay in hopes that the changes in the underlying stock price or index price will increase the option's market value before the option expires.

Careful
If you don't close out your option position when you invest in index options, your option will expire worthless.

The more time you have before an option expires, the more of a premium you pay. The less time you have until expiration the less the premium will cost you. Think of it this way. The more time, the more of a chance the stock price will move accordingly. The less time, the less of a chance it will get to where you want the price to go!

I'm a Little Short

You also should learn about when you short an option, which applies the same theory as when you short a stock. When you short a stock, you don't own the stock but rather borrow the shares from the brokerage firm. You first sell the stock at a price and hope to buy back the shares at a lower price. Keep the following in mind, and watch out for the risks:

➤ If someone sells a call or a put and it is the opening transaction, meaning it is the first transaction done, he or she is shorting the option. When the person does this, it is known as writing an option and the person is called a call or *put writer*.

➤ If a call option is exercised (by the buyer), the call writer (the person shorting the call option) must sell the stock to the call buyer at the strike price. Therefore, *the writer of a call* does not *want the price of the stock to go up*.

➤ If a put option is exercised (by the buyer), the put writer (the person who shorted the put option) must buy the stock from the put buyer at the strike price. Therefore, the *writer of a put* does not *want the price of the stock to go down*.

Secret
If an option is going to expire in-the-money, make sure you close out the transaction. If you don't, your option will be exercised for you and you could be forced into buying or selling shares of stock. Your broker should notify you, but just make sure you are aware.

Judging the Overall Risk

Table 30.1 recaps the risk potential of various option transactions. Make sure you're aware of the risk you're incurring before making any investment.

Table 30.1   The Risk Scale

When you...	Maximum Profit	Maximum Loss
Buy a call	Unlimited	Premium paid
Buy a put	Strike price less premium paid	Premium paid
Write a call	Premium received	Unlimited
Write a put	Premium received	Strike price less premium received

The Least You Need to Know

➤ If you buy a call option, you want the stock to go up. You're buying the option to buy the stock (call it in) at a specific price.

➤ If you buy a put option, you want the stock to go down. You're buying the option to sell the stock (put it out) at a specific price.

➤ If you write a call, or short the call, you don't want the stock to go up.

➤ If you write a put, or short the put, you don't want the stock to go down.

➤ The biggest risk involved in investing in options is losing all of your initial investment.

Part 7
Make That Money Grow

One of my favorite books, Think and Grow Rich *by Napoleon Hill, has the best line I've ever read, "Opinions are the cheapest commodities on earth." You can always get an opinion on a stock, bond, or mutual fund investment from anybody. There are millions of opinions on investing: research report opinions issued by brokerage firms, rating agencies, survey companies, newsletters published by financial gurus and market wizards, and a host of TV programs telling viewers what they should and shouldn't sink their money into.*

But the message to me, at least, in that book, had to do with knowing that the repetition of information and sheer determination is half the battle to achieving your goals. My goal, for you, is to help you make your own personal decisions about financial information so that you have control over your financial destiny. If you are easily influenced by the opinions of others, then all of the knowledge and investment smarts you have learned just went down the tubes.

You have the investment smarts to make your own decisions. This part tells you how to use that knowledge to make your money grow!

Chapter 31

Your Investment Portfolio from $100 to $10,000

In This Chapter

➤ Discovering that there are investments for everyone

➤ Finding what $100 can buy you

➤ Seeing what your investment portfolio might look like

Now that you have all this financial information stored away in your brain (which is probably ready to burst and ooze out of your ears), it's time to see how to assemble an investment portfolio. This chapter will help you finalize your investment decisions—no matter how much money you have to invest—assuming that you have settled your personal finances *first* (such as reducing your debt and getting your finances organized).

Where to Begin

I've given you an education about what types of investments you can buy and the philosophy that you don't need a lot of money to start. The world of making a lot of money is available to everyone, rich *and* poor.

Making money on Wall Street requires you to think about what kinds of investments are suitable for you. All of you who read this book have different levels of income and net worth, so the same investment portfolio that works well for me might not work out as well for you. I might be more of a risk-taker, and your investment approach may fall under the more conservative side.

I know you all want more from your investment programs. Some of you just want an investment program. The investment portfolios you are about to see are just guidelines. There aren't any secrets or any financial formulas to calculate. Any decision about how an investment portfolio is constructed is *your* decision and ultimately your responsibility. These are just suggestions. Your personal goals are different from anybody else's, but we're all looking for the same thing. It's not necessary to get rich, but we should all make our money work as hard for us as we do for it.

> ## Bet You Didn't Know
>
> If you have less than $100 to start out with, don't worry. There is still an investment for you—the dividend reinvestment program. Some DRIPs, such as Exxon, allow shareholders to begin investing with TEN BUCKS! For more information about companies that allow you to begin with less than $100, subscribe to *The Drip Investor*. For information, call (219) 931-6480.

The $100 Portfolio

If you are just starting out, congratulations and welcome to making money on Wall Street. You have motivated yourself enough (and I hope I helped a *little*) to start an investment program. Don't worry that you're starting out with only $100 a month or even every other month. Instead, focus on how you're going to make that $100 and any additional contributions grow. The idea is to start with $100 and continue adding as much as possible on a consistent basis. The more money you add, the more the magic of compounding can go to work for you!

The following investments are just suggestions. If you want to get your feet wet, these are a great way because most of them require no minimum investment amount, depending on which company you choose to invest in.

➤ **Money market funds or accounts.** The safest way to build your capital is to invest your $100 if the fund company or bank allows you a low minimum deposit. In exchange for little to no risk of principal, you'll earn a low, competitive rate of interest.

➤ **Automatic investment plans.** In exchange for a little more risk, take your entire $100 and invest it in an automatic investment plan. This type of investment allows you to automatically and electronically have a set amount of money transferred from your bank account (or money market fund) to the mutual fund of your choice. Start your automatic investment plan with your $100 deposit and pick an amount (such as $30) that you can work with to add subsequent investments. Then watch your money grow!

➤ **Dividend reinvestment programs.** In what is commonly known as a DRIP, you can invest your $100 and buy shares of stock without going through a broker. In order to diversify your portfolio, a good way to start is to choose three different companies that offer DRIPs with low minimum deposits and very few transaction fees. Divide up your $100 three ways (you choose the amount) to get your DRIP program started. If possible, add at least the minimum amount allowed each month to the program.

> **Secret**
> If you want your $100 to benefit from the magic of compounding, your best bet would be to invest in an automatic investment plan or a dividend reinvestment program. Money market deposit accounts are safe; however, they pay low rates of interest.

➤ **Savings bonds.** You can invest your entire $100 in a $200 savings bond because you only have to pay half of the face value of the bond upfront. Plus, if you use the $200 when you redeem the bond toward college tuition, you may be eligible for a tax break.

The $1,000 Portfolio

When you can make your $100 turn into $1,000 or even if you are fortunate enough to start off with $1,000, here are a few avenues you can pursue. Remember, since some investments require initial minimum deposits of $1,000, you'll have to fully invest your $1,000. Otherwise, make sure you diversify your portfolio and allocate a certain percentage to each investment. The allocation percentage depends upon your investment objective (growth or income) and your level of risk.

➤ **Money market mutual funds.** Typically, the minimum initial deposit requirement to open money market mutual funds is $1,000. If you're a conservative investor and need liquidity (the ability to get at your cash quickly) from your investment portfolio, consider depositing your money in a money market mutual fund.

➤ **Stock and/or bond mutual funds.** Unless you go through an automatic investment plan, many stock and bond funds require an initial deposit of $1,000 to invest. If your objective is growth, consider a stock growth fund for your $1,000. If your objective is income, consider a not-too-risky bond fund (no junk bond funds or commodity funds) for your $1,000. In either situation, make additional contributions on a monthly basis to take advantage of dollar cost averaging.

➤ **Automatic investment plans.** Because you can start with as little as $50 a month, allocate a portion—such as $50 or $100 a month—of your $1,000 to this plan. In fact, you could allocate $50 a month to a stock fund automatic investment plan and $50 a month to a bond fund automatic investment plan. This way you are diversifying your portfolio. Your other choices include a domestic stock fund and an international stock fund, an aggressive growth stock fund and a balanced fund. Whatever the mix, make sure it's the right one for you!

➤ **Dividend reinvestment plans.** Your $1,000 can be spread across several different DRIP stock programs. Each stock you select depends upon your investment objective (growth or income) and your risk tolerance. As an example, you could invest $100 in ten different stocks, five growth stocks and five income-producing stocks, or you can invest $200 in five different stocks. The allocation strategy is up to you, but make sure you research the stocks you choose, monitor company news and performance, and that your decision is in line with your objectives.

➤ **Savings bonds.** If you're planning on using the $1,000 for college tuition some day, you can invest all $1,000 in a $2,000 savings bond and possibly get a tax break. However, because savings bonds are conservative, those of you who want to earn higher returns should consider only allocating a portion of your $1,000 to a savings bond.

The $5,000 Portfolio

Now that you have accumulated $5,000, you can either keep doing what you've been doing, or take on a little more risk by allocating some of your money into the investments listed below. The idea is to diversify your portfolio, so all of your money doesn't get put into just one investment.

➤ **Money market funds—for cash needs.** Cash needs are those little "emergencies" that pop up, such as when you are laid off (not when you need to go to Las Vegas to "get away from it all" for a weekend). Most investors keep a portion of their portfolios in cash, anywhere between 10 and 30 percent.

Bet You Didn't Know

Most financial advisers require that you keep between three and six months' worth of living expenses in a money market account for emergencies, such as loss of a job or home.

➤ **Families of mutual funds.** Now you can choose several different types of mutual funds. Because you meet the minimum initial deposit requirements, consider investing $5,000 in five different funds. You can choose from aggressive stock funds, growth stock funds, balanced funds, and international funds. Five funds aren't too many *as long as you are diversified in your holdings.*

➤ **Automatic investment plans.** If you have been following this plan, continue to take advantage of dollar cost averaging. You don't need to sink all $5,000 in this plan; however, make it a point to increase your monthly contribution.

➤ **Foreign stock mutual funds.** The risks are greater, but the reward is, too. In 1993, the average international stock mutual fund returned slightly above 40 percent. I don't advise sinking *all* your money into this sector because of the risks involved. The more aggressive you are in your investment objectives, the more money you can allocate to these types of funds.

➤ **Stocks.** You can start but be careful. You have enough money now to actually buy 100 shares of stock, but the risks involved are greater. You don't necessarily have to sink all $5,000 into stocks, but for those of you searching for growth, a long-term growth stock with stable performance history might be a good choice. If dividends are the name of your game, consider researching companies that provide good, steady income. In either event, you can allocate your $5,000 among a few different stocks—just make sure you do your homework! (Refer to Chapter 5 for a refresher course.)

The $10,000 or More Portfolio!

Ten grand. Congratulations. Keep chugging along, you're doing great. Remember, a quitter never wins and a winner never quits! Don't get caught up because there are more zeros after the one in your investment portfolio now. Investment success requires long-term planning.

➤ **Money market funds—for those emergency needs.** Make sure you have a portion of your portfolio allocated to money market funds to help cushion any financial blows (such as a lay off or a market crash). Keep a percentage of your $10,000 in cash that you feel comfortable with, but not too much so you don't take advantage of higher returns elsewhere.

> **Secret**
> Add to your positions. If you currently own 100 shares of Bells and Whistles stock and want to invest more money into the same company, you would buy more shares. Therefore, you would be adding more shares to the number you already own.

➤ **Mutual funds—stock and bond funds and foreign funds.** All types of mutual funds are available to you now. If you currently are investing in mutual funds, consider allocating a significant portion to each fund. If you are new to this ball game, make sure you are well diversified and that you meet your investment objectives.

➤ **Automatic investment plans.** If you consistently do this, it's habit-forming. Keep up with your automatic investment plan. At this point, you may wish to increase your monthly contributions.

➤ **Stocks.** Make sure you have done your homework, and that you're keeping commissions low. If you're happy with the performance of your stocks and you are investing for the long term, you may want to *add to your positions.*

➤ **Fixed-income securities.** Depending on the direction of interest rates, consider looking into these now. Remember the minimum investment requirement for each fixed-income security, the risks involved, and the tax ramifications. For example, $10,000 buys a Treasury bill, but since $10,000 is all of your portfolio, investing only in a T-bill wouldn't follow the guideline of diversification. Keep in mind the higher degree of risk, the higher the return. If you are concerned with safety of principal, you can always look into a bond fund instead.

What about options and futures trading as you make more money? It's up to you, as long as you know what risks are involved. As my mother always taught me, "When in doubt, don't."

The Least You Need to Know

➤ It doesn't take a lot of money to make money.

➤ If you want to reach financial security, then you have to make your investment portfolio grow. Do it slowly and mainly over a long-term period.

➤ You know the 10 percent rule that I constantly drilled into everyone's head in the beginning of the book? Use it as a means to add to your investment portfolio.

Chapter 32

Tips on Year-Round Tax Planning

In This Chapter

➤ Learning a few basics about tax planning—year round

➤ Breaking down your taxation on all investments—profit or loss!

➤ Knowing how some investments are timed

The last item on your to-do list right now is worrying about this year's or next year's tax deadline, right? (Unless it is that time of year right now, and you're knee-deep in receipts with your accountant sleeping on a cot in your living room.)

Knowing sound tax strategies is an integral part of your investment planning, and this chapter can be a big help. After all, the more money you make in investing, the more you'll have to pay Uncle Sam. By putting smart tax strategies into effect now, you can avoid hassles come tax time—and keep your hard-earned cash in your pocket.

Understand that this information is *not* meant to replace sound tax planning advice from your accountant or tax adviser, but rather give you a basis from which to draw upon for your tax planning needs.

Adding Up the Pluses and Minuses

Memorizing last year's tax rules would be your worst kind of preparation. Why? Because things are always a changin'. Even in 1997, Congress passed a new tax law structure that affected many personal tax situations.

You should know that what bracket you fall under and how you structure your investing still requires you to be careful! If you find yourself paying more in taxes every year, don't wait until the last minute to look for some cash. You might end up having to sell some stock shares for only a slight profit, or even a loss. If you start squirreling away some extra money right now (in fact, set up a money market account specifically designed to meet your tax bill in April), the easier it will be.

Also, if you are self-employed, go in for a financial check-up immediately! If you're making estimated payments, increase them. If you're employed full-time, either have your boss increase your withholding or put some dollars away every month in a money market account earmarked for your tax payments. Every little bit helps.

Tax planning doesn't just concern the wealthy. You might find yourself in a new tax bracket if you planned your investments properly and made a few profits along the way.

Do It in June, Not April

Just as Bernard Baruch, legendary stock trader and millionaire, said to buy straw hats in winter and snowsuits in July, so should you begin your tax planning the June before your taxes are due! Sure, April is ten months away, but you know what our mothers always tell us. The early bird gets the worm. Assessing your tax situation when everything is a bit more relaxing allows you to take the time to make a more thorough review of your investments and how they could affect your taxes.

Go Tax-Free

One consideration, as you learned in Chapter 27, is if you find yourself in a higher tax bracket, consider investing in municipal bonds. As your tax rate increases, the value of tax-free investing increases, too. Compare yields that you would earn from a municipal bond to those of a taxable investment. (To figure this out, as you recall, make your tax bracket a decimal, subtract it from 1, and divide the tax-exempt yield by the result.)

For those consumers who'll be in a higher tax bracket, tax-free investments are especially advantageous. An investor in the 31% tax bracket buying AAA-rated, 20-year tax-free bonds which yield 5.21% would have to get a yield of 7.55% on a taxable investment to equal the tax-free investment's yield. Now, if that investor is bumped into the 36% tax bracket, the same municipal bond yield would be equivalent to 8.14% on a taxable investment.

Listen folks, no matter what tax bracket you fall under or how small your investments are, if you are planning to make your investment objectives work for you, you need to know about tax planning strategies. Familiarize yourself with any change in the tax rules and be sure to consult with a tax adviser. Tax planning is one area where it is definitely worth paying for the advice.

No Pain, No Captital Gain

When you buy low and sell high, you get a profit. That profit—known as a capital gain—has to be reported to the IRS. And when you buy high and sell low, you get a loss—a capital loss. That amount of loss must be reported to the IRS as well. Why would you want a loss? You'll see why in a minute.

To make tax preparation easier on you, make sure you record all of the prices at which you bought and sold your investment securities. Usually, a brokerage firm will have this information, but make sure you do too, in your financial records. Keep copies of all of your confirmation statements for all of your transactions.

In the month of January, you will receive a 1099 form from your brokerage firm. This form will tell you what you currently own and what you sold during the year for either a profit or a loss. Typically, the 1099 will not reveal at what price you bought the securities or if you indeed realized a profit or a loss. That information is up to you to supply. If you are organized, you should have it.

The capital gains listed on the 1099 represent *only* the capital gains that the company paid out to shareholders. You must add this figure to the capital gains or losses you incurred from your other trades. The total amount is the net capital gain or loss that is to be listed on your tax return.

Profits = Capital Gains

Profits are known as capital gains. On your 1099, there should also be a section reporting any dividends and/or capital gains that were distributed to you during the calendar year. Those must be reported to the Internal Revenue Service on your tax return.

Before the Tax Reform Act of 1986, if you held an investment security for more than a year and then sold it, it is reported as a long-term capital gain. If you owned it for less than a year, it needs to be reported on your tax return as a short-term capital gain.

But times have changed with the new tax laws passed in 1997. The new laws provide that assets sold within the first year of ownership will be classified as

Secret
Even if you are covered by an employer-sponsored plan (and you don't get the tax break for an IRA contribution), still set up an IRA for yourself. The interest and capital gains (profit!) that you accumulate in the account are not taxable until the money is withdrawn.

short-term, and profits will be subject to tax at an individual's ordinary income-tax rate (same as before).

Those assets held for at least a year and a day, but not more than 18 months, will be subject to a maximum capital gains rate of 28%, and those assets held for at least 18 months and a day will be taxed as long-term assets, at rates no higher than 20%.

What if you have a loss? I mean, what if you picked the biggest loser of all time? It's called a capital loss. No investor likes losses, but there is a bright side. Losses may reduce taxable income. Any action that you can do which reduces reportable income results in saving you money. That's where the positive side of having a capital loss comes in; you can either reduce your taxable income or reduce your capital gains.

Dividends and Interest

Dividends that you receive are known as income. Therefore, any dividends that you receive from owning an investment is taxed as regular income.

Interest payments you receive from bonds, certificates of deposit, money market deposit accounts, and savings accounts—with the exception of municipal bonds—are fully taxable at the federal level. The additions to this rule are the following:

➤ Municipal bond interest is exempt from federal tax, but often is subject to state and city tax, depending upon the issuer.

➤ U.S. Government Agency bonds are taxable at the federal level but exempt from state tax. However, Fannie Mae and Ginnie Mae bonds are subject to tax on all three levels—federal, state, and local.

Bet You Didn't Know

One of the best ways to accumulate capital gains and defer paying taxes on them is to set up an Individual Retirement Account (IRA). Not only are you able to deposit tax-deductible contributions up to a certain limit, you can also accrue interest and capital gains tax-*free* until they are withdrawn.

It's All in the Timing

There are two things in life that could really turn sour if you get the timing wrong. Jokes and taxes.

Timing when you buy and sell investment products does have an effect on your financial situation, either by putting you into a different tax bracket or by getting you a bigger tax refund in the mail. Don't limit yourself to reading these words. Always consult a tax adviser if you have any tax-related questions.

Timing your decision to sell an investment is just as important as choosing the right time to buy an investment. If, for example, it is mid-December and you have a stock that you want to sell at a loss because it isn't performing well, but you already have accumulated the maximum capital losses for the year, you could do two things:

Secret
If your goal is to reduce your taxable income and/or offset any capital gains, consider selling the investment to get the capital loss even if you already have the maximum capital loss requirement. The amount will be applied to the following year's tax return.

1. **Sell the additional stock for a loss and "roll over" the loss to the next tax year.** Since you already have the maximum capital loss you can claim on your tax return, the loss generated from the additional sale of stock (or any other investment) would have to be applied on the following year's tax return.

2. **Don't sell the additional stock for a loss until after January 1.** If you don't sell the stock, then any losses incurred will be applied to the following year's tax return.

For example, if you have already accrued the maximum in capital losses for the tax year, it's already December 20, and you're considering selling off more stock at a loss, do so *if your objective is to reduce your taxable income or if it is to net against a large capital gain you will have next year*. If your objective is to make a profit, make sure you do your homework to find out why the price of the investment is down from where you bought it to determine whether or not you should hold on.

In either event, any loss that results from the sale of additional stock (or any other investment) can be applied to the following year's tax return *if and only if* you have already met the maximum loss amount in one calendar year.

What if you were to incur a capital gain when you sold the investment and the gain bumped you up into the next tax bracket? You could wait until after January 1 to take the gain and apply it to the following year's tax return. Make sure you consult a tax adviser to select the best strategy.

The Least You Need to Know

➤ Start evaluating your tax situation right now. Find out what tax bracket you are in. Even if it's the middle of July and April 15 is not for another nine months, there's no better time than the present.

➤ If you are organized in your taxes, you have better control over your investment strategies. You'll know when to take a capital gain and an even better time to take a loss.

➤ Always, and I repeat, *always* consult a tax adviser if you have any complicated tax issues.

Shareholder Freebies

The companies listed in this appendix give shareholders the opportunity to "cash in" on ownership. Each company or mutual fund provides some perks in one form or another. These perks range from free boxes of cereal to coupons for discounts at theme parks—hours and hours of entertainment for the whole family. Remember, shareholder perks also include dividend reinvestment programs because you are able to purchase shares directly from the company, thereby foregoing brokerage commissions.

This appendix is based on information gathered from companies. Because there are many others that offer perks and freebies, I highly recommend you read the latest edition of Gene Walden's *The 100 Best Stocks to Own in America* (Dearborn Financial Publishing), in which he goes into extreme detail about these perks and other pertinent company information for potential shareholders.

If you become a shareholder, you must either call or write the company to inform them that you are a shareholder in order to receive the freebies. This listing does not constitute a recommendation to purchase stock in or bonds issued by any company included in the list.

Anheuser Busch Companies, Inc.   You get free beer samples and taste-tests if you attend the annual meeting. You may also receive discounts to theme parks they own, such as Busch Gardens.

Bristol-Myers   New shareholders receive product packs which include shampoos, toiletries, and some over-the-counter drugs.

Campbell Soup Company   In addition to providing free foods, the company sends its shareholders coupons in its quarterly and annual report.

Deluxe Corporation   The leading printer of bank checks and deposit slips, this company treats shareholders to dinner if they attend the annual meeting.

Emerson Electric Company   A dividend reinvestment plan is available to current shareholders with minimums as low as $25.

Federal Signal Corporation   This company manufactures sirens and warning lights for emergency vehicles. A dividend reinvestment program is available to shareholders.

General Mills Corporation   Mostly known for its label on cereal boxes, this company provides shareholders with a product pack of cereals, cake mixes, and coupons if they attend the annual meeting.

H.J. Heinz Company   New stockholders who own at least 30 shares receive welcome gifts, like a crock pot.

International Dairy Queen   DQ, as it's commonly known, provides shareholders attending the annual meeting with samples of its ice cream products.

Johnson & Johnson   You'll receive a gift pack of hygiene products if you attend the annual meeting.

Kellogg Company   New shareholders get coupons for free groceries.

The Limited, Inc.   Shareholders may receive coupons with discounts for clothing.

McDonald's Corporation   If you attend the annual meeting at Hamburger University in OakBrook, Illinois, you get a complimentary meal and a tour of the University.

Nike, Inc.   Shareholders get to have dinner with Michael Jordan—just kidding! You do receive some promotional materials if you attend the annual meeting.

PepsiCo, Inc.   Shareholders get to have dinner with Cindy Crawford—just kidding again. If you attend the annual meeting, you do receive some soft drinks, food products, and coupons.

Quaker Oats   In their quarterly dividend checks, shareholders receive coupons for discounts on products.

Ramada, Inc.   Shareholders get discount coupons for overnight hotel accommodations.

Sara Lee Corporation   Shareholders who attend the annual meeting receive sample products (perhaps a pound cake?) and coupons for products, too.

Tambrands, Inc.   This company offers a dividend reinvestment program to current shareholders.

UST, Inc.   This company offers shareholders samples of its product line, including pipe cleaners and smokeless tobacco, at its annual meeting.

William Wrigley Jr. Company   Shareholders receive Christmas gift boxes of gum.

No-Load Mutual Fund Companies

Provided below is a list of some of the largest no-load mutual fund companies. You may wish to contact several companies to ask them what types of funds they have—refer to Part 3 for review—and if they could please send you some information.

For a comprehensive guide that lists detailed information, including customer service hours, telephone switching privileges, and minimum investment requirements, I prefer the current edition of *The Handbook For No-Load Fund Investors*, Sheldon Jacobs, P.O. Box 318, Irvington-on-Hudson, NY 10533, (914) 693-7420. This guide is enormous—almost 600 pages in length—yet very easy to understand. Also, in Chapter 17, there is a list of mutual fund newsletters and rating services that you may wish to subscribe to.

Benham Funds
1665 Charleston Road
Mountain View, CA 94043
(800) 321-8321

The Berger Funds
210 University Blvd.
Suite 900
Denver, CO 80206
(800) 333-1001

**Sanford C. Bernstein
Fund, Inc.**
1 State Street Plaza
New York, NY 10004
(212) 504-5069

Blanchard Funds
41 Madison Avenue
24th Floor
New York, NY 10010
(800) 922-7771

Bull & Bear Funds
11 Hanover Square
New York, NY 10005
(800) 847-4200

Capiello-Rushmore Funds
4922 Fairmont Avenue
Bethesda, MD 20814
(800) 343-3355

Dean Witter Funds
Two World Trade Center
New York, NY 10048
(800) 869-3863

Dreyfus Funds
EAB Plaza
144 Glenn Curtis Blvd., Plaza Level
Uniondale, NY 11556
(800) 829-3733

The Evergreen Funds
2500 Westchester Avenue
Purchase, NY 10577
(800) 235-0064

Fidelity Funds
82 Devonshire Street
Boston, MA 02109
(800) 544-8888

Founders Funds
2930 East Third Avenue
Denver, CO 80206
(800) 232-8088

Gabelli Funds
One Corporate Center
Rye, NY 10580
(800) 422-3554

Gateway Funds
400 TechneCenter Drive
Suite 220
Milford, OH 45150
(513) 248-2700

Harbor Funds
One Seagate
Toledo, OH 43666
(800) 422-1050

The Highmark Group
Highmark Funds
1900 East Dublin-Granville Road
Columbus, OH 43229
(800) 433-6884

IAI Mutual Funds
3700 First Bank Place
P.O. Box 357
Minneapolis, MN 55440

Invesco Funds
7800 E. Union Avenue
Suite 800
Denver, CO 80237
(800) 525-8085

Janus Funds
100 Fillmore Street
Suite 300
Denver, CO 80206
(800) 525-3713

Lexington Funds
Park 80 West, Plaza Two
Saddles Brook, NJ 07662
(800) 526-0056

Merriman Funds
1200 Westlake Avenue North
Suite 700
Seattle, WA 98109
(800) 423-4893

Montgomery Funds
600 Montgomery Street
San Francisco, CA 94111
(800) 572-3863

Neuberger & Berman Funds
605 Third Avenue
New York, NY 10158
(800) 877-9700

Nicholas Family of Funds
700 North Water Street
Suite 1010
Milwaukee, WI 53202
(800) 227-5987

Oakmark Funds
Two North LaSalle Street
Suite 500
Chicago, IL 60602-3790
(800) 476-9625

The Pierpont Funds
461 Fifth Avenue
New York, NY 10017
(800) 521-5411

T. Rowe Price Funds
100 E. Pratt Street
Baltimore, MD 21202
(800) 638-5660 or (800) 225-5132

SAFECO Mutual Funds
P.O. Box 34890
Seattle, WA 98124-1890
(800) 624-5711

Scudder Funds
P.O. Box 2291
Boston, MA 02107-2291
(800) 225-5163

SteinRoe Funds
P.O. Box 1143
Chicago, IL 60690
(800) 338-2550

Stratton Funds
Plymouth Meeting Executive Campus
610 W. Germantown Pike, Suite 361
Plymouth Meeting, PA 19462
(800) 634-5726

Strong Funds
One Hundred Heritage Reserve
P.O. Box 2936
Milwaukee, WI 53201

Twentieth Century Funds
4500 Main Street
P.O. Box 419200
Kansas City, MO 64111
(800) 345-2021

United Services Funds
P.O. Box 781234
San Antonio, TX 78278-1234
(800) 873-8637

USAA Funds
USAA Building
San Antonio, TX 78288
(800) 382-8722

Vanguard Funds
P.O. Box 2600
Valley Forge, PA 19482
(800) 662-2739

Federal Reserve Banks

If you want to purchase Treasury securities through the Treasury Direct system, you can contact any of the 12 Federal Reserve Banks and their U.S. branches listed below. Additionally, each Federal Reserve Bank and its branches will provide you with free brochures about Treasury securities and savings bonds.

Alabama
P.O. Box 830447
Birmingham, AL 35283
(205) 731-8500

Arkansas
325 W. Capitol Ave.
Little Rock, AK 72203
(501) 324-8275

California (Southern)
950 S. Grand Avenue
Los Angeles, CA 90015
(213) 683-2300

California (Northern)
101 Market Street
San Francisco, CA 94120
(415) 974-2330

Colorado
P.O. Box 5228
Denver, CO 80217
(303) 572-2473

District of Columbia
20th Street and C Street, NW
Washington, DC 20551
(202) 452-3000

Florida
P.O. Box 929
Jacksonville, FL 32231
(904) 632-1000

Florida
P.O. Box 520847
Miami, FL 33152
(305) 591-2065

Georgia
104 Marietta Street, NW
Atlanta, GA 30303
(404) 521-8653

Illinois
230 S. LaSalle Street
Chicago, IL 60604
(312) 322-5369

Kentucky
P.O. Box 32710
Louisville, KY 40232
(502) 568-9236

Louisiana

525 St. Charles Avenue
New Orleans, LA 70130
(504) 593-3200

Maryland
502 S. Sharp Street
Baltimore, MD 21201
(410) 576-3300

Massachusetts
600 Atlantic Avenue
Boston, MA 02106
(617) 973-3805

Michigan
160 W. Fort Street
Detroit, MI 48231
(313) 961-6880

Minnesota
P.O. Box 291
Minneapolis, MN 55480
(612) 340-2345

Missouri
925 Grand Blvd.
Kansas City, MO 64198
(816) 881-2000

Missouri
P.O. Box 14935
St. Louis, MO 63178
(314) 444-8793

Montana
100 Neill Avenue
Helena, MT 59601
(406) 447-3800

Nebraska
2210 Farnam
Omaha, NE 68102
(401) 221-5500

New York
160 Delaware Avenue
Buffalo, NY 14202
(716) 849-5000

New York
33 Liberty Street
New York, NY 10045
(212) 720-5000

North Carolina
530 E. Trade Street
Charlotte, NC 28202
(704) 358-2100

Ohio
150 E. 4th Street
Cincinnati, OH 45202
(513) 721-4787

Ohio
1455 E. 6th Street
Cleveland, OH 44101
(216) 579-2490

Oklahoma
226 Dean McGee Avenue
Oklahoma City, OK 73125
(405) 270-8652

Oregon
915 S.W. Stark Street
Portland, OR 97208
(503) 221-5932

Pennsylvania
Ten Independence Mall
Philadelphia, PA 19106
(215) 574-6680

Pennsylvania
717 Grant Street
Pittsburgh, PA 15230
(412) 261-7802

Tennessee
200 N. Main Street
Memphis, TN 38103
(901) 523-7171

Tennessee
301 8th Avenue North
Nashville, TN 37203-4407
(615) 251-7100

Texas
2200 N. Pearl Street
Dallas, TX 75201
(214) 922-6000

Texas
301 E. Main Street
El Paso, TX 79901
(915) 544-4730

Texas
1701 San Jacinto Street
Houston, TX 77001
(713) 659-4433

Texas
126 E. Nueva Street
San Antonio, TX 78295
(512) 224-2141

Utah
120 S. State Street
Salt Lake City, UT 84130
(801) 322-7844

Virginia
701 E. Byrd Street
Richmond, VA 23219
(804) 697-8000

Washington
1015 Second Avenue
Seattle, WA 98104
(206) 343-3600

Financial Exchanges

If you ever have the chance to visit a financial exchange, take the opportunity to do so. The action you will see on the trading floor of any financial exchange will amaze you. Some traders hold trading cards to keep a tally of the day's trades; others run back and forth between trading desks and phones as quickly as possible. All financial exchanges are like this with the exception of the NASDAQ, where there is no centralized trading floor or trading pits. Listed stocks are traded via a high-tech telephone and computer system.

New York Stock Exchange (NYSE)
11 Wall Street
New York, NY 10005
(212) 656-3000

Commonly referred to as the "Big Board," the NYSE represents the exchange where the largest, most well-known stocks trade. If you wish, you may contact the NYSE for any brochures about the stock exchange and the specific stocks that trade there.

American Stock Exchange (AMEX)
86 Trinity Place
New York, NY 10006
(212) 306-1000

Mostly medium-sized and small-sized growth company stocks are listed here, and, just like the NYSE, you can either write to them or call them for further information about the exchange.

NASDAQ National Market System (NASDAQ NMS)

Even though there is neither a specific address nor a physical financial exchange, stockholders of companies listed on NASDAQ can still find their quotes in the financial section of newspapers. Formerly known as the OTC market (the Over-The-Counter market), this "exchange" began its high-tech trading and quoting system in 1972.

Other financial exchanges include the following: Boston Stock Exchange, Chicago Mercantile Exchange, Chicago Board Options Exchange, Midwest Stock Exchange, Montreal Stock Exchange, and Philadelphia Stock Exchange.

Money Talks—Learn the Language

Accrued interest   This is the interest collected on a bond since the last interest payment was made. The buyer of the bond pays not only the market price but also the accrued interest. This should be shown on a trade confirmation.

Agency bonds   These are IOUs made by an issuer that is typically a government agency. They don't have the full faith and credit of the U.S. Government like Treasuries do, although they are just one notch down on the risk scale from Treasury securities.

American Stock Exchange (AMEX)   This exchange is one of the leading financial exchanges in the world. It is located in New York City. Medium-size and small-size growth company stocks trade here. It also has the largest market for foreign securities in the U.S.

Analyst   Sometimes referred to as a financial analyst, this is a person who has been trained to investigate all of the facts concerning a stock, bond, mutual fund, future or option. An analyst often gives opinions and advice to help a potential investor decide what to do.

Annual report   This is a financial statement issued by a company that shows all of its pluses and minuses, including whether the company made a profit or not.

Annual or annualized return   Expresses the rate of return for a time frame that is greater than one year. The rate of return is calculated in terms of a twelve-month period.

Annual yield   The amount of money, percentage of return in dividends, or interest an investor receives from an investment. This figure is then calculated on an annual basis.

Appreciation   That fake smile you put on your face when your in-laws bring over the Christmas fruitcake, or in the investment world, it's known as price improvement.

Asked or offering price   The lowest price which any seller will accept for a security that you want to buy. You, as the buyer, would buy the investment at the asked or offering price.

Asset allocation   How you carve up your investment pie. Represented usually in percentages, such as the percentage you have in stocks, bonds, mutual funds, and so on, which then makes up your investment portfolio.

Assets   What you own. Easy enough, eh?

At a discount   Below par value, typically $1,000, in the world of bond investing. If a bond is selling at 95 ($950) and par is 100 ($1,000), then the bond is selling at a discount.

At a premium   Above par value, typically $1,000, in the world of bond investing. If a bond is selling at 105 ($1,050) and par is 100 ($1,000), then the bond is selling at a premium.

At auction   Where to buy antique furniture—oops, sorry. How Treasury securities are bought. For a list of places to buy Treasury securities, refer to Appendix C.

At par   Equal to face value, which is usually $1,000.

At the close   The final few milliseconds when the trading day stops. You can also put in an order to buy or sell a security "at the close." You would get the best price possible in these last few trading seconds.

At the market   Market order.

At the opening   Opposite of at the close. You would get the best price possible if you were to buy or sell a security exactly when the market opened.

Averages   Also known as indices. The Dow Jones Industrial Average is the most commonly known. They represent a way of measuring the trend of security prices.

Averaging down   The practice of purchasing the same security as the price continues to tank, thereby being able to buy more shares. Very risky.

Balance sheet   Found in the annual report, it lists the pluses and minuses of a company. You should make one for yourself, too!

Balanced funds   A mutual fund that diversifies its securities by purchasing many kinds of stocks and bonds.

Basis point   A measurement of change, whether up or down, in the current yield equal to one 1/100 of 1% on bonds or bills.

Bear market   A market where prices drop rather sharply. Pessimism, growing unemployment, and sometimes a recession are common. Opposite of bull market.

Bid and asked   A quote.

Bid price   This is the highest quoted price that any potential buyer will pay you for a security that you are trying to sell.

Big Board   New York Stock Exchange.

Block   An exceptionally large chunk of stock purchased, typically 10,000 shares or more.

Blue chip   The stock of a leading company which is known for superior management. Blue chip stocks are mostly listed on the Dow Jones Industrial Average.

Bond   An IOU issued by corporations, the U.S. government, foreign governments, state and city municipalities, and government agencies. These entities borrow money from investors and promise to pay them back in full at a later date plus interest.

Bond quality ratings   Tells whether or not you get a gold star from the rating agencies.

Broker   A person who handles your order to buy and sell securities and is paid a lot of money to do so.

Bull market   An advancing market, where everything is on the upswing. Opposite of a bear market.

Business cycle   A regularly recurring period that all businesses go through. Shows where the country is in terms of recession, depression, recovery, and expansion.

Buy order   An order to buy a security that you specify.

Call   An option that gives the option holder the right—but not the obligation—to buy the underlying stock.

Callable   A feature on a bond that says the issuer can redeem the bond before maturity.

Capital gain or loss   Profit or loss from the sale of an investment.

Cash dividend   A dividend paid on an investment in cash or by check.

CDs   Stands for certificates of deposit. These products represent a fixed dollar amount that has been deposited with a bank (usually) for a fixed period of time at a predetermined rate of interest.

Closed-end fund   Opposite of an open-end mutual fund. The fund's shares are traded on a securities exchange where the number of shares outstanding is limited.

Closing price   The price at which the final transaction of a security took place on a particular business day.

Commodity exchange   An organization of traders who buy and sell contracts for future delivery of commodities, such as grain, sugar, coffee, gold, and soybeans.

Common stock   An investment that represents ownership interest in a corporation.

Compounding   It is a mathematical process of finding the final value of an investment when the compound interest is applied. It's a matter of taking the interest earned on the interest earned on the principal investment. Get out your calculators!

Consumer Price Index   It is one economic report that is looked upon as the best indicator of inflation.

Corporate bond   A bond issued by a corporation. The corporation borrows the money from the lenders (investors) and promises to pay them back their "loan" at a specified date plus interest.

Credit rating   Typically used in describing the credit risk involved in a bond investment. Indicated by a letter, usually given by one of the large credit rating companies, such as Moody's and Standard & Poor's.

Current yield   Annual bond interest divided by the market price per bond.

Cutting a loss   Getting rid of it, honey, before it's too late. It is the decision to close out an unprofitable market position and take the loss involved before it gets too big.

Cyberspace   The Internet, World Wide Web, you name it. The "place" through your computer and a modem hook up, you can research all kinds of information, including financial information, as well as perform online transactions.

Cyclical stocks   Stocks that move in the same direction as the business cycle. When business conditions are improving, cyclical stocks tend to follow and vice-versa.

Day order   An order to buy (sell) an investment, which, if not executed, expires at the end of the trading day.

Deficit   The money the government—or even a company—pays out in excess of what it takes in over a given period.

Depression   A prolonged period of sharply reduced business activity. Typically characterized by high unemployment, low production, and a major drop in consumer buying.

Discount   In the world of bond investing, it is the amount by which a bond sells below its face value. If the face value of the bond is $1,000 and it is selling for $950, it is selling at a discount. Opposite of premium.

Discount rate   The interest rate the Federal Reserve charges to member banks for loans.

Diversification   The spreading of investment funds among classes of securities and localities in order to distribute the risk. Don't put all of your eggs in one basket.

Dividend   The proportion of a company's net earnings paid to its stockholders.

Dividend yield   Expressed as a percent. Divide the dividend payment by the market price of the stock.

Dollar cost averaging   This is when a fixed dollar amount is invested on a periodic basis into one or more investments, thereby enabling the investor to average the purchase of shares (if it's a stock or mutual fund) over the long haul.

Dow Jones Industrial Average   Also referred to as DJIA. A popular gauge of the stock market based on the average closing prices of 30 blue-chip stocks.

Due date   Maturity date.

Earnings per share   This is a company's net income minus preferred dividends divided by the outstanding shares of stock. Also known as EPS.

Equities   Refers to ownership of property, such as having equity in your home or owning stocks.

Eurodollars   Deposits of U.S. dollars at banks and other financial institutions outside the United States.

Ex-dividend   A divorced dividend. No, really, it is the date where the buyer of a stock must own the stock in order to receive the dividend.

Execute an order   To fulfill an order to buy or sell a security.

Expiration date   The last day on which a stock option may be exercised.

Face value   The value of the bond that appears on the face of the bond. Remember, face value is *not* an indication of market value.

Fannie Mae   Chocolate-covered cherries, chocolate-covered peanut swirls...oh, sorry. Stands for Federal National Mortgage Association.

Federal Reserve System   The central banking system of the United States made up of 12 Federal Reserve banks and supervised by the Federal Reserve Board.

Financial statement   Another term for balance sheet.

Fixed-income investment   Income from an investment (usually bonds) which remains constant and does not fluctuate.

Fluctuations   Variations in the market price of a security. Means it goes up and down.

Forward contract   Contract where two parties agree to the purchase and sale of a commodity at some future time and at a specific price.

331

Freddie Mac   Nickname for the Federal Home Loan Mortgage Corporation.

Fundamental analysis   Analysis based on factors such as earnings growth and value.

Futures contract   A transferrable agreement to make or take delivery of a commodity during a specific month under the terms and conditions established by a federally designated contract market (the exchange).

Ginnie-Mae Pass-Thru Securities   An investment that has its principal and interest payments collected on mortgages that are in specified pools passed through to the investors in the Ginnie Mae securities. Ginnie Mae stands for the Government National Mortgage Association.

Graduated payment mortgage   A mortgage that carries a fixed interest rate, but the monthly payments are lower at the beginning and gradually increase to a fixed level after five to ten years.

Gross Domestic Product   The market value of the country's total output of goods and services.

Growth stock   The stock issued by a corporation whose earnings have increased consistently over a number of years.

Hedging   The temporary purchase or sale of a contract (either futures or options) calling for future delivery of a specific quantity of an investment at an agreed price to offset a present position.

Index   In economics, it is a statistical benchmark or yardstick, if you will, expressed in terms of percentage of a base year or years. In investing, it is a basket of securities that are averaged to come up with a number that is used as a benchmark.

Index fund   A fund comprised of securities which will produce (hopefully) a return that replicates a designated securities index.

Individual retirement account (IRA)   An account that allows you a way to save money on a tax-deferred basis.

Inflation   A phase of the business cycle characterized by changing economic conditions, including sky-high prices and a loss of purchasing power. If you've been to the grocery store recently, you'll know what I'm talking about.

Interest   The amount a borrower pays a lender for the use of his or her money.

Interest rate risk   When interest rates rise (fall), the market value of a bond declines (rises). Interest rate risk is associated with these fluctuations.

In-the-money   In options investing, it is the striking price that is below the market price of the stock.

Investment objectives   Before you invest, you need them. They should be long-term, risk/return objectives developed principally from careful consideration of what you want to do with your money and where you want to go.

Investment portfolio   A securities portfolio.

Lender   I need money. You let me borrow it. You are the lender.

Leverage   A condition where you get the maximum bang for your buck.

Liabilities   The amount of money that you, a company, or the government owes to others.

Limit order   An order to buy (sell) a stated amount of a security at a specific or better price.

Liquidity   When you have sufficient cash available at the time you need it. The ability to get at your money quickly. If you need money but you can't sell your investment because there isn't a buyer, the investment is said to be illiquid.

Load   The commissions and sales charges associated with a mutual fund. Opposite of no-load.

Market order   An order to buy (sell) a security at the best price possible.

Market price   The last reported price at which an investment sold.

Maturity   The date on which a loan comes due and is to be paid off.

Mortgage-backed securities   Bonds which are a general obligation of the issuing institution but are also collateralized by a pool of mortgages.

Mutual fund company   A company that uses its customers' deposits to invest in securities of other companies through their mutual funds and pools the money together into a fund that is based on specific criteria, such as investment objectives and risk tolerance.

NASD   Stands for the National Association of Securities Dealers. Organizes and enforces the rules of fair practice among the brokerage industry.

NASDAQ   Stands for National Association of Securities Dealers Automated Quotations. A techno-geek automated information network which provides brokers with quotes on securities (typically stocks).

Net worth   The total amount of equity/assets that you have after you calculate what you own against what you owe.

New York Stock Exchange   Known as the NYSE or the "Big Board," this is an exchange where hundreds of securities trade every day.

No-load fund   A mutual fund that does not carry any commissions or sales charges.

Noncallable securities   Securities which cannot be redeemed before the date of maturity.

Odd lot   An amount of stock bought (sold) that is less than 100 shares.

Offer   The price at which a person is willing to sell.

Online banking   The process of completing your banking business (paying bills, transferring money between accounts) through the use of your computer and a modem hookup.

Open order   An order to buy (sell) at a stipulated price which remains effective until it is executed.

Opening price   A security's price at the first trade of the day.

P/E Ratio   Price earnings ratio. This measures whether a stock is overvalued or not. You take the stock's market price and divide it by its current or estimated future earnings.

Par value   This is the amount to be received in cash at maturity of a bond.

Point   A point means $1. If XYZ Company stock rises three points, it means it rises $3.

Position   Think of it as a market commitment of what you hold. If you own 100 shares of stock, the 100 shares are your position.

Preferred stock   Securities which represent an ownership interest (like stock) but have preference over the other shares in terms of dividends.

Premium   The amount by which a security sells over its face value.

Price   The market value of anything being offered for sale.

Prime rate   The minimum rate on bank loans set by commercial banks and only given to its top business borrowers. A benchmark used by consumers to determine loan rates.

Principal   The dollar amount of your initial investment on which you earn interest.

Profit   The money that you have remaining after all costs of either operating a business are paid or when you buy low and sell high.

Prospectus   A legal document that explains the complete history and current status of an investment security.

Purchasing power   The goods and services that you can buy given any amount of money. If there is inflation, you will have a loss in purchasing power of some goods.

Put option   An option that gives the investor the right—but not the obligation—to sell the underlying security.

Quote   "I think, therefore I am." Oh, in investing? It is the highest bid to buy and the lowest offer to sell a security.

Rally   A quick rise following a decline in the general price level of the market.

Reserve requirements   The amount of money that banks are required to keep in their vault per Federal Reserve bank rules.

Return   The amount of money that you receive annually from an investment typically expressed as a percentage.

Risk   Any chance of loss.

Round lot   When you buy 100 shares of stock, that is known as a round lot. It's a unit of trading. (See also *odd lot*.)

Rule of 72   A mathematical formula used to determine how long it takes to double your money. Divide the rate of return by 72. Your answer will give you the number of years it takes.

Safekeeping fee   A fee that a bank or brokerage firm will charge its customers who keep their stock and bond certificates in the vault.

Savings accounts   An account in a bank or savings and loan that earns a pretty low rate of interest.

SEC   Stands for Securities and Exchange Commission. This is a regulatory agency started by Congress in 1933 to help protect you, the investor.

Security   Note, stock, bond, or any type of investment product.

Settlement date   The date on which the final consummation of a transaction takes place and when the money is due.

Short sale   This is a trade made by investors who believe the market is going to take a tumble. They borrow the stock from the brokerage firm that is selling at its current price. These investors hope that the stock will drop in price so they can buy back the shares.

Socially reponsible mutual funds   These are mutual funds that invest in companies that have a greater social or moral quality.

Speculation   A risk taken in order to achieve a greater return.

Spread   The difference between the bid price and the asked (offering) price.

Standard & Poor 500   Also known as the S&P 500. This is an index made up of a basket of 500 stocks that is considered to be one of the most well-known gauges of stock market movement.

Stock   A certificate of ownership. See *common stock* or *preferred stock*.

Stock split   A division made of the stock (decided upon by the company's board of directors) to either create more shares or reduce the number of shares (which is known as a *reverse stock split*).

Stockholder   If you buy stock, you are a stockholder.

Stop order   An order to buy (sell) at a price above (below) the current market price.

Street name   Securities belonging to a client of a brokerage firm registered in the name of the brokerage firm.

Technical analysis   An approach by market wizards (with graph paper who chart price movements and volatility) to determine the best time to buy and/or sell a security.

Total return   The aggregate increase in the value of the portfolio resulting from calculating all of the pluses and minuses.

Trader   A person who actively buys and sells investment securities.

Treasury bills   Also referred to as T-bills. These are short-term IOUs from the government. Maturities range from three months to one year.

Treasury bonds   Also referred to as T-bonds. These are the government's longest-term IOUs. Maturities range from 10 years to 30 years.

Treasury notes   Also referred to as T-notes. These are the government's medium-term IOUs and maturities range from two years to ten years.

Underlying security   The shares of stock (or other security) subject to the exercise of an option.

Volume   The total number of shares traded during a given period.

Wealth   What you are working to accumulate. Think fortune, riches, treasures.

Wilshire 5000 index   An all equity, very broad-based index comprised of 5,000 stocks.

Yield   The return of an investment expressed as a percentage.

Yield curve   A visual illustration and representation of the term structure of interest rates.

Yield to maturity   The return provided by a bond to its maturity date.

Zero-coupon bond   A bond which has no interest payments that you buy at a discount. You should receive the face value of the bond upon maturity.

Index

Symbols

10 percent rule
  calculating amount to
    invest, 43-44
  income in investment
    vehicle, 78-79
12b-1 (SEC) fees on mutual
  funds, 157
100 Highest Yield Report on
  CDs, 117-119
401(k) retirement plans,
  contributing, 44-45

A

ABA (American Banking
  Association) numbers,
  automatic deductions,
  162-163
accumulating
  house down payment, 31
  money in IRAs, 32
  tuition for college, 31-32
adjustable rate mortgages
  (ARM), 256-257
agency bonds
  agriculture, 256-257
  bond dealers, 260
  education, 256-257
  housing, 256-257

investors, 259-260
pricing increments,
  259-260
purchasing, 259-260
transportation, 256-257
allocating
  investment portfolios,
    48-51
  investments into liquid
    accounts, 101-102
America Online, 64
American Association of
  Individual Investors, 55
  risk analysis, 55-56
  website, 64
American Municipal Bond
  Assurance Corporation
  (AMBAC), municipal bond
  companies, 274
American Stock Exchange
  (AMEX), 325
  contact address, 325-326
  "curb exchange,"
    187-188
  type of stocks, 325-326
amortization of mortgages,
  256-257
ancient Greece, banking
  origins, 100
Anheuser Busch Companies,
  315
annual report versus
  prospectus, 67

annual returns, perfor-
  mance information,
  65-66
ask price (stocks), 189
asset allocation, 81
  determining, 82
  historical gains and
    losses, 82-84
  risk tolerance, 82
  selection factors
    age, 82-84
    risks, 82-84
    time horizon, 82-84
asset management accounts
  features, 107-108
  initial deposits, 107-108
assets, calculating, 37-39
"automatic building capital"
  (ABC), 163
automatic deductions
  from checking accounts,
    investing, 161-163
  implementing, 162-163
automatic investing plans,
  163
  portfolios
    $100 range, 304-305
    $1000 range, 305-306
    $5000 range, 306-307
    $10,000 or more,
      307-308
average annual return,
  performance information,
  65-66

E

Protection Act of
1970, 124
selling process on New
York Stock Exchange
(NYSE), 186-188
shares, 25
shorting, 200-202
stock splits, 209
stop limit orders,
190-191, 207
stop loss orders, 207
stop orders, 190-191
swindles, avoiding,
222-223
*The 100 Best Stocks to
Own in America* (Gene
Walden), 315
ticker symbols, 62
types
cyclical, 198
growth, 196-197
income, 197-198
initial public offerings
(IPOs), 198-199
undervalued versus
overvalued, 199-200
versus bonds, 233-234
stop limit orders, 190-191,
207
stop loss orders, 207
implementing, 208
modifying, 208
stop orders, 190-191
Stratton Funds, 319
strike price (options), 294
STRIPs, 265
Strong Funds, 319
supply and demand, law of,
in stock market, 211
suspending dividend
payments, 181
swindles
investments, avoiding,
222-223

National Association of
Securities Dealers
(NASD), 222-223
National Futures Associa-
tion, 222-223
Ponzi schemes, 221-223

T

T. Rowe Price Funds, 319
website, 32
"taking a long position"
(futures contracts),
289-290
Tambrands, Inc., 316
tax planning
1099 forms (IRS), 311
brackets, 310
capital gains, 311
capital losses, 311-312
dividend income, 312
estimated payments, 310
interest payments, 312
municipal bonds,
310-311
profits, 311-312
records, organizing,
36-37
reduction strategies,
310-311
timing your buys and
sells, 312-313
withdrawls from IRAs,
312
technicians
price patterns, 27
telephone switching,
134-135
*The 100 Best Stocks to Own in
America* (Gene Walden),
315
The Berger Funds, 317
The Budget Kit, financial
software, 34-35

The CNNfn Lipper Mutual
Fund Report website, 170
*The Directory of Dividend
Reinvestment Plans*, 218
The Evergreen Funds, 318
*The Handbook For No-Load
Fund Investors*, 317
The Highmark Group, 318
The Hulbert Financial Digest,
226-227
The Limited, Inc., 316
The Motley Fool: Finance
and Folly website, 64
The Mutual Fund Almanac,
170
The Pierpont Funds, 319
The Wall Street Journal,
63-64
website, 62
The Wealth of Nations
(Adam Smith), 16
ticker symbol, in newspa-
pers, 62
TIGRs, 265
tiered rates, 103
timing
and tax planning,
312-313
market cycles, 84-85
trade deficit, 23-24
trading closed-end mutual
funds, 137-138
tranches, collateralized
mortgage obligation
(CMO), 261-262
Treasury bills (T-bills)
as component of U.S.
debt, 246-247
ask price, 247-249
auction frequency, 249
auction times, 249
bid price, 247-249

U

V

W

X - Y - Z